EVERYWHERE
WE WENT

EVERYWHERE WE WENT

Ben Dirs

**SIMON &
SCHUSTER**

London · New York · Sydney · Toronto · New Delhi

A CBS COMPANY

First published in Great Britain by Simon & Schuster UK Ltd, 2011
A CBS COMPANY

Copyright © Barmy Army Limited, 2011

The right of Barmy Army Limited to be identified as author
of this work has been asserted in accordance with sections
77 and 78 of the Copyright, Designs and Patents Act, 1988.

1 3 5 7 9 10 8 6 4 2

Simon & Schuster UK Ltd
1st Floor
222 Gray's Inn Road
London
WC1X 8HB

www.simonandschuster.co.uk

Simon & Schuster Australia
Sydney

Simon & Schuster India
New Delhi

A CIP catalogue record for this book
is available from the British Library

ISBN 978-0-85720-835-4

Typeset by M Rules
Printed and bound by CPI Group (UK) Ltd, Croydon, CR0 4YY

To sports fans everywhere who
support their team regardless

If you would like to find out more about the Barmy Army, and what we offer, or if you have any stories you think might be suitable for future books, please visit our website www.barmyarmy.com

Contents

Acknowledgements

To all the Barmy Army members I interviewed for this book, I extend my heartfelt thanks – there are too many to mention individually, but to a man and woman you were generous with your time, patient with my questioning and giving with your stories. Many others relayed your tales via email and I am extremely grateful you took the time to put them down in writing.

I must also thank the former England players and my BBC colleague Jonathan Agnew for their views on the Barmy Army phenomenon. In addition, I am massively in debt to the many cricket writers who have been quoted in this book – whether positive or negative about the Barmy Army, their views were invaluable in being able to chart the movement's narrative arc.

Thanks, too, to my editor Ian Marshall and my agent David Luxton, who was as supportive as ever. But most of all I am indebted to the Barmy Army's co-founder and driving force, Paul 'Leafy' Burnham, who was with me every step of the way during the writing of this book. Having handed me your 'baby' to look after, I only hope I haven't dropped it.

Ben Dirs, August 2011

Introduction

Of course, it is always callous to compare sport with war, but the story of how the Barmy Army began has parallels – as absurd as it might sound – with the early days of the Cuban Revolution: a small, ragtag band of men lands in a largely hostile country, packs on backs, shorts and flip-flops instead of army fatigues, wielding bottles of Victoria Bitter rather than Molotov cocktails. And then the march begins . . .

Across Australia they yomp, picking up like-minded Englishmen and women along the way – all in support of what must at times have looked like a doomed cause. In one respect it was: the cause being the England cricket team they so loved – but which was so very ordinary at cricket. But in another respect it was not doomed at all: while the Barmy Army – or, more correctly, the proto-Barmies – did not create the template of what the British sports fan should be, it built on the idea of the British sports fan as the patron saint of the lost cause. I must have heard it a thousand times in the researching of this book: 'The Barmy Army supports the England cricket team whether it is winning or losing.'

Indeed, while the motto of the SAS is 'Who Dares Wins', the motto of the Barmy Army might be 'Through Thick and Thin': no cause is a lost cause for the Barmy Army.

It was this baffling faith in a malfunctioning England cricket team that led the Australian media to dub these England fans the Barmy Army in the first place, during the Ashes series down under in 1994–95. Mike Atherton's side was getting a shellacking on the field, but their fans kept on coming back for more and they kept on singing. The Aussie media loved them – the British press pack was not so sure. Scratch that – for the most part they hated them. According to the grey-haired hacks clad in shirtsleeves and ties, some of whom had been covering the game since the days of Dexter and Cowdrey, cricket was a spectacle to be supported in reflective and respectful silence. *Test Match Special* commentator Christopher Martin-Jenkins opined the Barmy Army 'demeaned English cricket'. Ian Wooldridge, the *Daily Mail*'s veteran and venerable chief sportswriter, suggested they be gassed.

As the Barmy Army swelled in numbers over the next few years, winning over people as far afield as the Caribbean and New Zealand along the way, the criticism from the British press grew louder. While there were those who appreciated this new brand of more vociferous cricket support – with its songs and chants and focus on partying and booze – others were unable to differentiate the Barmy Army from the English football hooligans whose speciality was smashing up cities and terrorising people across the globe. The only thing was, the Barmy Army did not smash up anything and people across the globe seemed to love them. Then, when it became clear the Barmy Army did not fit the stereotype that had been foisted upon it, critics started to complain it had become not ragtag enough. 'An exercise, not just in forced jollity and willed high spirits, but in merchandising opportunism' was how one cricket writer summed the Barmy Army up during the disastrous Ashes tour of 2006–07. 'Corporate, publicity-hungry and, above all, really annoying.'

The truth was, the Barmy Army had become so big by the mid-2000s, with 25,000 members as part of its subscription fanbase, a level of organisation had become a necessity. Not that the England players minded. For the most part, the Barmy Army's heroes, if at times a little perplexed, have always been appreciative. Michael Vaughan, captain of England during the glorious Ashes series in 2005, when his side regained the Ashes for the first time in eighteen years, called the Barmy Army his 'twelfth man'. And then, when the Barmy Army morphed from the ultimate underdogs supporters' club to fans of perhaps the best Test side in the world during the victorious Ashes tour of 2010–11, the previously unthinkable happened and the British press followed suit. When Scyld Berry, *Wisden* editor and cricket writer very much of the old school, gave the Barmy Army his blessing, it was as if the Barmy Army had passed through the proverbial eye of the needle and become part of the cricket establishment.

While the England and Wales Cricket Board (ECB) remained reluctant to cement links in any official form, the Barmy Army had become a synonym for any England support abroad. The revolution, finally, had come to pass.

This book is the tale of how a handful of cricket tragics grew into arguably the most famous band of travelling supporters in the world. It is not a history as such, for that would not capture the spirit of the movement, but, rather, the stories of those who have been there, seen it, done it and bought the Barmy Army T-shirts. The main thread running through it is England's Ashes series down under: Australia is very much the Barmy Army's spiritual home and the Barmy Army remains very much a touring brand, with Test cricket its focus. But the book also makes stops in South Africa, the Caribbean, Pakistan, Sri Lanka, New Zealand and Bangladesh. India being such a vast country and such a vast subject, it was decided justice could not be done to it and that perhaps it deserved a book of its own, somewhere down the line.

But most of all, this book is a tribute to a certain strain in the British character: one that revels in fun and humour, absurdism and irreverence – and, perhaps above all, adversity. Call it the Blitz spirit; call it singing when you are not necessarily winning; call it shrugging, smiling, cracking open a beer and partying on through when other fans, in the same situation, would be booing and hissing – or not there at all.

1

In the beginning ... Australia
1994–95

When the Australian media christened the Barmy Army on the 1994–95 Ashes tour, they can have had no idea just how barmy some of those England fans would end up. Sent half mad by booze, dope and the never-ending partying, by the publicity and attention. But more than that, sent half mad by an unquenchable loyalty to their team. It was this fierce loyalty that first attracted the attention of the Aussie press pack. Bored with writing about a one-sided series, in which a very good Australia side were lording it over a very ordinary England team, the Aussie journalists started sniffing about for subplots. And they could hardly miss the ramshackle band of England supporters, whose unswerving support for its team, in the face of much heartache on the field of play, was as baffling to the hosts as it was endearing.

A frequent criticism of the Barmy Army in its modern

form is that it is contrived, stage-managed and lacks spontaneity. But in the beginning it was organic, more of a spirit or energy than something you could bottle and label. And it was also necessary, a reaction to the rather unpolished barracking of the Australian fans, who were as boorish in victory as the England fans were sanguine in defeat. Paul 'Leafy' Burnham and Dave 'The General' Peacock, two of the three Barmy Army co-founders along with Gareth Evans, were there from the start and remember when the Barmy Army was not the Barmy Army at all, but a tight-knit, hedonistic gaggle of backpackers with a shared passion for all things sport, cricket in particular, and, above all, the England cricket team.

'I had played for a cricket club in Bedford for many years, I loved cricket and loved watching it almost as much,' says Peacock, a recruitment director from nPower. 'My earliest memory was being taken to The Oval to watch Ian Botham take ten wickets against Australia. So it was always the dream to watch England in Australia. When I was offered redundancy I took six months off and then I travelled with two mates to America, Fiji, New Zealand and finally arrived in Australia in September of '94. We went to see the Melbourne Cup, watched the rugby league Grand Final and a few days before the first Test got a bus up to Brisbane from Melbourne and checked in to the nearest backpackers' to the Gabba. When we got there, there were several other young English lads, predominantly football fans, but who were all up for the cricket. We got straight on the beers and I could feel something brewing.'

'That tour was a bit old-fashioned in that there were maybe six or seven domestic fixtures outside of the Tests, so there was lots of time for the British community to get to know each other,' says Burnham, a former British Airways cargo agent who had decided to spend three months watching England, having inherited some money from his dad. 'From hanging out in the same backpackers' or the same bars, we were then all thrown together at the Test matches. There just happened to be a lot of like-minded people on that tour who had decided to go and watch the whole of the Ashes series, and as the tour progressed more and more of us got together and it grew into something big.'

While the England fans were expectant, England's players and management were singing from a different hymn sheet. Things had descended into chaos before a ball had even been bowled in the series. After mixed results in the warm-up matches, strike bowler Devon Malcolm went down with chickenpox, then there was a spat between the chairman of selectors Raymond Illingworth, throwing barbs from back in Blighty, and skipper Mike Atherton over the selection of veteran batsman Mike Gatting for the first Test in Brisbane. When Burnham bumped into a few of the England team after a defeat by New South Wales, it was evident that England were a beaten outfit before the Test series had even started.

'We were in the bar of the team hotel in Newcastle,' says Burnham. 'Tufnell, "Goughie" [Darren Gough] and Martin McCague were lined up at the bar, with Mike Atherton sitting nice and quietly at the other end. Gough was rushing around like a blue-arsed fly trying to find out about his wife, who was expecting to give birth at any minute. Ray Illingworth, for whatever reason, wouldn't let him use the hotel phone, so he was running round trying to get together some coins for the payphone, and going nuts because it kept on cutting out. Meanwhile, McCague was clearly feeling low because of all the abuse he'd been getting [McCague, who grew up in Australia, was famously dubbed 'the rat who joined the sinking ship' by Sydney's *Daily Telegraph-Mirror*] and Tufnell was raring up, saying he was going to bring over some of his Middlesex mates because of all the abuse he'd been getting. It was a real snapshot of the state of mind of that England team at the time – and, in hindsight, of how much more professional things are today.'

The first delivery of that Ashes series followed the trend of the previous three and set the tone for the next few months – indeed, the next twelve years: England seamer Phil DeFreitas was the bowler, Australia opener Michael Slater the batsman, and the ball was smashed to the boundary for four. Things did not get much better for England on day one. Slater, feasting on some insipid England bowling, and his skipper Mark Taylor took Australia to 87 without loss at lunch. Up in the stands, the England fans were also under siege.

'The Aussies got off to a flyer and after tea they were still piling on the runs and no one was really singing,' says Peacock. 'We started getting a bit of abuse, not very intelligent stuff – "England are shit", "when are you going to give us a game", kids' stuff really. I'd been to all the football grounds in England following Chelsea, had a few songs up my sleeve and some of the other lads joined in.'

'The songs and the banter were very much in retaliation for the way the Australian fans were supporting their team, which was in a very arrogant, cocky, over-patriotic way, more in line with English football supporters than the style the Barmy Army would pioneer,' says Burnham. 'There was a situation where I went to a game in Newcastle, New South Wales, and we were sitting on a Union flag. We went off to get some drinks, with two girls who were attending their first game of cricket, and when we came back we were told an Australian had pissed on the flag. The same day they had a blow-up doll with a banner on it saying "Phil Tufnell's Wife". Tufnell had some personal problems before he went on that tour, and that kind of abuse was out of order, over and beyond acceptable behaviour from a cricket crowd.'

Tufnell and the Aussie fans had history. On the previous England tour down under, in 1990–91, the Middlesex spinner had become a figure of much fun for his substandard fielding, ramshackle appearance and regular bust-ups with the team's hierarchy, leading to some infamous exchanges down on the boundary. Some of it was genuinely witty, including the time an Aussie fan shouted out: 'Lend me your brain, "Tuffers", I'm building an idiot.' Some of it, however, was just downright nasty. As Tufnell recalls: 'I remember someone asked me for my autograph and when I went over they slapped a minced beef and onion pie on my head. Which I thought wasn't very nice. I can remember it dribbling down my face.' According to Tufnell, even the umpires got in on the act. In Melbourne, Tufnell claims, as Australia were pressing towards victory on day five, he walked past the umpire and asked how many deliveries were left in the over. The response? 'Count 'em yourself, you Pommie ****.'

Fast bowler Angus Fraser admits that the abuse from Aussie fans could be so extreme that there were days when he felt like climbing over the hoardings and 'doing an Eric Cantona'. 'Standing in front of Bay Thirteen at the MCG or The Hill at the SCG was not a pleasant experience. You would get pelted with fruit, bottles, food or little balloons filled with urine that exploded on impact. You were also advised, under-standably, not to accept a drink from anyone on the boundary edge. There was plenty of verbal abuse too. I wish I had a pound for every time an Aussie fan shouted at me: "Who's shagging your wife while you're here, mate?" or "I hear she cooks a good breakfast".' The barracking might have coars-ened, but in truth little had changed since Harold Larwood's day. 'A cricket tour in Australia would be the most delightful period in one's life, if one was deaf,' said Larwood, hero and

villain of the notorious Bodyline series of 1932–33. His captain, the imperious Douglas Jardine, was even more to the
point: 'All Australians are an uneducated and unruly mob.'

Derbyshire quick Devon Malcolm, however, is keen to
point out that some Australian fans had a softer side. 'I
remember in that series an Australian came up to me and
gave me a little plaque of a British bulldog,' recalls Malcolm.
'He said to me "You got beaten, but you always gave one
hundred per cent, and we appreciate that." That meant a lot
to me. I've still got it, on the dashboard of my truck. I never
had a problem with the Australian fans. There would be the
odd comment when you were fielding on the boundary, but
what I found was that they liked hard cricket and they liked
players who gave their all. I had a good rapport with them,
I charged in ball after ball, gave a hundred per cent and I
played with a smile on my face, even when things weren't
going too well. Which, on that tour, was a lot of the time.'

Not surprisingly given his treatment at the hands of some
sections of the Aussie support, Tufnell was thrilled to now
have this raucous army of England supporters fighting his
corner up in the stands. 'England have always had good
travelling support all round the world,' says Tufnell, 'but the
first time I really became aware of this new phenomenon
was during a one-day game in Sydney before Christmas,
when The Hill was still there. I don't know whether it was
necessarily the Barmy Army but we had a fantastic game and
fantastic support. There were rows of Union flags flying,

people chanting and singing, and there was a sense it had become more unified. On previous tours there had been pockets of people, but in '94–'95 it became a bit more under one banner.'

The buccaneering Slater was out shortly before the close of play on day one, dismissed by the part-time seam of Graham Gooch for 176, and Australia were 329 for four at stumps. But while England's players had melted on that first day, their hardcore fans had begun to glow in the Brisbane furnace – and not just their foreheads. Peacock explains: 'A guy called Monty had been to the World Cup in 1992 and had done a song, "Ball and Chain", which went:

We came with backpacks, you with ball and chain,
    ball and chain.
We came here with backpacks, you with ball and
    chain.'

Hardly Noël Coward, but likely to wind up the Aussies all the same. 'So we sparked that up, us and some lads in Nottingham Forest shirts, and we walked past the Aussie fans on the Brisbane Hill, dragging our feet as if we were in balls and chains. When we got back to the tea bar, the pocket of England fans, there were probably only about forty at this point, gave us a standing ovation.'

'There's a lot to be said for making fun of someone rather than getting verbally or physically aggressive,' says

Burnham, 'because the only way they can really beat you is by coming back with something funnier or wittier. And the best thing is, the Aussies were incapable of doing so. By the end of the tour Dave was standing up and waving a twenty-dollar or fifty-dollar note at them and offering them as a prize to any Aussie who could come up with something original and funny. I don't remember there being any winners. On that day the locals were throwing stuff at us, pouring beer over us, but we just kept giving more banter back, we were completely undeterred.' And what did the Gabba's locals eventually hit back with, besides lukewarm Tooheys? 'They basically had two songs: "Aussie Aussie Aussie, Oi Oi Oi!" and "Pommies take it up the arse, do dah, do dah".' Compared to the natives, the England fans sounded like quick-witted members of the Westminster Cathedral Choir.

Shane Warne took eight for 71 in England's second innings as the hosts ran out winners by 184 runs. But the contrast between Australia's comprehensive victory and the effusiveness of the England fans had set a precedent: the Barmy Army now existed in embryonic form.

'From "Ball and Chain", other songs developed,' says Peacock. 'I quickly got the nickname "The General" and even at Brisbane during the early part of the tour, local journalists were asking how and why we were travelling, because they knew as early as that that this was a poor England team. And once we'd developed some sort of identity, everyone

started to group up at the tea bar every day and a few more songs, mainly football ones, would start up.'

As well as generic Aussie-baiting, that first Test saw the singling out of individual players, with fast bowler Craig McDermott given a shellacking. 'He took six wickets in our first innings, but in the second innings he bowled loads of no-balls, so he was absolutely ripe for abuse and got a battering from the England contingent,' says Peacock. 'So pretty much all the facets of what would become the Barmy Army style of support were already in place in Brisbane – patriotic songs, songs about Australia, songs about specific players, drinking beer in the sun, meeting new people, and having a huge amount of fun.'

There followed six warm-up matches before the second Test in Melbourne, plenty of time for 'The General', 'Leafy' and Co. to conscript more recruits and add to the repertoire. 'From three at Brisbane, to the second Test in Melbourne there were about a hundred people singing songs,' says Burnham. 'Everywhere we went we wanted to sing songs. We were on holiday, we were in that mindset, and the more time we spent together the more old tunes were recycled. Gradually we brought in words more appropriate to the cricket, so that songs that had perhaps originated on the football terraces became part of the cricket atmosphere. We just had so much more time than at football, seven-odd hours of five days in a row, so songs would develop, we'd sing them in the pub in the evenings and then bring them along to the game the next day.'

'Basically, England were crap,' says Barmy Army veteran Ian Golden. 'Every run on that tour was a celebration, every England century a victory, all we had was our sense of humour – something the Aussies were seriously lacking. We had a ditty on that tour:

'We never win at home and we never win away,
We lost last week and we'll lose again today,
We don't give a fuck 'cos we're all pissed up,
England Cricket Club, OK.

That pretty much summed up that tour.'

Adds Peacock: 'We parked ourselves very close to Bay Thirteen [the area in the Melbourne Cricket Ground where the rowdiest Aussie fans traditionally congregate] and as things started to go to shit in the Test match, we started singing West Coast Eagles songs because they had beaten Melbourne teams in recent Aussie Rules Grand Finals [the Eagles had become the first non-Victoria team to win the AFL premiership in 1992 and repeated the feat in 1994]. The MCG was the home of Aussie Rules, and we had the front to go in the middle of their bay with our songs and flags. I remember Sergeant Read, who was the copper in charge, making life quite difficult because, although there was no trouble whatsoever, we were a new phenomenon in Australia and the locals didn't quite know what to make of us.'

'The reason one man despises the Barmy Army is the very reason another embraces it,' explains Scott Heinrich, editor of the Fox Sports website in Australia. 'It is so completely different to what we are used to in Australia. Do a straw poll among fans in Australia and different people might describe the Barmy Army as annoying, distracting and arrogant – though probably well-meaning. When the Aussies saw the Barmy Army launching into "Who we are, where we come from" for the twenty-ninth time, most regarded it as an unwanted distraction, a vestige of what they saw as the terrace hooliganism that apparently marked British soccer in the 1980s.

'That's not to say Aussie crowds are well-behaved. Ask Muttiah Muralitharan, Harbhajan Singh or Monty Panesar [all of whom have been singled out for racist abuse down the years] for proof of that, but the idiotic few are the exception to the rule. And that unwritten Aussie rule is that you go to the game to watch the game. Sure you cheer, sure you talk about it with your pals, sure you have a beer, but you don't hunt in packs, you don't wear your team's footy strip as a statement of identity and you don't break into song every five minutes. And you most certainly don't sing about yourself. Half a dozen tinnies, a Mexican wave and the odd rendition of "Oi, Oi Oi" is about as wild as most get. Australian sport lovers see themselves as voyeurs, not participants. Streakers aside, of course.'

Alongside the Aussie-baiting standards ('Captain Cook only stopped for a shit' and 'If you've all shagged an Aussie clap your hands' are considered classics of the genre) sprang up songs tailored to individual players, with the rampant Warne inevitably bearing the brunt. In more recent Ashes series, Ricky Ponting would also come to recognise that a verbal coating from the Barmy Army was the ultimate mark of respect.

'Warne has had more songs written about him than any other player, because he's just so good,' says Burnham. Adds Peacock: 'Let's just say he didn't get the respect back then that he got at The Oval in his last Test in England, when we all sang "We wish you were English" to him. At the time he was a young, talented bowler who was taking loads of English wickets. But you know what? Most of the songs just weren't that funny back then.' The *Melbourne Age* recorded that on day four there were 'maybe a hundred lads, bouncing and chanting to a conga rhythm, fists punching the air, hips swinging, singing: "Shane Warne's got no wickets, Shane Warne's got no wickets, la la la la ..."' On day five, Warne took a hat-trick, England were skittled for 92 and Australia triumphed by 295 runs.

Adam Carroll, or 'Streaky' as he is known to his friends, sums up the feelings of most England fans when it comes to Warne, the bogeyman they could not help falling in love with. 'Warne had the Indian sign over us,' says Carroll. 'He was pretty much at his peak then, he'd run through us in the second innings at Brisbane and you just knew that when he really wanted to turn it on, when his team really needed him, he was always going to be there. But he was a good bloke as well. He took a lot of stick from us, but he'd played cricket in England as a kid, got to know the English way and he knew it shouldn't be taken personally.

'So there were always mixed feelings when it came to "Warney". He was a wonderful player and it's great to be able to say "I saw Shane Warne play cricket and take a Test hat-trick". But we were playing so poorly and there was also a resigned feeling among some: "Is this how it's going to be for the whole tour?" I think most people had realised even at that early stage that, cricketing-wise, it was going to be a struggle.' It wasn't only the England fans who had realised this. Patrick Smith of the *Sydney Morning Herald* was scathing in his criticism of the tourists: '*Wisden* should count England wickets as half,' he wrote. With England 2–0 down and with only three Tests to come, there were already signs that the Aussies' minds were wandering.

Resigned or not, with every on-field humiliation the proto-Barmies became more focused and galvanised in their support. As well as insane, barmy, according to some dictionary definitions, can also mean 'full of yeast'. When Burnham, Peacock and Co. hit Sydney, things started frothing over. Recognising that the England fans had become a story in themselves, Peacock sought to brand the hardcore, getting two hundred T-shirts printed bearing the legend 'We came here with backpacks, you with ball and chain', replete with a Union flag and 'Ashes tour 1994–95' on the back. 'We were flogging them down O'Malleys, a backpackers-cum-pub, for twenty dollars a pop and we were selling thirty or forty of them a night,' says Peacock. 'I'd already spent most of my redundancy money, so it was just a way of keeping the finances ticking over.' With hundreds of new recruits joining every day, Peacock was soon back in the black.

'Sydney was ten times as big as Melbourne, and that's when it really took off and we started getting media attention,' says Burnham. 'We were all able to get together on the Sydney Hill, which made us more noticeable. The smaller groups who had been making up their own songs were now able to join together and the singing and chanting was relentless. England played well, Darren Gough got his famous fifty before lunch [on day two], and then took six for 49 in Australia's first innings. It was felt that Australia were fortunate to end up being saved by bad light, salvaging a draw.'

England's improved display in Sydney provided their fans with the opportunity to sing about their own players for once, with Yorkshire's irrepressible paceman Gough the recipient of much love from the travelling faithful. Burnham says: 'It wasn't all anti-Australian, we also had songs to encourage the England players. One I remember, sung to the tune of "Lily the Pink", is:

'We'll drink a drink a drink,
To Goughie the King the King the King.
He's the saviour of our cricket team,

He's the greatest cricketer
That the world has ever seen.

Darren Gough was the first hero of the Barmy Army, and the Aussies also loved him, he's probably the only England player they would have wanted in their team.'

Tufnell, who had actually had a fair bit of success in the first two Tests, bagging nine Australia wickets, was a folk hero for the England fans. Variously described in the media as a larrikin, a rogue and a rascal, Tufnell made no attempt to alter their perception of him: he loved a drink, he loved a fag, and if he hadn't been good enough to play for England, he probably would have been up in the stands singing and chanting with the Barmies.

'The songs kept us going,' says Tufnell. 'You'd be standing there at four thirty in the afternoon and they'd be 300 for two or something and all of a sudden you'd hear "Everywhere we go", and instead of standing there with your soul in your boots you'd be thinking, "Come on then, boys, keep going, keep going, they're keeping it going, we've got to keep it going and try to get a couple out." The MCG can be a bit of a lonely place when the Aussie batsmen are on top so it's always nice to have a bit of your own stuff going on in the crowd, it was great to have them.' And does Tufnell remember any songs specifically penned for him? 'They did have one, something along the lines of: "Phil Tufnell's having a party, bring some spliff and a bottle of Bacardi ...'''

Malcolm, who had taken only one wicket in Melbourne after replacing Martin McCague, agrees. 'You'd be out in the field at the MCG, with eighty thousand people up in the stands, but it was lonely at times,' he says. 'There were times when we might have been forgiven for slipping into a little bit of a depression when things weren't going too well, but the Barmy Army always kept us cheerful. All of a sudden you'd look up and see them cheering you on and that would keep you going.'

While England's performance at the Sydney Cricket Ground was laudable, the fact remained the tourists were staring down the barrel with two Tests to play. Even most of the English press had already given up hope. Martin Johnson, then of the *Independent*, wrote of the catalogue of woes afflicting Mike Atherton's team, compiling two lists: Missing in Action (i.e. been ruled out of games) and Wounded But Fit for Duty. 'List 1: Atherton (bad back), Stewart (broken finger, twice), Thorpe (groin, hamstring, dehydration), Crawley (calf), White (side muscle, tour over), DeFreitas (calf, hamstring, groin, you name it), Gough (hamstring, foot, tour over), Malcolm, Benjamin (both chickenpox), Udal (broken thumb), McCague (shin fractures, tour over). List 2: Gatting (cut mouth), Hick (sciatica), Rhodes (finger), Tufnell (neck, hamstring).' Johnson added: 'England still stand a chance of becoming the only touring side in history to return with a totally different side to the one that set out, and have now consulted so many specialists that they could yet bankrupt the Test and County Cricket Board when they present their end-of-tour medical bill.'

With the series pretty much done and dusted in most people's eyes, sections of the press started truffling for stories from beyond the boundary. 'The Aussie media had got a bit fed up with how easily England were getting beaten so we became a little subplot,' explains Burnham. 'They found out we'd all shelled out about five grand to be there and travel around, and they just couldn't work out why all these people were spending all this money on such a poor England team. So they christened us the Barmy Army.' Peacock remembers things a little differently. 'We were already singing "Barmy Army", along with "Everywhere we go", which were both old football songs. Even at Melbourne we were all singing "Barmy Army" incessantly and jumping around, like we were on the football terraces back home, and the Aussie media picked up on it.'

Football fans had indeed been belting out 'Barmy Army' all over English grounds for many years before the chant became a brand. There was even a short-lived band in the 1980s called The Barmy Army, who released one themed album, loosely based on football, called *The English Disease*. But Burnham is strictly correct in that it was the Aussie media who picked up on the chant and turned it into a label.

It is doubtful the *Daily Mail*'s sportswriter Ian Wooldridge was *au fait* with the English dub scene, but he would have thought the title of the Barmy Army's album highly appropriate. 'Wooldridge didn't like what he saw,' says Peacock. 'He saw a group of fans standing around in football tops singing songs and pointing. He wrote what turned out to be a fantastic article about us, suggesting that we should all be gassed. It was laughable, we were just having a brilliant time.

Adds Adam Carroll: 'The British press decided early on that we were football hooligans who happened to be following the cricket. But it was the other way round – we were cricketing people who happened to also support football in the winter. You don't spend thousands of pounds to watch an entire tour if you don't like Test cricket. We knew that noise at cricket matches was previously unheard of, to the extent that we were doing it, anyway. It wasn't unprecedented, though, because of the bells and the whistles of the West Indian fans in England in the seventies and eighties, but it still wasn't the done thing. Even some of us in the Barmy Army, while not exactly uncomfortable with it, were thinking "how is this going to go down?" But most of it was good-natured. I vividly remember an occasion at the SCG, when we were all sitting up on The Hill and this chap in a suit walked past pushing a baby in a pram. He came past two or three times and as he went past we'd all give it a big "Sssh" and start singing "Rock-a-bye Baby".

'So our reaction when we heard about Wooldridge's article was: "Why are you saying that? We're here, we're supporting the team, the team are obviously trying to feed off it, what an awful thing to say." Obviously if someone comes out and says "I don't like what you do and I don't think it's right", fair enough. But to say we should be gassed? Come on.'

'To be honest, when the Barmy Army first started on that tour, the general impression was that these guys were bloody hooligans,' says Malcolm. 'But when you got up close to them you realised these were genuine bloody people, professional people, not hooligans at all. They were loud, yes, but they were just having a bloody good time.'

However, England fast bowler Angus Fraser, who had not played in the first two Tests but who took a five-fer in Sydney, admits some members of the England team were more enamoured of this new style of cricket fandom than others. 'I don't think every player was inspired by that type of support,' says the former Middlesex man. 'I'm pretty sure "Athers" didn't particularly warm to them because he had quite a serious cricket head on when he was captain. But others, like Alec Stewart, Graham Thorpe, Darren Gough and "Tuffers", who would be out drinking with them a lot of the time, got into them. And maybe they had more of a football background. I don't mean that snootily or anything, but they enjoyed having that football-type support, whereas others were a bit more cricket-minded in the way they felt the game should be watched and followed. Maybe they felt that the raucousness, dare I say it, wasn't quite cricket. But each to their own, and the majority were extremely positive about the Barmy Army.'

Fraser's recall is correct; England skipper Michael Atherton was largely unmoved. 'I can honestly say I didn't give the Barmy Army a lot of thought,' says Atherton. 'I didn't really think much of it, they were just supporters who had come to support the team. I never thought of the Barmy Army as any different or more special from the husband and wife who bought their tickets separately and sat in the ground watching the cricket quietly. The Barmy Army were a little bit more colourful and a little bit more humorous, but they were all the same to me. There may have been a keenness from some of the players to have songs written about them, but not from me. You play for your country, you play for your team-mates and you play for the people that support you. But I wouldn't single out the Barmy Army, all the England fans demanded our gratitude.'

However, Stewart, who did not feature in the final three Tests after suffering a broken finger, was indeed an enthusiastic convert. 'I'd been aware of this new type of support back at the 1992 World Cup in New Zealand and Australia,' says the Surrey legend and lifelong Chelsea fan. 'It might not have been under the Barmy Army banner, but that's when the songs and chants started. But it was in '94–'95 that it got bigger and bigger and more organised. And what the Barmy Army weren't was just a group of football fans up for a singsong. They were people who understood the game and had a passion for the game but at the same time enjoyed all hanging out together in the ground and creating a football-style atmosphere, within a friendly environment.

'At the same time, the people you may call traditional cricket watchers offer just as much support but in a different style. Cricket is a traditional game but it's also moved forward with the times, which is great. There's room for every type of cricket fan, whether it's the group of thirty lads in their twenties who want to drink beer and have a singsong or the retired couple who have decided to spend some well-earned money to support the team. Every single supporter is highly valued and appreciated by the team. But what I will say is this: when the boys were knackered, whether we were winning or losing, knowing the Barmy Army would continue to support us was a massive boost.'

While Stewart's assertion that there is room for every type of cricket fan was a reality in that Ashes series, the truth is that the old and the new made uneasy bedfellows. During the Melbourne Test, the members' pavilion hosted members of English county teams, not all of whom were amused: this new breed professed to be fellow Brits, but as far as some of the old school were concerned, they might as well have been aliens in their midst. 'They are not cricket fans,' Roger Davidge, a sixty-four-year-old retiree from Northamptonshire, was quoted as saying in the *Melbourne Age*. 'This element follows British sport around the world. We've been banned from soccer in Europe. I make a point of sitting on the opposite end of the ground. The chanting. I don't like the chanting.'

Wooldridge's piece had caused a diplomatic incident in Melbourne. On the first day of the Test, the Australian Cricket Board (ACB) was entertaining English dignitaries when the England fans started running through their full repertoire of ditties. The English dignitaries, apparently, were horrified. In his next column, Wooldridge wrote about an alleged conversation he had with Graham Halbish, then the chief executive of the ACB. On being asked if these uncouth England fans could be evicted under any law, Halbish allegedly replied: 'I would love to see them gassed, but unfortunately that is not possible under Australian law.' Wooldridge added: 'This is a wholly politically incorrect remark and I support him. Our cricket may have been less than superlative on Monday but it was this small, banal bunch of louts in the crowd who really let our country down.' Whether it was mischief-making on the late Wooldridge's part we will never know, but Halbish strenuously denied ever making the now notorious 'gassing' remark in the first place.

Whatever Wooldridge's intentions were, his piece backfired spectacularly. 'I [Peacock] wrote a letter that I intended to go to Wooldridge and gave it to Michael Herd of the *Evening Standard*. Obviously, it never made it to Wooldridge as Herd printed it in his own paper. The headline was: "TIES OR NO TIES, THE BARMY ARMY LOVE THEIR CRICKET". So now all the other journalists started interviewing us in Sydney and we had a platform to show that we were not drunken louts, we were proper cricket fans just having the times of our lives. As for the Australian media, they couldn't believe it: "This guy in England thinks the England fans should be gassed? These guys are great." The Barmy Army became a phenomenon because of Ian Wooldridge.'

Perusal of Australian newspapers at the time tends to back up Peacock, although there were dissenting voices. Bob Millington of the *Melbourne Age* described the Barmy Army thus: 'You can always pick them out in the TV shots, poor sods: they are the blokes who have taken off their shirts to cop a good walloping of UV on their pasty torsos.' But that appears to be as negative as the coverage got. For the most part the cuttings reveal a mixture of bafflement, curiosity and amusement, and a feeling that the Barmy Army were generally a positive thing for the series and the game. 'The Poms might have been getting a caning at the wicket but on the terraces they've got what it takes,' said the *Melbourne Age*. 'The Poms have got variety: mass chants, question-and-answer routines and the bouncy, nonsensical repetition of "Barmy Army", over and over, for up to fifteen minutes at a time. By way of response "Aussie Aussie Aussie, Oi Oi Oi" is pathetically lame.' Peter Roebuck, former Somerset captain turned erudite Australian cricket writer, was an unexpected supporter: 'Nor did the Barmy Army ever lose voice or hope,' he wrote after the final day of the Sydney Test. 'Their contribution was acknowledged by the players almost every time a wicket fell. Really, it has come to something.

Australians all around were observing how loud the English are, and how much they drink. For a hundred years, it's been the other way around.'

'We were doing six or seven interviews a day with the Aussie media, we were even on the Aussie news,' says Burnham. 'They found us highly amusing: "We're stuffing the Poms, let's have a look at this lot singing all these songs about the Queen and Captain Cook." We filled in space that the England team weren't filling. It was something that was very British, that ability to laugh at ourselves, and something we should all be proud of. Meanwhile, the English press thought we were just a bunch of football fans, as you would do from a distance because of all the football shirts and the raucous nature of some of the songs. There was definitely a football feel to that first tour and there were a lot of football shirts and a lot of football chanting. And there was a rawness to it because we weren't as fine-tuned as we are today.'

'Perhaps the British press thought it was all a bit like football, because of the chants and the songs,' says Tufnell. 'I'm sure there are some people who would rather just sit in the sunshine, watch a bit of a cricket and have a snooze, but that's up to them. Everything has its place. Lord's has that sort of buzz, but I always preferred places with a bit more atmosphere, somewhere that was a bit more of a laugh, a bit more raucous.'

Peacock admits many of the Barmy Army on that tour would fit the description of the 'general sports fan', many of whom would have been at the football World Cup in the United States instead, if England had qualified. 'There was a typical England fan on that tour, mainly defined by what football team he supported,' says Peacock. 'We had Sean McGiff from Stoke City, who would always sing "Delilah", we had two lads from Spalding who were Man City fans, there was also Mark "Chopper" Randell, who was a big Tottenham fan. A lot of us had come from the football terraces, but there was never the bad side of football fandom. There were some lads who, in a different environment, might have been getting involved in football-style support: not all of them, but some of them, were a little bit naughty. There was never any animosity, though, it was more a case of "this is the best thing I've ever done in my life". There was no one squaring up to us in the pubs, the Aussies were all too bemused by us, singing our songs and having fun despite our team getting stuffed out of sight. We were loving it, it was just an unbelievable time.'

Carroll argues that the support for the England team was unswerving precisely because most of the Barmy Army came from a football background. 'I've been an Ipswich supporter all my life, and you don't continue supporting a team like that if you only want good times,' he says. 'Most of the Barmy Army supported teams from lower down the leagues. When you support a team like Ipswich you want to win, of course you do, but first and foremost it's about supporting the team through thick and thin. We got a lot of "Why are you still following them? They're crap." But it says a lot about the English character, that winning isn't the be-all and end-all.'

Burnham points out that while the Barmies made a point of keeping security and the police on side, there was a steady stream of Aussies being ejected from the SCG for behaviour deemed unacceptable. 'A lot of the Aussies would retaliate by throwing missiles and getting aggressive,' says Burnham. 'But I think they [the Australian security and police] liked us. We were capable of having a drink and having good fun without aggression, we enjoyed their company, and that was a big factor in how things have evolved down the years.'

On reflection, that the Barmies were not smashing grounds up is hardly surprising. As Burnham points out, the Barmies decked out in football shirts cannot have been that into their football because the Ashes would have taken out a great chunk of the season. Also, whereas football hooliganism had been largely a working-class pursuit, that 1994–95 Ashes tour coincided with cheaper air fares, increased spending power among the British middle classes and, subsequently, backpacking and gap years becoming the norm. All of a sudden Australia did not seem so far-flung, and certainly not for young professionals, many of them shift-workers, many between jobs and many with plenty of cash to burn. Burnham, a public school-educated son of an engineer and teacher from Sunbury, who was thirty at the time, was no more a football hooligan than Ian Wooldridge. It is just that he liked a few too many beers and a singsong, interspersed with plenty of swordsmanship.

'We almost became an 18–30 type operation,' admits Peacock. 'Once you were in town, Paul and I would be the ones organising which pub everyone would meet at, and that pub became the base from which the Barmy Army operated. Our status as minor celebrities meant that local girls often came to our parties. We felt we were like sailors coming into a port.'

If Sydney was where the Barmy Army was born, it was in the small city of Bendigo, Victoria, where the officers and rank and file discovered exactly how big their baby had become in such a short space of time. 'There was just so much cricket on that tour,' explains Peacock. 'There were State games, one-day games, games against Aussie "A", games against Aussie students. We were travelling back and forth between New South Wales and Victoria so often that in the end Firefly, the bus company, were giving us free tickets.

'On one particular occasion, England were playing Victoria in a friendly in between the third and fourth Tests. About fifteen of us all stayed in the same hostel and when we went to the game there was an unbelievable media presence, because our profile had been building so dramatically after the Sydney Test, the local paper did a three-page feature on us: "The Barmy Army comes to Bendigo". We were presented to the crowd during lunch on one day, the bouncers at the nightclub would call us to the front of the queue, and we got drinks bought for us; it was just incredible to get that kind of welcome. After the game we were in the local pub and we were chatting to Aussie players Dean Jones and Paul Reiffel. They hadn't been involved in that particular Test series, so they were as intrigued about us as the Aussie media had been. There was a lot of camaraderie between us and the opposition players as well.'

'It was probably at this time that it became obvious the media coverage and local expectations were getting a little bit out of control,' admits Dave Woodley, who was also there from the Barmy Army's inception. 'It seemed as if the whole of Bendigo was waiting for the Barmy Army to arrive. Most of the core touring party were staying at a pub in the town called the Brian Boru, and the landlord and regulars were doing a great job of making us feel welcome. Obviously, they knew they'd probably take more in three days than they normally would in three weeks.

'During the games the local cricket club organised our own, specially roped-off Barmy Army VIP area from which to watch the game, and we ended up signing loads of autographs for the locals. They also arranged free entry and free lager from the beer tent. And if that wasn't enough, Phil Tufnell was handing out cartons of fags among the crowd.

'Towards the end of our stay, it was agreed that an Ashes pool contest would take place, a straight run of singles matches between Barmy Army members and regular punters. On the night of the competition the landlord produced a trophy to be awarded to the winners, made from the sawn-off ends of three pool cues and a cue ball, put together to look like a set of stumps being knocked over. I can't remember the exact scores, but I'm pretty sure that was one Ashes contest that we won.' Burnham puts the finishing touches to the story. 'The agreement was that the losing team would have their flag burnt out the front of the bar while singing the other country's national anthem, so it was that all the Aussies stood around a burning Aussie flag singing God Save the Queen.'

While the Bendigo welcome was further proof that the Barmy Army had well and truly stamped itself on the public consciousness, the fourth Test in Adelaide was where it discovered its identity. 'The first time we really became aware of them was in Adelaide in 1994–95,' says BBC cricket correspondent and *Test Match Special* commentator Jonathan Agnew. 'They found a separate area for them on the grass, sponsored by Mitsubishi, and they had suddenly developed into this rather ramshackle, but recognisable, body, by now identified by Barmy Army T-shirts. Pre-Barmy Army, England fans did their own thing. There have always been backpackers and travellers, but as far as organised tours were concerned they were all in that middle market until the Barmy Army came along and showed people there was an alternative way of supporting their team.'

Keen to shrug off the label of football yobs that sections of the British press had slapped on them, the Barmy hardcore had taken steps to forge an alternative image. 'We got fed up with people calling us football fans and that's when we printed off our own shirts for Adelaide,' says Burnham, who had completed a degree in recreation and business studies before travelling down under. 'They arrived on day three and we'd sold four and a half thousand shirts by the end of the next Test in Perth. That's when things started getting big and we started taking ourselves seriously.'

Tim Knight still runs T-Shirt City in Adelaide and vividly remembers the day Burnham turned up in his shop and ordered the first hundred shirts. 'The first thing he said to me was: "We need some shirts, mate, I've got a few friends over following the cricket,"' says Knight. 'But it was a phenomenon, we had to bring five or six people in to work through the night. I admired the way these few guys took this small idea and made it into something so big. What they pulled off in that one week was an amazing feat.

'When they first walked in that day I thought, "These guys are just so fanatical." They just seemed so determined that they were going to personally turn English cricket around: it was a case of, "Hey guys, we want to win, we want to make things happen." I'd heard how fanatical the English soccer and rugby fans could be, but cricket had never been supported in this way, in terms of the songs and chants and the determination they put in. England now have a pretty special side, and I think that's in part down to the fact the Barmy Army have demanded they reach those levels.'

Burnham's assertion that the Barmy Army got 'serious' in Adelaide might send shivers down the spines of those who like their fun and jollity to be spontaneous and unprescribed, but Peacock maintains the organisational hand was a deft one. 'The level of organisation was pretty informal back then, but it was no different to what we do today,' he says. 'What worked in 1994 is the same as what worked on the Ashes tour in 2010. We had a base in every city, we had a party in the evening, we had the T-shirts. When you're on tour, you just want to be in a pub with your mates having a laugh. We formalised what we did as that '94–'95 tour went on, but what we did back then is pretty much what we do today.'

Burnham agrees, and also thinks the variation and quality of songs is what made 2010–11 so positive for the Barmy Army. Coincidence or not, '94–'95 England pulled off a stunning victory in Adelaide. Gatting scored a ton in England's first innings before debutant Australian Greg Blewett notched an unbeaten century to give his side a healthy first innings lead. At the end of day four England were 220 for six and the following day the *Adelaide Advertiser* went with the headline: 'AUSSIES POISED FOR THE KILL'. 'If there was going to be a winner you would have expected it to be Australia,' says Carroll. 'We were six down in the second innings at the start of play, but DeFreitas came out and started slapping them about in the morning [he made 88, his highest score in Tests], Malcolm and Chris Lewis bundled Australia out for 156 and we ended up winning by

106 runs. So the *Adelaide Advertiser* got it slightly wrong.'

'I'd like to think that our support did help in Adelaide, with the players knowing that we were there cheering them on,' says Burnham. 'We got a blast out of Malcolm [the paceman took four for 39 in Australia's second dig, including a spell of three for 13] and Tufnell took an amazing catch on the boundary and came running over to us on the Adelaide Hill, just as Graeme Swann did when we sealed the Ashes in Adelaide fifteen years later. That Test match set the tone for the future. We knew after that that if we got it right, we'd help the boys and we've had regular feedback from players ever since that day to support us and our efforts – and we've never been a good enough cricket side to turn down any extra encouragement, even if it's only one per cent.' The mercurial Malcolm, who could be lethal one day, lamentable the next, was certainly grateful. 'The Barmy Army definitely lifted me that day,' says Malcolm. 'They put an extra yard of pace on me, make no mistake. If the players could have lifted our games as much as the Barmy Army did, maybe we would have competed on a more regular basis.'

Unsurprisingly, Tufnell, not noted for his spectacular fielding, remembers that catch to dismiss Michael Slater well. 'Slater had gone for the hook, the ball just kind of stuck and there was a great moment when I turned round to the Barmy Army and pumped my fist and they all came rushing down,' he says. 'We had great support down there. Whether it was a contributing factor to us winning or not, I don't know. But it was lovely to know that even though we hadn't been doing so well before then, everyone was still turning up, everyone was still following us around.

'There was a little bit of bafflement among the players at the level of support, but that's what us Brits do, isn't it? We like travelling around, we like a party, we like enjoying ourselves. The Australia supporters and the Australia players couldn't believe it. They were thinking, "Bloody hell, how do we shut these blokes up? We keep beating them and they keep coming back for more." We always felt a little bit disappointed for them, because when I went down there, we came across very good Australia sides and we didn't play particularly well. But the England fans were always there for us. And when we did put in a performance and manage to win a Test match here and there, it made it even sweeter. We sort of thought to ourselves, "We're trying to pay you lot back a little bit." That's the way I thought about it, anyway.'

While the Barmy Army had anointed him their leader and the T-shirts bore his name, Atherton did not share Tufnell's view. 'I never really thought of it as us owing them anything,' says Atherton. 'It's a wonderful thing to do, follow your team around a nice place like Australia, particularly back then, when it was about three dollars to the pound. It was tough, but we weren't getting flattened 5–0, the games were competitive in their way, albeit we never came close to winning a series. That said, it was great to see the reaction when we did win a game. I remember that catch from Tuffers, with the

Barmy Army massed behind him, and their reaction which was fantastic. And then back at the hotel, there were hundreds of supporters. It was special to have that kind of support.'

'Adelaide was amazing,' says Peacock, who laid $20 on an England win before the start of the final day's play at odds of 10–1. 'Phil DeFreitas smashed eighty-eight on the last morning and I'll never forget Devon Malcolm getting Steve Waugh first ball. When Tufnell took that catch, there was a football-style terrace bundle and we all ended up spilling over the advertising hoardings. And when Malcolm took their final wicket we all steamed on to the pitch, like when your football team get promoted. Alec Stewart beckoned down to me and "Chopper" and we were led through the members' area, through the players' dressing room and on to the balcony. Singing songs arm in arm with Stewart and Neil Fairbrother for the Barmy Army below, songs we'd been singing all tour – that's probably the highlight of my sporting career. And that's when the bond between the Barmy Army and the players was cemented.'

Far from being appalled by the Barmies' celebrations, the local press were enthralled. 'The Barmy Army more than compensates for skipper Michael Atherton's public poker face,' said the *Adelaide Advertiser.* 'In other circumstances, the Barmy Army would be characterised as "lager louts". Maybe it's the civilising influence of cricket, maybe it's just us as charming hosts, but the Barmy Army has been a slightly dishevelled credit to itself and has added colour and interest to the series. I'd have the Barmies before the Swedish tennis fans any time. What's more, they've been so well-behaved – and I admit this is risky – I doubt even the celebrated French kick-boxer Eric Cantona would have cause for complaint.'

Indeed, the Barmy Army was generating so many column inches by this stage that there was a sense, even among some England players, that it was hogging a little too much of the limelight. 'There were times when you thought, "Is the Barmy Army becoming about itself?"' says Fraser. 'Are they here to sing about themselves and promote themselves rather than the team they're supposed to be following?' And even from the eye of the storm, Burnham could see his point. 'The Barmy Army at one stage was almost getting too big for its boots,' says Burnham. 'People were asking why people weren't writing about the England cricket team. From the point of view of the Australian media, it was because they had already written everything, which was basically how bad they thought the England team were.' We weren't going out to get press coverage; it just happened that way because there was little else for them to write about.

Despite the reservations of some in the England set-up, that evening the bond that had been formed between play-ers and fans set hard. The *Adelaide Advertiser* reported: '"Jingle bells, jingle bells, jingle all the way. Oh what fun it is to see England win away, Oh!" That was the chant which continued into the early hours of this morning as 200 members of the Barmy Army celebrated England's fourth Test win at the Adelaide Oval yesterday. The Lord Raglan Hotel in Waymouth Street was swamped by a mass of sunburnt Poms early last night, eager to soak up the atmosphere following an unexpected win.'

Included in the 'mass of sunburnt Poms' were many of the England players, every bit as delirious as their supporters at recording their first Test victory on Australian soil since 1986. Peacock recalls: 'The Lord Raglan was absolutely rammed, full to the rafters by about half past eight. It was a Monday night and the landlord didn't normally open, but we went and spoke to him and persuaded him otherwise. We bought a few copies of the *Advertiser*, with the 'AUSSIES POISED FOR THE KILL' headline, and decorated the windows. And the landlord took as much money that night as he normally would in two or three weeks, we cleaned him out. Fairbrother came in, Gatting, Steve Rhodes, Stewart, Tufnell obviously, Graham Thorpe, and it was all going off. I remember Atherton came to the door, had a look around, decided it was too noisy and went back to the team hotel. But the others stayed all night and we drank them out of everything. It was probably the best night I've ever had.'

'We had a great time after the Test match in Adelaide,' agrees Tufnell. 'Everyone came up to the old pavilion straight after the game, some of the Barmy Army came up on the balcony, and we were throwing down beers from the dressing room. In the old days, if you won a Test match, you went out and had a party with the fans.' Fraser adds: 'There was always a social element back then, and we certainly had a drink that night after the Adelaide win. The ritual was always the same: it began with several beers at the ground, then the hotel. A quick shower and change would be followed by an enquiring visit to the hotel bar, which would usually be where the party started. We would then head off to the Barmy Army's favoured watering hole. We didn't go drinking with the Barmy Army because we felt we had to. We wanted to. The players enjoyed the fun, the songs, the revelry – and the free booze. We wanted to celebrate special moments with people who it meant just as much to.'

'That Adelaide Test was one of the best times I had as an England player,' says Malcolm. 'Some of us players couldn't understand why the England fans kept on supporting us. Playing out in Australia and fielding all day in the heat was always tough, and then to add insult to injury we had the press telling us how rubbish they thought we were. But when we looked up into the stands and you'd see these guys still pulling for us, cheering and shouting when things weren't going very well, we'd look at each other and say "Jeez, this is unbelievable." And the joy on those boys' faces that we'd won a game was so beautiful to see. They were so grateful when the England team occasionally shone and put up a bit of a fight. It was great to get close to them, to see the passion in the people who had been cheering us on for five days.'

'That the players turned up that night was greatly appreciated,' says Carroll. 'I remember at one point Tufnell standing on the table singing "If you've all shagged an Aussie clap your hands", including actions, which went down fantastically. He was exactly what you expected him to be, absolutely in his element. Mike Gatting, although one of the older heads, was also getting involved. I remember him starting the "Everywhere we go" chant, forgetting the words and almost getting laughed out of the pub. I caught up with him last year at The Oval and his eyes misted over when I reminded him of that night. There was a genuine affection between the fans and the players back then, a feeling that we were all in it together.'

With the series now poised at 2–1, there was all to play for in the fifth and final Test in Perth: England could not win the series, but having been thrashed in the previous three, a come-from-behind draw would have represented something of a triumph. 'We did go mad about that win in Adelaide,' says Ian Golden. 'In Perth we were selling T-shirts saying "Victory in Adelaide, I was there". I remember one Aussie commenting to me, "One win and you lot go mad." Well, yes, we did, but why shouldn't we?'

'By now we were a media sensation,' says Peacock. 'We were on *A Current Affair*, which is a big Australian magazine show, we were the leading item. Every newspaper and every magazine wanted to talk to us. I think the Aussies liked the fact we won in Adelaide because at least now it was a competitive series.' Indeed, England's win drew applause from the unlikeliest of quarters. Australian Prime Minister John Howard, always keen to prove his blokeish credentials, commented, 'I think people were very happy to see the fight and backbone and commitment from the England team that perhaps wasn't there before.' Former Australia captain and scourge of the English Ian Chappell added: 'Thank heavens for a competitive Test match.'

The prospect of squaring the series led to a *Wacky Races*-style dash across the continent, with England fans scrambling any and all forms of transport to get them to their chosen destination. 'After the victory in Adelaide the boys were singing "Go West to the WACA", which inspired a lot of Barmies to want to get over to Perth,' says Burnham. 'A load of them went by train,' says Peacock. 'We had a real character on the train from Adelaide to Perth called "Essex Col". He had previously been a quiet member of the group until one day he shaved his head and started singing "I've got no hair but I don't care 'cos I'm from England". That was all he used to do, it became his party piece. Somehow, Denis Compton, who was in first class, invited him and some of the other lads to join him for the journey and they drank with him pretty much all the way from Adelaide to Perth. He was unbelievably kind, funny and generous to them. He loved the Barmy Army and we loved him. At the same time as Ian Wooldridge was saying these boys should be gassed, there was an England legend giving us his time and his company and enjoying our company as well.'

'There were a few eyebrows raised when we all got on the train,' says Carroll. '"Oh my God, what do we have here?" But we were all pretty well-behaved. And then when we stopped off in Kalgoorlie we had our first "Don't you know who we are?" moment in the station pub. We told them we were the Barmy Army, that our photos were in all the papers and demanded free beer. And we actually got free beer. That's how ridiculous the whole thing had become. It sounds awful, but it had reached that stage where we were thinking, "We don't have to pay for our beer any more, do you want to be known as the pub that charged the Barmy Army?"'

Gareth Evans, who had quit his job in England a few months earlier and travelled to Australia with Burnham, remembers that by the time of the Perth Test, the Barmy Army hierarchy had started believing the hype. 'The commercial aspect originally had a prosaic side,' says Evans, 'in that by Adelaide we'd run out of money and maxed out on our credit cards. We started out by buying up sets of student tickets, separating them up and selling them individually and making some money that way. And then we struck upon the idea of getting a tour T-shirt done and it suddenly went nuts at the Adelaide Test. Then we got to Perth, where anything with the Barmy Army logo on it was flying off the shelves. We sold about three thousand shirts in five days in Perth, and from having no money, suddenly we had about thirty thousand dollars sloshing around. It all got very big in a short space of time – we were buying, selling, working our nuts off, going out in the evening and having a good time and the media were heavily involved. It all got a bit crazy and we probably got a bit over-excited ourselves, because we decided to trademark the name to protect the brand. I had an old friend from university days who was a lawyer and worked in that field. I called him when he was working at Cannes for Madonna to ask him to prioritise the Barmy Army trademarking in Australia and England. So we spent probably about ten thousand dollars sorting that out as well, thinking what was going on in Australia could be replicated in the UK as well, which didn't turn out to be the case.'

Despite a ton from Graham Thorpe, who topped 400 runs in the series, England were steamrollered by a refocused Aussie side at the WACA, with Australia's bullish fast bowler Craig McDermott taking six for 38 as England were dismissed for 128 in their second innings. 'After 25 days, it was over,' wrote Roebuck in the *Sydney Morning Herald*. 'England had been outplayed once again, given another thrashing ... in some respects, the Barmy Army has helped because it has provided the sort of uncritical support needed by a losing team. English cricket is too full of egos and Clever Dicks, and service is in short supply.'

Not that the Barmies were much interested in post-mortems; they had partying to do. The England players, too, ground into the dust by a ruthless opponent over the course of four chastening months, only had lager in mind. It was the perfect marriage, and Dave Woodley tells how the bond had grown so strong that Barmies had no problem gaining access to the players' inner sanctum. 'We knew beforehand that both Mike Gatting and Graham Gooch were playing their final Tests at the WACA, so we decided we should do something to mark the occasion,' says Woodley. 'A couple of "good luck in retirement" cards were purchased, a suitably congratulatory verse was composed and written in each and both were then passed around the Barmy Army contingent to be signed. The Test finished during the morning session of the fifth day, so me and my friend Adam hatched a plan in an attempt to hand the cards to our distinguished retirees in person.

'Everyone had been allowed on to the pitch at the end of play and plenty of fans were milling around the outfield, so Adam and I took advantage of the lack of order, made for the players' tunnel and the dressing rooms beyond, all the time expecting that we would at some point be intercepted by security. However, we got lucky and quickly found ourselves sat in the corridor that ran between the two changing rooms, still holding the cards. Several players came and went and after a while we had managed to catch both "Goochie" and "Gatts" and presented them with their cards.

'At this point we assessed our situation: we were between the dressing rooms, players from both sides were milling about and no one seemed about to throw us out. So after a quick discussion we agreed that we'd stick around and see what transpired. Not long after, Alec Stewart passed by and exchanged a few words, before noting that we didn't have a beer in our hands and asking if we'd like one. Obviously we accepted and "Stewie" disappeared into the dressing room, returning shortly after with a few cans of a well-known English bitter from the team's sponsor of the time. So Adam and I got plumbed in, supping on our beers and raking over the previous few months with any player that happened to pass by. All in all it was a dream end to our first overseas tour.'

'The England players appreciated being able to have a bit of banter and a drink without any serious cricket analysis,' says Carroll. 'Gullivers Tours and such like often stayed in the same hotels as the England players, and the players would say to us, "Every night we get in the lift and someone comes up and asks for a full analysis of the day's play, and we can't be bothered with it." They were young men, like us, and like us they just wanted to have a laugh some nights. Darren Gough, for example, was just a young lad, wide-eyed and on his first England tour, like us. We didn't mob them, we just talked to them as human beings and I think they appreciated that.'

Old warhorses Gooch and Gatting did indeed retire. Gooch, who had served England magnificently, especially towards the end of his career, had cut a mournful figure on that tour, fiddling and flirting where once he would have piled right in. Gatting, whose England career peaked and troughed, at least made a match-winning hundred in Adelaide, one in the eye for those who said he should never have been picked in the first place. But he and Gooch were hirsute symbols of the past. The beaming Gough, the mischievous Tufnell, the fresh-faced Thorpe, who represented England's future, chimed with the Barmy Army age. 'The only difference was that they were good enough to play for England and we weren't,' says Peacock.

Adds Peacock: 'That last night in Perth, we organised a party in a nightclub that was underneath the hotel where the England players were staying. All of the England team, without exception, turned up. It was absolutely rammed, there were probably eight hundred people in there. The only person that wasn't let in, as I recall, was John Etheridge, cricket correspondent of the *Sun*. "Chopper" had a few choice words for him because he'd said some pretty derogatory things about the England team. "Thorpey" was standing on the bar singing "There's only one Graham Thorpe" and swallow-diving into the crowd. If I remember rightly, he signed off by walking into a glass door. Stewart was there, "Goughie" and "Tuffers", of course. Even Atherton was there. They were good lads, very approachable. They had had a long and hard tour, been unsuccessful, but they'd appreciated our devotion, which had been as loud in defeat as it had been in victory.'

'The England players were appreciative, that's for sure,' says Fraser. 'They appreciated that people could be bothered to spend their hard-earned money and come all that way to support us.' Tufnell adds: 'In those days England used to go

49

all round the bloody country, up to Ballarat, Bowral, Bendigo, all over the place, and they followed us around the whole way. So you'd see the same old faces when you jumped out of the bus and you'd say "Hello, mate, how are you?" And he'd say "Yeh, not bad, I've travelled all the bloody way up here, so make sure you bloody win," or "I'm sleeping on a bloody beach, so make sure you put in a performance." So this bond grew between us and them.'

In 1994–95, the final Test meant the end of the tour. No wearisome one-day tournaments tagged on to the end as happens nowadays, they had already got all of the short stuff out of the way. So England's chastened players headed home straight from their drubbing in Perth, to be prodded, poked and gnawed at by tut-tutting members of the British press. For most of the Barmy Army, too, the party that seemed like it would never end was over. Redundancies blown, inheritances frittered, relationships shattered, minds gone awry – it was a party that had a hell of a lot to answer for.

'By Perth, when it had all gone crazy, there wasn't a lot of time to sleep and there was a lot of money flying around,' says Gareth Evans. 'It all became pretty full-on. Over a ten-day, two-week period I was getting an hour's sleep here and there, I was just getting by on adrenaline, caffeine, and so on. I started getting pretty paranoid and I ended up in the centre of Perth one night, I'd lost all the guys and I didn't know where I was. I was a bit scared and my mind was all over the place, and all I could think was I needed someone to help me. So to get the attention of the police I went up to a sports car and kicked it a few times, to set the alarm off. The next thing a policeman comes wandering over and he obviously thought I was a lunatic and arrested me for criminal damage. By this time "Leafy" [Paul Burnham] had found me and also the owner of the car, who he bunged two thousand dollars to cover the damage. But the police decided they wanted to prosecute anyway.

'Because they thought I'd lost it completely, they kept me locked up in a cell at the police station for twenty-four hours and eventually I got transferred to a secure place where all the nutcases go. There were recovering alcoholics there, drug addicts, but I ended up with all the real nutters in the maximum security wing. When I got there they injected me with something that put me to sleep for twenty-four hours and that's when I started to get better – they decided it was largely down to lack of sleep after all. After forty-eight hours they realised I wasn't that crazy, so they transferred me to an open area and after about four or five days they decided I was fine to go to court, where I got fined two hundred bucks, something like that. It was all a pretty surreal experience. But the really weird thing was, it turned out Phil Tufnell, who had been having a bad time with his wife back in the UK, which had obviously been splashed all over the press, had flipped in Perth as well and ended up in the same place for a couple of days. That's the sort of tour it was. It was a lot of fun, but so intense it sent people half round the bend.'

'Both "Yorkshire Gav" and I met Aussie birds that final night in Perth,' recalls Golden. 'While my fling lasted a mere couple of weeks, Gav married his, had kids, got divorced, moved to Coogee and opened up a bricklaying business – not all necessarily in that order.' 'We had plenty of casualties on that tour,' says Peacock, sounding like a gnarled veteran reminiscing about a stint in Vietnam. 'Some of the guys never came home, they ended up getting married. "Worcester Mark", "Fat Sam", the Palace fan, they both got married and stayed. "Yorkshire Gav" got shacked up, although he's now divorced. But a lot of the relationships went to rot. Why? Because that holiday we were on, you couldn't top that. Hundreds of us over from England, in the pub every day and every night, travelling together from A to B, in the media spotlight, it was immense. And when ninety-nine per cent of the England fans went home and you were left with your girlfriend, suddenly things weren't quite the same. All of a sudden you were living in another country and people were calling you a Pommie bastard. When you haven't got five hundred people backing you up, singing "God Save Your Queen" or "You're just a part of our empire", it's not quite as much fun any more.'

'I don't think it's lost anything,' says Carroll, 'I think it's improved as the years have gone on. But I don't think there will ever be that intimacy or closeness that was there in '94–'95 – twenty, thirty lads spending the best part of eight weeks together, day in, day out. And we actually converted a lot of people to cricket on that tour. People came along to watch, a lot of them females who had never seen a game of cricket before, who never would have watched a game of cricket if it wasn't for us. The Aussies all realised that there was actually a lot more than a game of cricket going on. There was an atmosphere, there was banter, and there was also plenty of fun to be had. Cricket did have a stuffy image back then, and still does, but we showed it didn't have to be about sitting in silence and chomping on cucumber sandwiches, it could be much more than that. I'm immensely proud to have been part of the start of the Barmy Army, it's something that will always live with me – "Wow, I helped create that, if only by just happening to be there." It was wonderful and something I will take to my grave. And anyone who was on that tour will say the same.'

2

Teething troubles ... South Africa 1995–96

Long before the Ashes tour of 1994–95 had ended, plans were already afoot for a Barmy Army invasion of South Africa the following winter. Immediately after England's famous win in Adelaide, Peacock was quoted in the *Adelaide Advertiser* as saying: 'It has cost around $10,000 to travel with the team, so it's not cheap, but we hope to go to South Africa.'

Call it chutzpah, call it wishful thinking, call it the ramblings of a very drunk man, but the fact is, Peacock, Burnham and Co. were true to their word. 'We went back home and, on the advice of one of the players' agents, set up Barmy Army as a trademark,' says Burnham. 'Then in March Barmy Army Ltd was born. But we soon realised what we had created was a tour community and it wasn't really something that could be replicated in England at that stage. We tried to repeat the success of the previous winter with the T-shirts, we did five hundred with a map of England and the West Indies tour dates on, but we hardly sold any. By the time we got to Lord's for the second Test, we still had about four hundred and ninety-nine left. It had seemed the logical thing to do, try to recreate the Australia tour back in England, but we didn't have it sussed. People watch cricket differently in England, they turn up to watch one day usually and that's it. Plus, the TCCB [Test and County Cricket Board] certainly weren't interested in supporting us at that time, we were a bit too left-field for them, and maybe a bit too volatile.'

England drew their six-Test series with the West Indies, despite a mountain of runs from Brian Lara and the threat of the visiting quicks. Graham Gooch and Mike Gatting had both been put out to pasture after the tour down under and fresh faces such as Nick Knight, Jason Gallian, Mike Watkinson and Dominic Cork were drafted in, with varying degrees of success: Derbyshire seamer Cork and Lancashire all-rounder Watkinson were included in the squad for South Africa, Knight and Gallian were not.

In 1994, South Africa toured England for the first time since 1965 and the visit was not without incident: England skipper Mike Atherton was lucky to escape with his job after television cameras caught him apparently roughing up the ball with soil secreted in his pocket during the first Test at Lord's; then came Devon Malcolm's devastating spell of nine for 57 in the third Test at The Oval, the unpredictable paceman, a bona fide 'rabbit', having been clattered by a Fanie de Villiers bouncer in England's first innings. That series was drawn 1–1, but an ever-improving South Africa were expected to provide a sterner test on their own turf. Not that the prospect of another series defeat deterred the Barmy hardcore. 'What we found is that people got such a buzz from the tour down under that they just had to go on the next,' says Peacock, 'so a lot of the guys who were in Australia ended up in South Africa. "Chopper" went to South Africa, "Streaky", "Monty", Paul, myself, so there was a lot of continuity.'

However, not everyone shared Burnham's philosophy that formal leadership equated to more fun. And, hardly surprising when people had shelled out thousands of pounds to travel halfway across the globe, not everyone was happy to be told what they could or could not sing or generally how to behave. 'After the '94–'95 tour there were lots of football fans and expats very keen to fly the flag and it was very volatile indeed with regards to some of the singing,' says Burnham, 'and that only alienated more of the British press.' But surely the British press, hardened by their battles with the Barmy Army the previous winter, had heard it all before? Not quite. Explains Burnham: 'You can actually get away with more in South Africa than you can in Australia, the South African fans seem to have more of a stomach for it. So for example the swearing, which we tried not to do in Australia, crept in – it was a case of when in Rome, do as the Romans do.

'One of the songs on that tour was:

'Allan Donald's illegitimate,
He ain't got no birth certificate,
He's got AIDS and can't get rid of it,
He's a Springbok bastard.

'Then there was:

'Jonty Rhodes is a child molester,
He's shagged kids from Leeds to Leicester ...

'I can't remember the rest of that one, although, to be honest, the South Africans found it hilarious. But when I heard them being sung for the first time, along with football songs like "No Surrender", it just seemed over the top. But there were a lot of people saying to me, "Who the fuck are you to tell me what we can and can't sing at the cricket?" I wasn't looking to be in charge as such, I was just trying to make sure the songs we sang in the grounds had a positive effect for England and we weren't going to wind up the opposition. So there was a lot of discussion going on about the songs, a lot of politics: there would be one group wanting to sing cricket songs and there would be another group wanting to sing dodgy songs about South Africans. It was hard work, there were loads of people with energy and enthusiasm but there was no structure there.'

Peacock, however, is happy to admit he did not share

Burnham's compunction, at the time at least. 'As far as I'm concerned, the Barmy Army started out as lads on tour: we're going to have a drink, we're going to sing lads' songs, we're going to support the team and have a good time. And that Allan Donald song, we all joined in, there's no getting away from that. And I'm not going to lie to you, we thought it was funny. In hindsight, it probably wasn't, it was offensive, but that's just the way it was back then.' Burnham adds: 'Spot on! If you can't beat them, join them. I chilled out and enjoyed the tour.'

Just as there were those who objected to people attempting to orchestrate their fun, there were also England fans suspicious of the motives of the Barmy Army officers. 'There was lots of talk at the start that we were only in it to make lots of money,' says Burnham, 'there were plenty of people that didn't like it. There was a perception in those early years that all we were doing was taking people's cash, getting pissed and watching the cricket. Now, we needed to make money to run the supporters' club, but it was never a commercial thing first and foremost, it was always about maximising the support for the England cricket team. And there was an awful lot of organising, albeit it was a great job description: networking, coordinating, that sort of thing. It's fun, you've got the sun on your back, and it's better than jumping on a train commuting to London every day. So there was a bit of jealousy, and understandably so, because, and I don't mind saying it, what a great lifestyle. Sometimes I get disappointed people don't realise the amount of work that goes into it. That said, you don't necessarily want them to know you're doing much work because you don't want it to seem organised and contrived, you want people to think it's spontaneous. As indeed it is – it just helps to have the best singers sat together, which is what we did.'

The first Test at Centurion Park, situated in the Pretoria suburbs, lasted barely two days. Thunderstorms are an almost daily occurrence in the Highveld in November, but this one was biblical by any country's standards: six inches of rain fell in forty-eight hours and the Hennops River, which borders the ground, burst its banks. Matthew Engel, writing in the *Guardian*, described the weather conditions as being like 'an explosion at an ammunition dump'. The shame for England was that they had made their best start to a series abroad for four years, with Graeme Hick making an imperious 141. *Test Match Special* commentator and *Daily Telegraph* cricket correspondent Christopher Martin-Jenkins described the innings as 'Hick's best yet' for his adopted country. The situation rather summed up Hick's England career, which waxed and waned for the best part of a decade and was ultimately disappointing.

The match may have been a washout but two days was enough for the Barmy Army to get itself noticed. Wrote Engel: 'In a country which really did have a barmy army, and where the generals of it are on trial, this must cause some confusion.' Indeed it did. Tom Chesshyre, reporting for the

Sydney Morning Herald, wrote: 'South African supporters look on in utter amazement. One large Afrikaner, chuckling loudly, says: "We've never seen anything like these people. They're mad. Who are they?"'

Dave Turton was an expat Englishman in South Africa, and remembers his adopted countrymen were just as intrigued by the Barmy Army as they were by the appearance in their country of an official England team for the first time in thirty-one years. 'I, along with many other generally conservative South Africans, wondered what we were in store for,' recalls Turton. 'Everyone had been told about the Barmy Army after the tour down under the previous winter and the South African public couldn't quite get their heads round this story of beer-swilling, heavily tattooed football hooligans that they'd been sold. I must be honest, I wondered myself: Brits abroad, 25p a beer, blazing sunshine and the "Gentleman's Game". Something wasn't adding up.

'The beer-swilling bit was absolutely spot-on. Heavily tattooed? Some, not all. In fact, I formed the early feeling the "Rainbow Nation" version of the Barmy Army was going to have a lot of fun – with a couple of provisos: be warned, I thought, this is a nation full of conflicting beliefs, racial backgrounds, there's still a little tension around, so don't do anything silly or you might upset a few people and find yourself banished to Robben Island.

'Endearing yourself to South Africans normally means telling them their rugby team is untouchable, their cricket team only loses due to poor umpiring decisions, the scenery of their beloved country is like no other and that Castle lager is the best beer you have ever tasted. Well, "Leafy" [Paul Burnham] and the Army obviously didn't know about this. So just before tea on the first day of the first Test, a burly Englishman stood up in front of 10,000 people and started bellowing out the "Allan Donald's illegitimate" song, which finishes with the line "he's a Springbok BASTARD!" I was thinking, "What are they doing? This is madness! This could cause a riot!" Enter two hundred more voices ... "Jonty Rhodes is a child molester, he's shagged kids from Leeds to Leicester, he's so thick he's the village idiot, he's a Springbok BASTARD!" "Oh my God," I thought, "they're going to revoke my permanent residency" ... and then came more ... "Paul Adams is a Thalidomide, he can't bowl to save his fucking life, and he's shagging Allan Donald's wife, he's a Springbok BASTARD!" "Oh well, that's it," I thought, "my stay in South Africa has been short, but sweet." And to make things worse, my fellow countrymen by birth had made up a song that could only ever encourage Mr Donald to bowl the living daylights out of any English batsman. If people were fool enough to not think it was going to be a tough tour before then, it was sure going to get tough now.'

The Barmy Army's commitment was such that they still trooped to the ground every day, despite there being little or no chance of play. And it provided its members with a chance to become acquainted with the locals. 'After the first two days got rained off we were generally hanging around, talking to players and locals and supping a beer or three,' says Dave Woodley. 'On one of the days we were invited to join some local businessmen in their corporate hospitality box in the main stand for a beer and a chat. One of the walls inside the box had been painted white and over the previous few years had collected the signatures of pretty much every significant South African cricketer in black marker. By the time we left that box the wall had a number of Barmy Army autographs added to the collection, at the box owner's request. I repeat, it was not an act of vandalism.'

However, while the South African fans were generally welcoming, Burnham is correct in his assertion that sections of the British press were becoming more and more resentful. 'Sadly, the Test and County Cricket Board has no influence when it comes to picking their overseas supporters,' wrote Martin Johnson in the *Independent*. 'And there was depressing evidence from the electronic scoreboard yesterday – "BARMY ARMY!" it kept flashing up as the familiar band of inebriates launched into one of their mindless chants – that the South Africans regard this lot as even more cute than the Australians last summer. Then the Barmies were granted something akin to the freedom of Bendigo. Although it's a moot point as to whether the freedom of Bendigo qualifies as an honour, one can only hope that this time they get the freedom of something more appropriate. Just a suggestion, but there is an extremely large disused mining hole in the middle of Kimberley.'

One man who might have been expected to share Johnson's view was England team manager Ray Illingworth, who had a reputation as a curmudgeon, even by the standards of his native Yorkshire. However, all it took for the Barmies to get him on side was a jar of his favourite condiment. 'During the tour game against Orange Free State in Bloemfontein we were having a chat with Illingworth on the outfield, about cricketing issues and the tour in general,' says Carroll. 'You could get that sort of access to the players and management in those days. He was quite candid about issues including travel and his hatred of hotels and various player problems. But his biggest beef was the lack of mint sauce to go with his lamb. He wouldn't let it lie – "Bloody useless," he kept saying, "all you want is a bit of mint sauce with your lamb" – he went on and on and on about it. I remember looking at him and thinking, "If that's your biggest worry, then things can't be so bad."

'So we did a tour of the local supermarkets and eventually hunted some mint sauce down. The next morning we called Dominic Cork over and said, "Can you tell Ray to come down, we've got something for him." About twenty minutes later he wandered down with a look on his face as if to say "What the hell am I walking into here?" and we presented him with this jar of mint sauce on the outfield, in front of the pavilion. We had photos taken, he had a great big grin on his face, and afterwards he turned to us and said: "Knowing my luck, they probably won't serve me any more lamb for the rest of the tour." At the Durban Test, Dave "Wooders" Woodley shouted to him, "Oi Ray, what about the mint sauce?" and he chucked down one of the England shirts as a thank you.'

From Bloemfontein, the Barmy Army decamped to Johannesburg, where they would witness one of the greatest rearguard actions in Test history. Not exactly the Battle of Rorke's Drift, but as close as you can get with bats, balls and linseed oil. England skipper Mike Atherton won the toss and put South Africa in and the hosts responded to England's generosity by reaching 211 for two. However, with Cork producing some late swing and finishing with figures of five for 84, South Africa lost their last eight wickets for only 121 runs. England, however, were unable to take advantage on day two. Only the pugnacious Robin Smith provided any real resistance, the South African-born batsman making a typically gutsy 52 in England's total of 200. Even at that early stage, Martin-Jenkins was predicting that 'England are facing the probability, if not yet the cast-iron certainty, of going one down in a rubber for the sixth time in their last seven series'. Barmy Army or Masochistic Mob? Take your pick.

Brian McMillan scored 100 not out in South Africa's second innings as the hosts declared on 346 for nine, a lead of 478. At stumps on day four, England were 167 for four in their second innings – Atherton 87 not out, Smith unbeaten on 11. Martin-Jenkins wrote: 'For all Mike Atherton's indomitable excellence, Jack Russell's record of 11 catches in a Test looks like being the only thing for which England will remember their first Test in Johannesburg for 31 years.' Martin-Jenkins, who on a future England tour of South Africa would opine that the Barmy Army 'demean English cricket', had not banked on a late-night guerrilla intervention by Burnham and his boys. 'Stroh rum is probably the most potent alcoholic drink you can imagine,' explains Peacock. 'It's rocket fuel, petrol, and would send some people half mad. Anyway, we were out after that fourth day, drowning our sorrows, when in walked one of the South African players with his agent. There were these three expats in Johannesburg playing cricket and they had drunk a tray of Stroh rums between them in the bar the night before. Anyway, these boys challenged him: they said if we drank a tray of Stroh rum, he had to drink five glasses. Obviously, the player didn't think they'd do it, but they did. And so did he. That night we were four wickets down and all of us were resigned to losing, so we didn't think much of it at the time. We just thought he had been a bloody good bloke for coming out and having a few drinks with us during a Test match.'

Atherton reached his ninth Test hundred courtesy of a hook for four off the bowling of Donald. Off came the skipper's helmet, up went his arms, but surely it was a hollow triumph. Smith's departure forty-five minutes before lunch brought Jack Russell to the crease, and while England's quirky wicket-keeper had proved a nuisance to opposition bowlers plenty of times in the past, nobody expected him to last the distance. Then came the moment Barmy Army veterans still offer as proof that they were partly responsible for saving the Great Johannesburg Test. When Russell hadn't made too many, he was dropped by the very player who had been drinking the rum. Indeed, it soon appeared as though the entire side must have been drinking the potent spirit, so many catches did they drop. 'At the time we didn't think too much about it,' says Peacock, 'but as the day went on, a buzz started going around the Barmy Army: "Bloody hell, we got him on the rum last night and he dropped Jack Russell."'

Atherton and his faithful batman Russell were still there at the end: Atherton batted for almost eleven hours for his 185 not out, Russell faced 235 balls for his unbeaten 29, scoring from only fourteen of them. The Miracle of Johannesburg was complete. The match-saving partnership chimed with a set of fans imbued with a love of heroic escapes, from Dunkirk to Colditz to *Escape to Victory*. For members of the Barmy Army, Atherton and Russell, subconsciously or not, represented Churchill's 'few', holding firm against a hostile and numerically superior foe. Just as they might have seen themselves.

'There's definitely a bit of that in the British soul or the British psyche,' says Atherton, 'a glorifying or mythologising of the rearguard action. My view of England supporters is that they're pretty generous to you, even if you're losing, if you're the kind of player who shows that he cares and that you're giving your all. Not that I was aware of the crowd that day, or whenever I was batting. There were little moments, when I got to fifty or a hundred, when I raised my bat and soaked up the applause of the crowd. But then I went back into my little bubble, I was watching the ball and everything else was irrelevant.'

While Atherton may not have been consciously aware of the crowd, Devon Malcolm, who took four for 62 in South Africa's first innings, is convinced his skipper was feeding off the Barmy Army's positivity, as if by some form of osmosis. 'That was a phenomenal escape from Mike Atherton and Jack Russell,' says Malcolm. 'How did they get away with that? But what I do know is that they both took a huge amount of positive energy from the Barmy Army that day. The rest of the team was the same. We were all sat up in the changing room for the first and second sessions and nobody moved, we wanted to transmit our energy down to "Athers" and Jack Russell and the Barmy Army were doing the same. I think that day said something about the British character, that love of escapes, that determination when things are going against you.'

'Atherton is spot-on, it's the not trying that any England supporter can't stomach,' says Adam 'Streaky' Carroll, for whom the tour of South Africa would be his last as part of the Barmy Army. 'On the previous tour of Australia, we just realised we were outgunned, from the moment we opened the bowling with Martin McCague and Phil DeFreitas in the first Test at Brisbane. We knew we didn't have the best team and in that situation you just want some fight. If we'd ever got the inkling that people weren't trying, we probably would have jacked it in long before that trip to South Africa. The feeling was, we were giving it our all, can we not have something in return? We sensed early on that he wasn't that happy about it being "Atherton's Barmy Army", but we didn't worry too much about that. Although we never got a sense that Atherton had any great love for us, we loved him anyway. That day we knew we were watching a piece of history – an "I was there" moment. Usually it's not until afterwards that you think, "Cor, I saw something special there today." But we actually knew we were watching something great. That innings was Atherton at his best: gritty, determined, doing everything he could to hold the team together, which he spent most of his career trying to do.'

'There came a point when the Saffers realised we were going to get out of jail and they started leaving the ground before the close,' says Peacock. 'I remember they were leaving and we were chanting "We can see you sneaking out!" And when "Athers" and Russell saved it we all invaded the pitch, so all that was left was a few hundred England fans all singing the song from *The Great Escape*, celebrating the draw as if it was the most famous victory. I remember catching up with Jack Russell just before he went under the little cage to get into the pavilion and he thanked us for our amazing support. I just thought that was incredible: he'd batted all day, saved a Test match for England, and he still had it about him to thank the Barmy Army.' Burnham adds: 'The South African authorities had to ask us to leave the ground in the end because we were still celebrating. "Athers" acknowledged us, and he didn't always smile at or react to the fans, "Stewie" usually did the fan bit for him. But we never really begrudged "Athers" for that. It was hardly surprising, as at times he almost took on teams single-handed.'

From the Wanderers, fans and players continued the celebrations at a nearby hostelry, with Atherton to the fore. 'I was always one who enjoyed the post-Test match parties,' he says. 'We'd played hard for five days and we were going to have a few drinks afterwards. I didn't really feel that bad after that innings at the Wanderers because I was on such a high and the adrenaline was flowing. As I recall, we stayed out pretty late, I was buzzing.' Which is not exactly how the Barmies remember it. 'We were all dancing in the pub,' says Carroll, 'Alec Stewart was there drinking his white wine spritzers, and I remember "Beefy" Botham being in the pub that night and him plying Atherton with drinks. After a couple Atherton was almost on the floor. But he stuck it out, he was fully into it, even if people were having to accompany him to the loo to make sure he didn't fall over.'

While there was a smattering of female Barmies on that South African tour, the overall vibe was still determinedly macho. South Africa, it seemed, offered all the opportunities for hedonism that Australia had – and the Barmies filled their boots. Says Peacock: 'The backpackers' we were staying in, in downtown Jo'burg, there were people getting shot round the corner – I'm not sure I'd be staying there now I'm forty-four years old. But at the time we didn't really think much about it. We were on a budget, but South Africa was dirt cheap, and we were having a good time. So we were sort of blink-ered to the fact that our backpackers' had razor wire and high walls and security guards and people warning us where not to go.'

The third Test of that historic tour took place in Durban, where once again the weather wreaked havoc. Atherton took what appeared to be the curious decision of dropping Devon Malcolm and Angus Fraser for swing pair Peter Martin and Mark Ilott, two bowlers who had taken ten wickets between them in ten previous matches. But the punt paid off, England's new-look attack taking advantage of an early start and overcast conditions to reduce the hosts to 139 for five on day one before bad light stopped play. With Kingsmead doing a very good impersonation of Headingley in March, day two followed a similar pattern. South Africa were reduced to 153 for nine before lunch, with Essex left-armer Ilott taking three wickets in his first three overs, before Allan Donald and Shaun Pollock combined for a restorative last-wicket stand of 72, the highest partnership of the innings. In reply, England disintegrated to 123 for five, Donald and Craig Matthews ripping through the top order. Alas, rain allowed for only thirty minutes' play on day three while days four and five were swept away completely.

As in Australia the previous winter, although for different reasons, the Barmy Army became an integral part of the series. While in Australia the Barmies had become a phenomenon largely because of the substandard performance of the England team, in South Africa they found themselves promoted to joint top-billing because of the substandard performance of the weather. After all, you could hardly ignore a train of Santas in Union Jack capes, splashing through puddles, swigging Castle lager, banging bongos and singing 'Let's all 'ave a disco'. In response, a bank of about a hundred black South Africans at Kingsmead broke into a chorus of the traditional Zulu song 'Shosholoza'.

The Durban media loved them, even when they were chanting 'we're going to nick your sweets and lollipops' at children beating drinks cans against the advertising hoardings in time with the bowlers' steps. Barmy Army member Allan Freeman was quoted in the *Independent* as saying: 'On the grassy banks there's lots of banter, banner waving and laughing. Both sets of supporters join in generating a superb atmosphere and the local paper even offers a year's supply of beer for the best banner of the day. Yet in England we're still told it's not cricket.' One English journalist referred to the Barmy Army as 'an unwanted military unit in this disciplined country'. Perhaps he should have asked the South African players. Recalls Peacock: 'Shaun Pollock [the nephew of legendary South African batsman Graeme, who had made his Test debut at Centurion] was fielding at fine-leg and "Chopper" kept waving a bat and pen at him and calling him over. Pollock finally came over and just as he was about to sign "Chopper" went, "No, not you, can you keep it and get your uncle to sign it?" I'm not sure Pollock was too happy, but we were all obviously pissing ourselves. About ten seconds into the New Year, at a party in Cape Town, "Chopper" actually asked Pollock for his autograph for real and, good man that he is, he put pen to paper and had a laugh about the whole thing. The players got it much more than the English media did.'

While to cricket traditionalists back in England the Barmy Army continued to be the most heinous thing to happen to the game since Bodyline, the uncomfortable truth for the cucumber sandwich brigade was that, in the space of just over a year, it had almost become part of the game's establishment. Burnham and Peacock had set the Barmy Army up as a limited company following the trip down under the previous winter, and more than 10,000 T-shirts had been sold by the end of the tour of South Africa. 'The demand for the shirts was incredible,' says Peacock. 'We sold them through the individual cricket unions and had all sorts of people buying them, including South Africans, Kiwis and Aussies. Even some of the more established English guys on the traditional tours bought them.'

The Barmy Army even started organising package tours on

the trip to South Africa, the first taking in the Port Elizabeth and Cape Town Tests. Thirty people booked on to the first package, with the emphasis on budget travel and fun. Accommodation was in budget backpackers (or at least it was meant to be), transport was laid on and cricket and hedonism were mandatory. The total cost undercut some of the more established tour companies by between £500 and £1000. 'We didn't try it again until Australia 2002–03 because it was so difficult,' says Burnham. 'The people we partnered up with got the hotel accommodation wrong and naturally the guys were very upset about it. Me and Dave showed them a good time, but we ended up losing money because we were only making £50 a head. It was such a difficult thing to attempt, you have to be an expert to do it. We tried it a bit too soon.'

'We took thirty lads over and it went really well in Port Elizabeth,' says Peacock, 'but in Cape Town the travel agent had booked us into student accommodation and it was shocking. We moved them to another place in town, and at night time it turned into a knocking shop, with prostitutes and drug dealers patrolling the place and rats running round. But it was still better than the university. It was a shame because we had a great product and had brilliant accommodation in Port Elizabeth, but it went to rat shit in Cape Town. And then we lost, and I guess people are more likely to be pissed off when you've lost.'

South Africa was also where the Barmy Army's charitable

work really took off. 'We were sponsored by Mitsubishi in Perth the previous winter and raised some money for local charities there,' explains Burnham. 'We started making quite a bit of cash out of the T-shirts in South Africa and the general feeling was that it wasn't fair that we took all of it, we should be giving some of it to charity. And that's been a strategy all the way through. At the end of that South Africa tour we challenged Soweto Cricket Club to a game that was shown on three different local TV channels – there was more press out there than players at one stage. The boys all paid to play and First National Bank covered our contribution and doubled it, and I think we raised about 10,000 rand. They opened up and scored about 250 and we had a young lad called Darren Stevens, who was only about eighteen at the time but who now plays for Kent, who got half of our runs. But we still ended up something like 100 for seventeen.

'Because of the types of countries we go to it seems appropriate to give something back. Sri Lanka, Pakistan and Zimbabwe, there's a lot of poverty in these places. It's really only Australia and New Zealand where you don't see any poverty, and even there we raised money for the victims of the Bali bombings in 2005 and the Chris Cairns Cancer Appeal. We did our supporters and members a big disservice by not speaking publicly before about all their marvellous help and financial backing. Wherever we are, at home or abroad, members and supporters are always keen to raise money for charity. We've collected well over £100,000 and a large chunk of that has gone to Leukaemia Research, not least because of Sir Ian Botham's tremendous work for it. Considering the poor rap we sometimes get from the press maybe we should have been shouting about all this charitable work a lot earlier.'

The fourth Test took place in Port Elizabeth, where, despite a second innings collapse by the hosts and more fiery bowling from Cork, the game petered out into a draw. But Dave Turton, who had been swept up in the madness created by his former countrymen, recalls that even bore draws were played out amid much carnage off the field. 'There was a huge after-Test party in a place called Cagney's Action Café – hardly the sort of place the England lads would have been used to, but as good as it got in South Africa in those days. I remember Robin Smith throwing out some dreadful moves on the dance floor and, at the end of the evening, four of the more senior players, despite my protestations, decided to go wandering into the night in search of a taxi. About twenty minutes later we drove past to see them thumbing a lift. I told them to get in and asked where the other one was. I was told that he'd found some "entertainment", that he was behind the petrol station and that he "could be a while". I took them back to the hotel where they fell out of the car, left all the doors open and stumbled off – no thank-yous or anything. So I thought, "I'm not having that," ran after them and made them come back to the car, close the doors and say thank you to the lady who had been kind enough to give us a lift. It felt quite good, asking them to mind their bloody manners.

'As for the fans, the Phoenix Hotel, which was the Barmy Army HQ in Port Elizabeth, was quite possibly the dingiest place that city had to offer. Situated in an area only frequented by hookers and junkies after dark, the rooms were cheap and the beers ice cold. It was the perfect place to convene after a long day at the cricket, so the Barmy Army took over and have done on every tour since. The walls of that particular hostelry have many stories to tell.'

Then came the final Test in Cape Town, which Robert Winder in the *Independent* described as looking like 'a fanfare to little England in the land of the palm-tree sunshine'. Winder continued: 'The Barmy Army yomped to the Cape with their banners, and Newlands was draped with touching tributes to faraway places: Preston, Hornsley, Buxton, Stevenage, Redcar, the Builders' Arms and, of course, Manchester United. Someone even waved a flag for Cambridge University – perhaps the skipper had friends in town.' However, the brave souls of Preston, Hornsley and Buxton, many of whom had flown in especially for the climax of the series, were to be sorely disappointed.

Atherton got a duck as Donald tore through England's first innings, taking five for 46 in the tourists' total of 153. 'Someone had stolen a life-size cardboard cut-out of Allan Donald in full flight from a local bank at the start of the tour,' says Dave Turton. 'Allan stayed with the lads for the entire tour, until the final Test in Cape Town, when he was set fire to.' But England were still in the game when their seam attack reduced the hosts to 171 for nine on day two, only for Dave Richardson (54 not out) and South African cricket's new poster boy Paul Adams (29) to put on 73 for the last wicket and give their side a first-innings lead of 91. Then came a crazy third day, when England threw away the series in the blink of an eye: four wickets were lost for two runs as Pollock ripped out the heart of Atherton's team, proof, if further proof were needed, that there was no more brittle team in world cricket than England, especially on the road. In a memorable postscript, Illingworth announced during his turn at the mic that his boys would be playing a hastily arranged day-nighter in Western Province the following day. 'Atherton looked absolutely livid,' says Peacock. 'We weren't exactly over the moon either. We all went up there the next day and we lost that game, too.'

For Devon Malcolm it had been a tour of attrition, on and off the field. The Derbyshire quick had always had a rough-hewn action, and when the mood took him and the confidence was high, it was an action that could cause devastation, as at The Oval in 1994. However, Illingworth and bowling coach Peter Lever wanted to tether Malcolm's raw pace to greater consistency, tinkering with his technique before and during the tour of South Africa. Malcolm, however, claimed the alterations resulted in a loss of pace and added pressure on his recently healed knee, and he therefore dispensed with them, to the management's chagrin.

'All I wanted to do was go out there and do what I'd done to the South Africans at The Oval in 1994,' says Malcolm. 'I knew I had the upper hand. But I had this disagreement with the management and I was very low on that tour, totally embarrassed, the confidence was on the ground. Even in the final Test match at Cape Town, the players in the changing room were saying to me, "Why didn't you give them [the England managers] a slap?" But that would have made me the bad man. Some people would have packed up and left, but I looked around and thought, "There are people out here who have been through a hell of a lot during the apartheid period, far worse than I had. These are people who stand up and fight, they don't give up." And, of course, I had the Barmy Army behind me as well. They stayed supportive, they knew what had been done to me was wrong. They kept telling me they thought it was terrible the way I had been treated and that gave me the strength to hang on.'

Malcolm certainly cut a confident, and dashing, figure with the local white population, who were astonished to see a black man stepping out in a tuxedo following the Johannesburg Test. 'That was just totally unheard of in South Africa,' says Dave Turton. 'All eyes were on Big Dev as he arrived at a local nightclub dressed like he was ready for a night out in the West End and proceeded to sip from a champagne flute. It was hilarious to watch the locals, the Afrikaners were in awe, and that is something I have never seen them be. That was great swagger from the big man, despite everything that was going on behind the scenes.'

'After the final Test I was walking across the ground and I heard "Dev! Dev!", and I looked round and you know who it was? Desmond Tutu! And he shook my hand and said "What a great man you are!" And I thought, where has this come from? But it was support like that that I got my faith and control from. There were only a couple of negative guys, everywhere around me there were positives – the South African fans, the Barmy Army, even Desmond Tutu. And you know what? I'm glad I kept my cool.'

3

Organised chaos ... Australia 1998–99

England went into the 1998–99 Ashes off the back of their first victory in a five-Test series for twelve years against a strong South Africa side the previous summer. But that did not mean anyone gave them a chance against Australia down under. Only one side – the West Indies – had won a series in Australia since England in 1986–87, and Aussie skipper Mark Taylor announced on series' eve that his side was 'at its peak'.

'Unless Shane Warne, Glenn McGrath and Jason Gillespie are all missing for the series, Australia will win comfortably,' said former Aussie skipper and perennial English-baiter Ian Chappell. Wrote Scyld Berry in the *Sunday Telegraph*: 'Even if every England player rises to the occasion – and Australia always exposes the character and cricket of at least one tourist – an England series win remains by far the least likely outcome. At the crunch Australia will have keen eyes on the prize, while England are all likely to be content with the knowledge that they have competed.'

Even the Barmy Army commander-in-chief expected little, which is never a great sign. 'There was quite a lot of optimism from some of the England fans because we'd managed to nick a couple of games in the 1997 series at home,' says Paul Burnham. 'And on paper they looked like closely matched teams. But Chappell was right, if they had only one of McGrath and Warne in their team, we were in trouble. They were two of the greatest players ever. If they played on song, we didn't have a chance, it was as simple as that, they were complete gods. So there was a realisation among most that if those two performed – and they pretty much always performed – that was pretty much that.'

As it happened, McGrath, Gillespie and Warne were all struggling with injuries going into that series – but, as ever, so were a host of England players. Senior batsmen Alec Stewart, Graham Thorpe and Michael Atherton were all dealing with niggles, while Surrey left-hander Mark Butcher ducked into a ball in a warm-up game at Perth and needed ten stitches above his eye. However, when Thorpe (223 not out) and Mark Ramprakash (140 not out) put on an unbeaten stand of 377 against South Australia, the highest partnership by any touring team in Australia in 136 years, it was cause for some optimism. Just don't mention the dropped catches and the iffy bowling, although the Aussie fans obviously did. Wrote Atherton in his column for the

Daily Telegraph: '"Bring back Tuffers, mate, he can bowl quicker,"' offered a wag from the Hill as Angus Fraser ran in to bowl on a "flattie" at Adelaide. I knew then that we were back in Australia with all its attendant delights.'

Numbers of England fans were significantly down on the previous Ashes trip in 1994–95, with the recent Caribbean tour, which had finished only six months before, and five Ashes defeats on the trot offered up as reasons. However, Vic Sowunmi, who had been recruited as Burnham's batman for '98–'99, bore no mental scars, seeing as he had no interest in cricket at all before that tour. 'Me and Paul went to uni together, he's always been cricket mad and bored me to tears about cricket this, cricket that,' says Vic. 'He announced he was going off to Australia and said "Why don't you come over and help me out for a few months?" I didn't always know what was going on – I didn't know what fine-leg or silly point was, for example. But in Australia it's such an everyman sport, it changed my perception of the game. I soon realised it was all about the whole show – you didn't have to watch every ball, there was a lot of banter in the crowd, and I never thought cricket could be like that. I enjoyed the atmosphere, the camaraderie, the songs and generally watching the Aussies get wound up. But most of all I enjoyed everyone being united. Over there as a black guy, it made me feel more British.'

Sowunmi was part of the Barmy Army commercial arm on that tour, selling T-shirts and other merchandise. And while the method was very Del Boy at times, the numbers were anything but. 'Paul said it would be a bit mental, but I didn't really know what he meant,' said Sowunmi. 'I just thought I'd be selling a few T-shirts and watching the cricket, but it was absolute chaos. We turned up in Brisbane and they had about a hundred boxes containing about five thousand shirts. We spent a lot of time wheeling and dealing out of suitcases, we were permanently being moved on, but for that reason it was also pretty exciting. In Adelaide, we organised a party in the Adelaide Gaol, and I was a walking flyer: I had my body painted on the front with a Union Jack and Barmy Army and "Party at Adelaide Gaol" written across my back. We were selling hundreds of T-shirts a day, "Leafy" [Burnham] must have had headaches trying to count the money. Everyone wanted one. I remember at Adelaide one of the umpires sent his wife over to buy one, because obviously he couldn't do it himself, and in Melbourne a driver stopped his tram and called us over to buy one, and none of his passengers seemed to mind.'

Sowunmi's other job was to keep Burnham, who would become so consumed by his role that he would forget to eat for entire days, out of harm's way. '"Leafy" would spend the whole time organising things,' says he, 'whether it was where to go for a drink at lunchtime or piss-ups after every day's play. That's all it was for three months, and I was quite glad when it was over, I lost a lot of brain cells and stomach lining in that time. I don't know how "Leafy" did it, he was under so much pressure. There were always people wanting to know this, that and the other, he was very stressed, wouldn't be sleeping for days. He was doing TV and radio interviews, and all the while getting smashed every day and night. Added to that, he was also a bit of a ladies' man, especially once he got a drink inside him. You could use the word insatiable. It must have been very difficult trying to be the heart and soul of the party all day and all night and trying to effectively run a business at the same time. So I was there to keep Paul on the straight and narrow a little bit, make sure he ate, make sure he didn't drink too much and got some exercise, sweated out some of the toxins and prepared for the next session.'

While McGrath was fit for the first Test in Brisbane, Warne and Gillespie failed to make it, with Warne announcing he was unlikely to be ready for the second Test either. For Alec Stewart's England, it was a huge psychological fillip. 'Without one of their two great match-winning bowlers, Shane Warne, for at least the first two Tests,' wrote the *Telegraph*'s Christopher Martin-Jenkins, 'they are vulnerable.' Not that Australia appeared too vulnerable on day one at the Gabba. Wrote Ian Chappell in the *Telegraph*: 'The Australians have heard much about the way this England team have improved but after seeing the way they performed in the last session at the Gabba, they could be forgiven for thinking: "What has really changed?"' Taylor, playing his 100th Test, won the toss and chose to bat, before England's bowlers made early inroads into Australia's batting, reducing the hosts to 178 for five. But Steve Waugh and Ian Healy, two of the grittiest whelks in Australia's order, combined to take their side to 246 for five at the close. On day two, both men made centuries as Australia took the game away from England with a first innings total of 485. Left-arm seamer Alan Mullally, who had grown up in Western Australia and played for Australia Under-19s, finished with figures of five for 105, but he had had to bowl forty overs to do so. And England had been woeful in the field.

Not that Barmy Army virgin Luke Jarvis minded – he hadn't been watching half of it. For Jarvis, over from Essex with two old schoolmates and for whom that Brisbane Test was his first following England abroad, that opening day had been a mind-bending introduction to the Barmy Army.

'It was 19 November 1998 when I arrived at the Brisbane Backpackers' Hostel, the day before the first Test kicked off,' recalls Jarvis. 'As soon as we had dumped our bags we hit the makeshift bar, where you could buy a slab of beer for $10, and started the inevitable small talk.

'It soon became clear that above the massed ranks there was a Barmy Army hierarchy. One or two could be heard proudly announcing they knew "The General", while others spoke of their Barmy Army battle scars with pride, telling stories of previous tours (the tour to South Africa the previous winter sounded brutal).

'On the walk to the ground the next day I thought the excitement was immeasurable, the Gabba is at capacity and we are ready to go … the rest of it is a blur. I know the singing started after about the second beer and the song repertoire will stay with me forever. Standing next to me was a bloke who started a rousing rendition of "Come play my game, psychosomatic Nasser Hussain", to the tune of The Prodigy's "Breathe". His mate then quickly followed up with an equally committed performance of

'His name is Super Gus Fraser,
He's sharp as a razor,
He bowls right-arm fast for England.
When he walks down the street,
All the people he meets say,
"Hey, Big Man, what's your name?"

And repeat. Amid all of the slightly more spontaneous songs there was of course the permanent war cry of "Alec Stewart's Barmy Army", the anthem for the tour.

'By the mid-point of the final session I had missed every wicket and almost every boundary. I had completely lost my voice. I had also spent the last twenty minutes singing a song about tins of salmon from Tesco. The highlight of the entire day however was just around the corner.

'The entire Barmy Army collective blew a gasket when darts player Bobby George was hoisted above someone's shoulders to lead us all in a song. With a beaming grin on his face, arms widespread and with a beer in one hand, he led thousands of us in singing "God Save YOUR Queen" to the Aussie supporters.'

On day three, Butcher, who had made nine runs from five previous innings in Australia, fired a splendid hundred and Nasser Hussain made a fighting half-century as England showed their opponents they were at least in a game. But on day four it was a case of same old, same old. While Australia's last five wickets put on 307 runs, England's managed just 60, and it was McGrath, who finished with six for 85, who did most of the damage. Michael Slater thundered a century in Australia's second innings before Taylor made a generous declaration, setting England a target of 348 from a minimum of ninety-nine overs.

On day five, England were reduced to 179 for six when Armageddon arrived twenty minutes before tea. England, who were being mauled, had been saved. 'That was the most amazing draw of all time,' says Burnham. 'They set us some ludicrous target [no side had scored more runs to win a game in Australia] and got us six down when the rain came in. We celebrated it like a win, mud-sliding down the hills, singing the theme from *The Great Escape*, it was unbelievable. We're very good at that, celebrating improbable draws like famous wins.' Still, the match had lasted long enough for Australia to open some festering wounds. McGrath extended his domination of Atherton, who he had now dismissed eleven times in his last fifteen innings against Australia. And Stuart MacGill, in the side instead of Warne, once again exposed England's weakness against sharp-turning leg-spin. 'The empire still breathes,' wrote John Harm in the *Australian*, 'although it is with the assisted breath of the intensive care ventilator.'

Only one England side had ever won a Test in Perth (Mike Brearley's in 1978–79) and on the eve of the match the TAB, the Australian equivalent of the Tote in Britain, put a full-page colour advertisement in the *West Australian* newspaper enjoining readers to 'Do Something Nobody's Done For Years – Bet On The Poms'. The irony is, you might have got half-decent odds on it finishing in two and a half days. England, without the injured Thorpe, were skittled for 112 and 191 as Australia romped home by seven wickets. John Harm wrote that England's 'ineptitude has been breathtaking and should lead to the inquisition to end all inquisitions'. From the sidelines, Warne announced England were already psychologically beaten: 'I wonder how many of his [captain Alec Stewart's] players will be able to look him in the eye and say: "Yes, skipper, I have given you everything." I'd want them to tell me they had been playing for all the people who care about English cricket, for the Barmy Army who have paid thousands to spectate out here.'

The crushing nature of the defeat at the WACA also led to some deep psychoanalysis of England fans in the Australian press. 'I thought about things English,' wrote John Harm.

'*Monty Python. Yes, Minister. It Ain't Half Hot Mum.* Prince Charles. *Ripping Yarns.* The English have not only learned to take the mickey out of themselves, they've started to believe in the myths which highlight absurdity and incompetence. These days the English resort to humour to condemn their own, and ultimately themselves. It's about self-loathing. The Barmy Army are an amusing bunch of seemingly intelligent, educated chaps. But, as is the way with their mythology, they choose to feign incompetence as a matter of style. Sitting with the Barmy Army is like being on the set of *Four Weddings and a Funeral.* It's wall to wall Hugh Grants. It's pretending to be hopeless, until such incompetence becomes real.'

Not surprisingly, the Barmy Army response from the psy-choanalyst's coach was a resounding 'bollocks!' 'All it shows is that we're good-natured people and we don't mind losing,' says 'Surrey' Mark Jacobs. 'We just don't have that "winning is everything" mentality. We enjoyed ourselves so much when we were losing, to the extent that some people might say since we've started winning it's spoiled it a bit. On a more basic level it shows we like having fun, winning or losing, and I'd say that's something to be proud of. I'm an AFC Wimbledon fan, and the best nights I've had are often after a defeat – when you've won, you've quite often not got any-thing to talk about. When you've lost there's so much to dissect. My first Test was the Cape Town Test in 1996, which we lost in three days. I was then at the game against Western Province, which we lost, and I then went to six out of seven one-dayers, and we lost all except one – and the game we won I missed. Then in the West Indies in 1997–98, I saw us win one one-day game and we lost all the rest. So it took me almost four years to see England win away. One guy went to about twenty games before seeing England win on the road, so all these guys whose first tour was Australia in 2010–11 don't know the half of it really. My first series win away was 2001 in Sri Lanka, six years after I started watching England away from home.'

The Adelaide Test at least gave the Barmies a chance to do what they do best, that is take advantage of any misfortune to visit the opposition. In the build-up to the match, news broke that Warne and Mark Waugh had accepted money from an Indian bookmaker in exchange for pitch and weather information during a tour of Sri Lanka in 1994. The Australian Cricket Board fined both players but hushed up the affair. The Australian press was scathing. The *Daily Telegraph* labelled the ACB's handling of the scandal 'a national disgrace' for which it should be 'eternally ashamed'. But perhaps the most cutting commentary was to be found in the letters pages of Australia's newspapers, which fairly brimmed with vitriol. 'Naive and stupid definitely,' wrote one fan in the *Australian*, 'but they left out greedy.' One fan went as far as saying he would now be supporting the tourists: 'So long, Shane and Mark, I'm off to join the Barmy Army.' With fans like that . . .

Warne was still absent for Adelaide, but Waugh was not so

lucky. He was booed, heckled and whistled on to the Adelaide Oval and having made a scratchy seven in thirty-six minutes, booed, heckled and whistled all the way back to the pavilion. 'We were giving him a fantastic amount of abuse, it was incessant,' recalls 'Surrey' Mark Jacobs. 'We even produced a special song sheet, and that's when we started singing the famous one about him, to the tune of "My Old Man's a Dustman":

'Mark Waugh is an Aussie,
He wears the baggy cap,
But when he saw the bookie's cash,
He said I'm having that.
He shared it out with "Warnie",
They went and had some beers,
And when the ACB found out,
They covered it up for years.'

'To be fair, on good days the Barmy Army can be funny,' commented the *Financial Times* in its editorial. 'This is Wildean wit compared with the one-word chant of "Ingerlund" favoured by football supporters.' While Waugh later admitted in his autobiography that he never really enjoyed his cricket after the incident [although he played on for a further four years], he would never condemn the Barmy Army for their actions, stating during the 2002–03 Ashes series: 'What's all the fuss about the Barmy Army? They deserve medals for bravery and patience rather than chastisement for over-stepping the mark. So what if they have been baiting and barking at Brett Lee? And so what if they allegedly upset a few locals with their attempts at "undermining" the Aussie team? Look, the English fans have paid very good money to come out here – many of them staying the full course – to support their heroes through thick and thin. So it's silly to condemn them for trying to rattle the Aussie players. It's all part of the modern Ashes scene. And I like it. I'm just amazed the Army have not turned on their own team.' It is doubtful he was so enamoured by some of the barracking meted out by his fellow Aussies. 'I don't have to pay anyone $6000 to tell me how hot it is today,' declared one banner on that first day.

And, my, it was hot. 'I was staying in the Cumberland Arms,' says Burnham. 'I remember hitting mosquitoes all night and the next morning the walls were covered in our blood. It was a real old dive, and there were people sleeping on balconies it was so over-booked.'

Robert Craddock of the Brisbane *Courier Mail* reported that after less than thirty minutes on day one 'Darren Gough's face was so red it looked as if it had been hit by a flying tandoori chicken'. In temperatures of up to 41°C, Australia's batsmen toiled to 266 for four, with Justin Langer reaching a second Test century shortly before the close. Langer was still unbeaten on 179 when England finished off the Australia innings for 391 the following day. In reply,

England were all out for 227, only Nasser Hussain (89 not out) and Mark Ramprakash (61) offering any real resistance as MacGill took a four-fer on a sharply turning pitch. At the end of day three, with Australia 314 ahead with nine wickets in hand and two days remaining, the bells of St Peter's Cathedral that rang out across the Adelaide Oval sounded the end of England's Ashes dreams. England had been pathetic, their last seven wickets falling for 40 runs before two more catches went down, making it fifteen chances spurned in less than three matches.

Slater made a lively 103 in Australia's second innings of 278 for five declared, before England disintegrated on a crumbling pitch on day five to slump to a 205-run defeat. 'Three Tests into the series, this England team have yet to show much heart for the fight,' wrote Simon Briggs in the *Guardian*. 'But you could hardly say the same of their travelling supporters. For the best part of an hour after Glenn McGrath & Co. had finished England off on Tuesday, the fools on the hill kept chanting away defiantly: "Barmy Army – Alec Stewart ... Barmy Army – Alec Stewart". The Ashes may be staying south once again, they seem to say, but the fans aren't finished just yet.' Dave 'The General' Peacock was quoted as saying: 'So what, we lost. There's more to it than the cricket. All these people are on holiday, they want to have a good time.' Fellow co-founder Gareth Evans was not quite so sanguine about England's plight: 'I get very depressed,' he said, 'more than most of them, I think. I couldn't have stayed there for the singing at the end.'

For the organisational arm of the Barmy Army, the third Test could quite easily be dismissed as the warm-up event. 'The Biggest Barmy Army Bash' took place at the Old Adelaide Gaol that evening, with about 1500 punters, most of them English, each paying $5 entry fee in aid of Leukaemia Research. The takings were presented to Ian Botham the following summer, as he began his latest fundraising walk for the charity. Among those patrolling the Adelaide Gaol was Jack Hyams, a new recruit at the age of seventy-nine. 'He was an absolute legend and we immediately made him president of the Barmy Army Cricket Club,' says Burnham. 'He's the leading amateur run-scorer in English history, with something like 130,000 runs and 170 centuries for various clubs in and around the London area, and apparently he made his first ton in 1934 [Hyams did indeed score his first century in 1934, the year Don Bradman hit 304 against England at Headingley]. He played against Jack Hobbs, Jim Laker, Denis Compton, Fred Trueman, and in the Second World War he was an aircraft gunner before running a pet shop. What a character, and we welcomed him with open arms.'

'I remember he fell asleep at the SCG and was lying on The Hill and someone laid a cardboard coffin next to him with RIP written on it,' recalls Andy Evans. 'The irony being that he had more energy than anyone else – he always used to say, "I'll have enough time for sleeping when I'm dead".

He'd be out on the dance floor in clubs and bars, he loved it. He won a disco-dancing competition in Melbourne, and I remember hearing him on the phone to his wife afterwards: "I'm in the outback, dear. Of course I'm not making a fool of myself." He came back that night with bruises and cuts down one side of his body where he'd been bouncing off walls all the way home. Remarkable man, he put plenty of the youngsters to shame.'

From Adelaide, the Barmy Army marched on Melbourne – or, rather, they would have done if they'd known which direction Melbourne was. 'For some reason we decided to set off in the dark,' recalls Burnham, 'me, Vic, Jack and Gareth's brother Andy, all jammed into this old Ford Falcon called "Bessie". We drove for about an hour through the pitch-black until we came to a sign that said Melbourne was about 100km further away than when we started. We'd taken the coast road and we eventually ran out of petrol at about 3 a.m. and had to sleep at a petrol pump for four hours. I remember Jack singing old war songs in the back to keep the spirits up: "When this bloody tour is over, oh how happy I will be; on the plane back to England, no more Aussie cheats for me; no more cheating Aussie umpires, no more catches off the grass ..."'

'"Bessie" was basically a death trap,' says Evans. 'At various stages the brake pads went and the radiator hose, it was a mess. One time we had a puncture, put a spare tyre on and drove very slowly to the next town, arriving just as the garage was about to close. Basically there was one bolt holding the suspension on, and most of that had been sheared off – if we'd hit something we probably all would have been dead. These two Aussie mechanics hammered away for a couple of hours while we cleaned their fridge out of beer. That's the way it was for most England fans on that tour, and all tours down under, everything was just done on the cheap – transport, booze, food, that was the ethos.'

The Melbourne leg of the Test series did not get off to an auspicious start. Footage of the Adelaide Gaol party and camera equipment were stolen from the Pint on Punt backpackers', while Sowunmi fell down a beer hatch in the backpackers' reception. Things got worse before they got any better. Day one at the MCG was a washout, but not before Taylor won the toss for the fourth time in the series and put England in to bat. Then, on the morning of day two, Atherton was dismissed for a duck by – you guessed it – McGrath, before Butcher followed to leave England tottering on 4 for two. Stewart, who had given up the wicket-keeper's gauntlets to Warren Hegg in order to open the batting for the first time in the series, and Hussain did a partial rebuild before Ramprakash joined his captain in the middle to steer the tourists to 200 for three. Australia, for the first time in the series, had a bloody nose. But it was soon wiped clean, as England's last seven wickets went down for 70 runs.

Darren Gough took five for 96 in Australia's first innings,

but the hosts, courtesy of a ton from Steve Waugh, still compiled a 70-run lead. 'Not for the first time Waugh seems to have broken England on his steel-rimmed wheel,' wrote Christopher Martin-Jenkins in the *Telegraph*. England lost two wickets before stumps – Atherton completed his pair – as Taylor's men tramped seemingly inexorably towards a 3–0 series lead. And how the Aussie fans loved it. 'The thing is, our Barmy Army are brilliant at giving stick because it's humorous,' says England fast bowler Dean Headley, 'although in all fairness, the West Indians are quite humorous as well. I remember standing on the boundary in Barbados and all I kept hearing was "Headley, I want ya . . ." and after about eight overs I plucked up the courage to turn round and there was this big, fat momma sat on the end of some bleacher in the hot sunshine, sweating away, and I thought "God, she'd eat me alive . . ."

'But the Aussies were different, they'd basically slate you, call you every name under the sun – but then what do you expect from the Aussies? It was pretty base stuff, they'd just swear at you, and that's why they've always found it hard to take on the Barmy Army because while the Barmy Army were making up clever songs about this and that, they were just calling you a wanker. They do clever things. Like when Justin Langer had a go at them in 2002–03, calling them all beer-swilling louts, the next day a load of them turned up in aerobics gear and started doing exercises up in the stands. That's genius.'

Headley was the central figure in the Miracle of Melbourne that unfolded on day four. Resuming on 65 for two, England could only manage 244 in their second innings, with Stewart, Hussain and Hick making fifties. Perhaps the most valuable runs, however, came from Mullally – the rabbit's rabbit – who crashed McGrath for two fours in a knock of 16. That still left Australia needing only 175 to win and a banner draped across the Great Southern Stand, stating that not even a dose of Viagra could stiffen England's batting, summed up the feelings of the home fans. However, Australia had a habit of falling short when chasing seemingly small fourth-innings targets – at The Oval in 1997, they fouled up chasing 124, although that was on a disintegrating pitch. In contrast, the pitch at the MCG was still a good one on day four, as demonstrated when Australia passed 100 for the loss of only two wickets. Then came the spark that turned the second innings into a bonfire. 'Australia were two wickets down and only needed 70-odd more to win,' recalls England skipper Alec Stewart. 'And then we had that little purple patch, which was all started by Ramprakash catching Langer at square-leg, a great one-handed catch. That's what got us in it to win it.' Taylor later agreed that was indeed the turning point.

However, Australia, who at that point were 103 for three, remained red-hot favourites. Then, with Australia on 140 for four, Headley produced one of the most dramatic spells in Test history. 'That was perhaps the most amazing spell of bowling

I've ever seen,' says Burnham. 'We got right behind "Deano" – every time he came in to bowl we were banging the seats and shouting his name and he kept on steaming in, over after over after over.' First, Darren Lehmann got a thin inside edge to wicket-keeper Hegg; eight balls later, Healy edged to Hick in the slips; three balls later, Damien Fleming was leg before to a ball of full length. That left Australia in a bit of a pickle, 35 short of the target with only three wickets left.

'The MCG on that final day was just awesome,' says Vic Sowunmi. 'Just being in the middle of all those white shirts, the adrenaline, the euphoria, it was a very powerful feeling, as if we were all part of something bigger. It was a real high and took a long time to come down from. To me it was all about togetherness in a foreign land, everyone being cool with everyone else, never any trouble, no bitterness or malice. I'm not really one for big crowds, but that was something else.'

'It's an easy thing to say that the Barmy Army are England's twelfth man,' says Stewart. 'But what I'd say is you'd rather have them on your side than against you. When you're out there on the field, it's you against the opposition, but any outside assistance is a big bonus. If you are tired, you are going through a tough time, it's been a long session and you can still hear the Barmy Army supporting you, it gives you that lift. And that final day in Melbourne we were tired, we had been going through a tough time and it had been a very long session, so we were especially glad of the support that day.'

At 7.22 and with Australia 161 for seven, only 14 runs short of victory, Taylor claimed the extra half an hour in order to finish off the game. The end of England's second innings twenty-nine minutes before tea meant the break was taken early and the evening session would now run to more than four hours, the longest in Test history. Stewart, his bowlers already flogged into the ground, was furious. But with shadows lengthening across the pitch and five victims already, Headley was happy enough to continue. 'We were all knackered so I didn't have too many thoughts going through my head by that stage,' says Headley. 'But there was a lot of adrenaline as we were on the brink of winning. They needed fourteen runs and we needed three wickets. All we knew is that we just needed to get one out because anything could happen with MacGill and McGrath.'

When play resumed, Headley duly dismissed one-cap-wonder Matt Nicholson and, just as Headley predicted, MacGill and McGrath fell in Gough's next over as Australia came up 13 runs short. 'There was something fitting about this,' wrote Ian Chadband in the *Evening Standard*. 'Throughout this tour, as throughout this match, he [Gough] has never given up, throwing himself about, bowling every ball as if it were going to be his last. No wonder the Barmy Army, which shares his passion of chasing lost causes with the same inde-fatigable enthusiasm, sees him as their spiritual leader.' 'That Melbourne Test was unbelievable,' says 'Surrey' Mark Jacobs. 'There were four or five thousand of us in the corner, hoping for a miracle more than anything else, and suddenly Ramprakash took that great catch and it all went off. Headley and Gough were out on their feet, they could hardly run, but every time they came down to us at the end of an over you could see them getting stronger again. I reckon the Barmy Army helped win that game.'

'I remember quite a lot had left and only the hardcore had stayed – and they got their money's worth,' says Headley, who finished with six for 60 in Australia's second innings. 'It wasn't necessarily that the Barmy Army put a yard of pace on me, but it was knowing I had the support there, up in the stands, that helped. For me, they were like a twelfth man. I was just in a state of oblivion at the end, I didn't know which end of my elbow I was meant to be pointing to be honest. I think there was euphoria afterwards, for me it was a case of taking it all in, going and partying with the Barmy Army afterwards at the hotel, it was all good fun. Melbourne was quite memorable, or not, whichever way you look at it. We partied with a certain group of supporters in a bar opposite our hotel. We were standing on the tables, drinking and singing and enjoying ourselves. I've always enjoyed their company, and without fans like that, you haven't got a game.'

While for many England players and fans the victory at the MCG was the definite high point of the tour, Headley sees things differently. 'Melbourne was big, but we played bloody well at Sydney,' says the Kent quick, 'and we were bloody unlucky not to come away with a 2–2 draw.' Headley took four for 62 as Australia were dismissed for 322 on day one at Sydney, but it is a day largely remembered for the heroics of Darren Gough. Just don't ask anyone in the Barmy Army about his hat-trick, the first and only by an Englishman in an Ashes Test in the twentieth century.

'I heard the hat-trick, I was selling T-shirts outside,' says Vic Sowunmi. 'But I do remember the noise being unbelievable.' Says Andy Evans: 'I could hear it – there was a cheer, then a bigger cheer, then a colossal cheer. What the hell was going on? I often used to spend the final session in the pub, because you couldn't get pass-outs at the SCG.' Says Graham Barber, who joined up with the Barmy Army in Melbourne: 'My reputation has grown in terms of what I see and what I don't see. I've got the best collection of unused Test match tickets anywhere in the world. I might make the first ball or the first hour, but when it comes to lunch you might not see me for dust.' Adds Giles Wellington, who had also caught up with the Barmy Army in Melbourne: 'It's a bit of a strange one, that "Goughie" hat-trick, because even though all the newspaper reports confirm the SCG was a sell-out, with an estimated 10,000 England fans inside, you'd be hard pushed to find a member of the Barmy Army who saw it. I remember walking back into town after the close and there were a couple of English blokes having this big argument about whether the hat-trick had happened or not, and it was left to me to tell them it had. Not that I saw it ...'

Burnham wasn't there either. He was outside recruiting, and had called for a gathering at the Captain Cook bar.

It had, indeed, happened: first, Healy tried to withdraw his bat from Gough's short, rising delivery and edged behind; second, MacGill, as at Melbourne, had his stumps splattered by a yorker; third, Colin Miller had his furniture rearranged by an absolute beauty, another yorker that swung away at the decisive moment. The England fans went ballistic and partied long into the night, believing a 2–2 series draw was now at least a possibility.

On day two, that optimism seemed misplaced, as MacGill, bowling in tandem with the fit again Warne, took five for 57 in England's first innings total of 220. Day three saw a remarkable innings from Slater, who made 123 in Australia's total of 184 (Headley bowled superbly again, taking four for 40). Only one man had ever scored a higher proportion of a completed Test innings: Charlie Bannerman, in the first innings of the first Test played, at Melbourne in 1877. Not that the Barmy Army was too impressed. 'Sydney was the Michael Slater run-out,' says 'Surrey' Mark Jacobs. 'He was miles out, it was embarrassing. The on-field umpire should have seen it, it should never have even gone upstairs.' Slater, then on 35, had been surprised by a Dean Headley throw from long-on, a direct hit at the bowler's end. Repeated television replays on the giant video screen suggested Slater had failed to make his ground by an inch or so, but he was given the benefit of the doubt by the third umpire, Simon Taufel. But for that decision, the hosts could quite easily have been skittled for double figures. England, who had lost every toss in the series and seen most of the luck go against them, found themselves on the wrong end of a bad one again.

Yet when Hussain and Ramprakash guided England to 104 for two at stumps, and with 183 more required to seal the win, it seemed it could be done. But not for the first time against Australia, and not for the last, they could not get it done. On day four, MacGill outshone his more illustrious leg-spinning partner Warne once again, finishing with match figures of twelve for 107 as England's second innings was wrapped up for 188, twenty-one minutes after lunch. Australia had won by 98 runs to seal a 3–1 series win. But as far as Headley was concerned, England could take more from the defeat in Sydney than victory in Melbourne.

'In Melbourne, Australia weren't quite at their best, but in Sydney they were expected to trounce us and that was the only game in that series when we really went toe-to-toe,' he says. 'Melbourne was great, but Sydney was the pinnacle of my career because I thought that was the best I've ever bowled. It wasn't an easy wicket, I had to work hard, and the atmosphere in that ground was incredible. That Test had the "Goughie" hat-trick, it had the crowd, we rocked and rolled Australia in the second innings, and who knows what might have happened if Slater had been given out. Whenever anyone asks me what my favourite ground in the world is, I always say Sydney. Favourite Test match? Sydney.'

Following one final shindig, the members of the Barmy Army, never great lovers of one-dayers, scattered their separate ways – physically battered and mentally bruised, like soldiers melting away from a battlefield. 'After that series I went up to Darwin to get away from it all,' says 'Surrey' Mark Jacobs. 'To be frank, it was a relief that it was over, I was absolutely knackered. You'd be standing in the sun all day, boozing morning, noon and night, and you'd just do the same thing over and over again. In the end, it just grinds you down.' It might be of some succour to Jacobs to know how much England's players appreciated his efforts.

'I felt sorry for the England fans at times,' says Headley. 'We've made big strides over the last ten to twelve years, but English cricket missed out on a lot of years because of poor selection policy and a lack of continuity in selection, and England's travelling fans bore the brunt of that. Most good sides that are built don't go round chopping and changing, and England have learnt that. What they have now is a real belief in what they're doing: English cricket at the moment is a nice place to be. It wasn't that the players on our tour didn't have the talent, it's just that they didn't have it collectively. I know that might sound daft – you might argue that eleven good players should make a good team – but not if all eleven are looking over their shoulders.

'It was quite an extraordinary experience being with the

Barmy Army. They were good fun, they were good-natured, they were boisterous, and they're a big part of cricket today, I would say synonymous with England tours nowadays. They like to have a good time and they don't want to sit there and not make a noise – I can't see how you can pay for a ticket and people can tell you you can't have a good time – but they're cricket lovers first and foremost. If I was given a chance to see just one more game, I wouldn't pick a game in England. I think I'd pick somewhere that was a lot more fun, all a little bit more light-hearted, all a little more raucous – let's say an Ashes Test in Sydney, where half the crowd are Barmy Army.'

4

Barmy Army under fire . . . South Africa 1999–00

If the South Africans had been ambushed by the Barmy Army the first time around in 1995–96, four years later they saw them coming. And while it would be a vast exaggeration to say the locals were on a war footing from the moment England's fans started streaming into Johannesburg for the first Test in November, there were guerrilla units spoiling for the skirmishes all across the land.

'That tour was bloody scary at times,' says 'Big John' Geagan, the Ilford giant who Barmy Army co-founder Paul Burnham describes as the outfit's 'unofficial security'. 'There was a day-nighter at the Wanderers [in Johannesburg] and the South African fans were coming round, getting on their phones and ringing up their mates to come and have a fight with us. It was pretty dicey stuff. "Chopper" started giving them abuse back but his stuff was quite witty and they didn't know how to react. So one of the blokes hit

"Chopper" from behind and he went down between the seats. I got involved and in piled this huge Afrikaner, and it took about ten of us to hold him down, but he was still lifting us up. I got a punch in, smashed him on the nose, and he didn't flinch. I hit him again, split his nose, and he still didn't flinch. He just got madder. Eventually security jumped in and pulled me aside and I ended up having to do a legger – in no shirt, because it had been ripped off, blood all over me – because they wanted to arrest me. The odd ending to that story is "Chopper" bumped into the bloke who started it all in the toilet, beat him up and the bloke ended up buying him a beer. How very South African – give them a kicking and they'll love you for it.' Off the pitch, at least.

The Test series had been billed as the Allan Donald and Mike Atherton Show in light of some coruscating duels between the two men on South Africa's tour of England in 1998. Their stand-off at Trent Bridge, when the two men went at it like a couple of stags, was magnificent theatre. On the first morning of the first match at the Wanderers, Donald looked a touched miffed at being awarded joint top billing. In a matter of seventeen deliveries, England were reduced to 2 for four: Atherton had his off-stump ripped out by a ball from Donald that jagged back alarmingly off the pitch; Nasser Hussain got a snorter from Shaun Pollock and was given out caught in the slips; Mark Butcher, too, edged to Mark Boucher behind the stumps; Alec Stewart was trapped plumb in front next ball. The scoreboard displayed the horror story in all its gory detail: one single and a leg-bye against four wickets down. They call the Wanderers 'The Bullring', but that morning 'The Abattoir' would have been more apt.

England debutants Chris Adams and Michael Vaughan could have been forgiven for fainting as they made their way to the middle, the stench of slaughter all around them. 'I said to "Vaughany" a nervous "what's happening?"' recalled Adams a few years after the event. 'And he said, "I haven't got a clue, I haven't faced a ball yet!"' Adams, who finished with 16, trebled the score with a boundary from his second delivery and Vaughan's guts held firm for long enough to help save his side from utter humiliation. His partnership with Andrew Flintoff was worth 52 runs, but England had still been routed: Donald finished with six for 53, Pollock with astonishing figures of four for 16 in 14.4 overs, as the tourists were skittled for 122. When bad light stopped play with sixteen overs remaining, South Africa were 61 for one. Daryll Cullinan scored a classy century on day two as South Africa kept hacking away at England's corpse, and a ballsy knock from Stewart on day three only delayed the inevitable (Atherton completed a pair). After seventy minutes on day four, England finally expired, the losing margin an innings and 21 runs. It had been as pitiful a start to an overseas tour as almost anyone could remember.

There was some respite for the Barmy Army with news that they may no longer have been the world's most irritating sporting fans, according to a journalist in Australia. 'High up in the southern stand in the Palais des Expositions the last two days sat "The Fanatics," wrote Bruce Wilson, reporting from a Davis Cup clash in Nice, in the Brisbane *Courier Mail*. 'The touring Australian tennis fans are in danger of supplanting England's Barmy Army as the world's most irksome and annoying bunch of travelling yobbo sporting clots. One of the troubles is the Australian players go out of their way to pander to "The Fanatics". They accused the French of cheating and they shouted insults at the French players – some very personal – all the time believing they were doing nothing more than being good Aussie patriots. It is time the players stopped encouraging them.' The Barmy Army hierarchy would have known how 'The Fanatics' felt; they had heard it all before.

There followed a one-dayer against a Gauteng XI before a four-day match in Durban against KwaZulu/Natal, which was bad news for Burnham and Co.: it was even more dangerous out on the open road than it was up in the stands. 'We almost had about three head-on crashes on that tour,' says Burnham, 'people were driving off their heads – not us, the South Africans. People used to flash each other to warn of police speed traps coming up, and one day John was at the wheel and I was acting the goat, leaning across and flashing everyone in sight. Unfortunately one of the cars I flashed was police and he spun round, chased us down and pulled us over. They dragged John out of the car, and all of a sudden I'm thinking, "Maybe I shouldn't have been doing what I was doing, they don't fuck about over here, he's going to prison." So I wandered over and started saying, "Sorry, mate, everyone flashes everyone over here, we're the Barmy Army, we were just trying to fit in." When he heard we were Barmy Army, all he was bothered about was getting a couple of T-shirts for his kids. That was that, I dug a couple out of the boot and he sent us on our way.'

England showed some spirit on day one of the second Test at Port Elizabeth, restricting the hosts to 253 for six at stumps. But on day two limited-overs specialist Lance Klusener, feasting on some insipid bowling by England, took the game away from the tourists with a classy 174 in South Africa's first innings total of 450. In reply, England were 139 for one at stumps, still 311 adrift. For the Barmy Army, it might have been just another day at the cricket were it not for more heavy-handed treatment from the locals. 'It was the first time I remember seeing him,' says Geagan. 'Apparently he had been in Australia the year before, but people just hadn't taken much notice of him. He was this old bloke, maybe in his late fifties, with grey-blond, straggly long hair. Feeble-looking bloke, decked out in this George Cross vest and top hat and waving a George Cross flag. Everyone was pretty much ignoring him that day, too, until a couple of Saffers did that old schoolboy prank – one of them knelt behind him and the other one pushed him over, and he went flying. To be honest, most of the Barmy Army probably thought that was quite funny, but then later in the day someone steamed over and rugby-tackled him. That almost started a riot, it was bang out of order – that's what the Saffers are like, they bully people – so we called him over, embraced him, took him into the fold.' And that is the story of how Vic Flowers – aka 'Jimmy Savile' – went from out-of-work carpenter from Oldham to the face of the Barmy Army, all in the time it took for a bevvied-up South African to think 'You know what, that bloke looks harmless, I think I'll take him out', before skewering him into the ground.

The second Test also provided the Barmy Army hardcore with an opportunity to mix with some of the black population, with a football match arranged against a local Port Elizabeth team. 'We had a cracking match against a local side and ended up having a drink with them in a shebeen [township drinking den],' says 'Big John' Geagan. 'That was a pretty big thing at the time, to be hanging out with the black community in their own environment, that wasn't really the type of thing white people did back then, and probably still don't do now.'

'The Walmer Township is possibly one of the most dangerous townships in the Cape,' says Dave Turton, a veteran of England's previous visit five years earlier. 'It was notorious for its gangs, subject to its fair share of documented murders, as well as non-documented ones, I guess. Our team played against the African Aces and the Barmy Army probably had fifteen players on the field at any time. "Jimmy Savile" in goal had to be seen to be believed and the Barmy Army got a thrashing like I've only ever witnessed of my beloved Derby County. After-match festivities at the local shebeen included lots of rather strange-looking foods (some of which I only later found out came from parts of an animal's anatomy we would normally dispose of), African dancing and lots of fun was had by all.'

For Vic Sowunmi, a black Englishman in South Africa, the visit to the shebeen turned out to be blessed relief. 'I'm sure they train their police dogs to bark at black people over there,' says Sowunmi. 'They are basically racist dogs, every time one would see me it would start salivating. I felt uncomfortable pretty much the whole time on that tour, to the extent that "Leafy" [Paul Burnham] felt a bit bad that he'd invited me along. I'd go into a bar or a hotel and the only other black people in there would be cleaning glasses or in the toilets. Pretoria was particularly horrible, people were shouting stuff at me the whole time. I felt like I couldn't look anyone in the eye, all the black South Africans were walking about with their heads down. And I'd be walking down the street with "Leafy", maybe with our arms round each other and having a laugh and people would be looking at us as if to say, "What are you two doing together?" The only time I really felt happy was in Soweto or when we were hanging out at the shebeen. They were the only places I felt unthreatened and safe.'

Having bagged a pair in the first Test in Johannesburg – in marked contrast to his monumental match-saving innings at the Wanderers five years earlier – Atherton notched his thirteenth Test century on day three, his first since taking one off the same opposition at Edgbaston in 1998 and England's first since Stewart's against Australia in Melbourne the previous December. 'At least, and at last,' wrote Stephen Brenkley in the *Independent*, 'the millennium version of new England refused to go without anybody realising they had arrived. Here were a team who somehow achieved the low-key ambition they have set themselves on this tour. They competed.' That just about sums up how low English cricket was at that time. On day five, Hussain, who had succeeded Alec Stewart as captain earlier in the year, scored a battling half-century, his second of the match, as England escaped with a draw.

The third Test match in Durban got off to a soporific start, with England scoring 135 for two on day one and finishing day two on 366 for nine. England declared overnight, Hussain having made 146 not out from 463 balls in ten hours and thirty-five minutes. 'Not even your one-eyed Barmy Army supporter,' wrote veteran South African cricket writer Trevor Chesterfield, 'would agree with Nasser Hussain's batting tribute to bad taste.' On day three, however, Hussain's innings suddenly looked like a potential match-winner: Andy Caddick – who could be Hadlee-esque one day, yet as ineffective as a club bowler the next – took seven for 46 as the hosts were skittled for 156 and forced to follow on for the first time in seventy-four Tests and the first time since isolation ended in 1992. But England's ascendancy was short-lived. Gary Kirsten scored a monumental 275 in his side's second innings – at 872 minutes it was the second longest innings in Test history – as the game petered out into a draw.

While at times the Durban Test must have felt like a stint in the trenches for the long-suffering Barmy Army, with all its attendant boredom, the trip down to Cape Town was the equivalent of going over the top. It even involved guns. 'We'd organised a Millennium Eve party in Cape Town ahead of the fourth Test,' explains Burnham, 'so as soon as the Durban Test was over we all piled into an old bashed-up car – me, Vic, "Big John" and Graham – and went on our way.' 'Big John' Geagan takes up the story: 'We were told not to drive through the Transkei [formerly an autonomous region in the Eastern Cape], but it cuts four hours off the journey and we would have missed the party otherwise. The Transkei was pretty much a no-go area for white people, just miles and miles of mud huts, so we stuck Vic in the front the whole way, so at least we had a black presence. At one point we stopped off at a petrol station in a little village and Graham, who was only driving because no one else could see by this stage, reversed and clipped an old woman with four kids. We thought we were going to all end up dead in a burnt-out car, we had to get out of there pretty quick.

'Anyway, having driven for seventeen hours and risked life

and limb, we arrived at this party and there must have been about twenty Barmy Army there – we hadn't pre-sold tickets and people had been turning up, seen that no one else was there and just left. The poor owner was expecting two thousand – he had "the longest bar in the world", literally two hundred bar staff, fairground stalls, the lot. But we ended up seeing in the millennium with about thirty other people. After a while we decided to head into central Cape Town and we all fell asleep in the back of the cab. When we woke up about an hour later, the driver still hadn't found the bar we wanted and when he finally did he asked for a hundred quid, which was about double what it should have been. So I chucked him fifty and told him to deal with it and all of a sudden he lost it, started shouting "You fucking English, give us the money" and threatening to call the police. Then, when I started writing his registration number down, he suddenly pulled out a gun and started waving it at us. I remember looking into his eyes and thinking I was dead. The others completely shat themselves and jumped over a wall, Vic was hiding in a bush. We moved the next day, but we didn't report it, just in case he came after us for revenge.'

If Burnham, Geagan and Co. sounded like men badly in need of a guardian angel, then their prayers were soon answered. 'I worked in the pavilion at Kent County Cricket Ground,' says Katy Cooke, an early female pioneer with the Barmy Army. 'Me and a couple of mates had been sitting around in the summer thinking about what we were going to do for the millennium, throwing around ideas – New York, Edinburgh, wherever – and Kent fast bowler Dean Headley overheard our conversation and said "Have you thought about Cape Town?" And we thought, "What a brilliant idea." Not really because of the cricket, but more because we knew it would be hot and a bit different. So we booked it up.

'While we were in Cape Town we decided to go along to the cricket, and on the first day of the Test the ground was absolutely heaving. We naturally gravitated towards the England supporters, who were all standing up on the grass bank, in the cheap seats. And naturally, being three girls, they were very nice to us. We had a fantastic day, drinking in the sun, and we went out with the Barmy Army in the evening. One of the guys made sure I got home OK that night, put me in a taxi – Cape Town wasn't really a place for a blonde girl to be wandering around on her own at night, and I was only twenty at the time. And the next day I got up and thought, "I want to go back to the cricket, that was wicked fun". So my two mates went to the beach and I went to the match with the boys. At the end of the second day I went back to their house in the suburbs for a party, because they had a pool in the garden, and from there I just got caught up in helping out, with stocktaking in particular. I remember someone had a parking ticket to pay on that first day and I generally started being a useful person to have around. They just weren't very organised, they were just a bunch of boys on tour. And that's the kind of person I am, I'm not very good at standing around doing nothing – if something needs doing, I'll do it. And I also don't like a messy house! There were about twelve boys living in a six-bedroom house, it was disgusting.'

That Cape Town Test was also the first for Tim 'Haffers' Haffenden, one of the Barmy Army 'Blazer Boys' and a founder member of the outfit's 'Dawn Patrol'. 'I picked up a blazer before heading out to Cape Town, to give the locals what they expect to see from an English gentleman abroad from the moment I step off the plane,' says Haffenden. 'I'm just fitting in with the stereotypical image they have, or at least used to have of us. It also works wonders in getting upgraded on the flight because it gives the impression you have money, so now I never get on a plane without one.' Haffenden has also been known to attend games in full St George knight's attire, once winning a fancy dress competition at the Wanderers and 2000 rands' worth of light fittings.

The 'Dawn Patrol' is a motley collection of individuals who meet up at around eight o'clock on the morning of a Test and proceed to drink heavily before attending the day's play. 'The first ever "Dawn Patrol" was also in South Africa,' says Haffenden. 'We were invited to a pub for early morning hospitality by a load of ex-directors of major companies such as Boots, British Airways and British Steel. These boys were all pushing a hundred years old and had all retired to South

Africa and had an exclusive little club which meant that they had to meet every Saturday morning in the boozer at eight o'clock for the first pint of the day. If one of them didn't show up then everyone else's beers would be put on their tab. They just invited us along because they were interested in meeting some of the Barmy Army that they had heard so much about on the telly and in the papers. So we all went along in fancy dress for a laugh and a tradition was born.'

Cooke and Haffenden were part of a massive invasion of England fans for that fourth Test, with the *Observer* noting: 'Not since Admiral Keith Elphinstone arrived in Table Bay in June 1795 with the British fleet at his back to claim the Cape for King and country have so many Englishmen invaded Cape Town simultaneously. The New Year Test has acted like a magnet to draw the Barmy Army, the Barmy Army's Almost As Silly Reserves, and hundreds of "ordinary" cricket followers to the foot of Africa.' The capacity at Newlands was 16,500 and a third of the crowd were backing Hussain's team. It was just a shame England served up such depressing fare. Donald took five for 47 as England were dismissed for 258 on day two, having been 115 for nought at one point. 'The compendium of England collapses includes a few surrenders statistically worse than the seven wickets they lost for 45 runs,' wrote John Etheridge in the *Sun*. 'But none should attract more vitriol. It was a performance that was staggering in its ineptitude and probably fatal in its consequences. The Barmy Army resorted to songs such as "We're the worst team in the world" and "We're so shit, it's unbelievable". It was meant to be ironic humour.'

Cullinan and Jacques Kallis both scored tons in the hosts' first innings of 421 before, on day four, England disintegrated again, mustering a pitiful 126 as South Africa wrapped up an innings victory. 'A new year, a new century, a few new faces,' wrote Frank Malley in the *Western Daily Press*. 'But it's the same old story for England's cricketers. Truly you could have cried for England's weeping willow of a cricket team as it creaked and groaned its way to another series defeat against South Africa in Cape Town. Another innings defeat, one more drop of misery in an ocean of under-achievement. As recently as Tuesday, the Barmy Army – the mad, raucous but somehow magnificently passionate travelling supporters – had sung "Jerusalem" as England's bowlers thundered in bidding to claw back the initiative surrendered by their inept batsmen. Their reward was to watch yesterday as England's batsmen fell like Zulus at Rorke's Drift – the heart of the team ripped out in 11 overs either side of lunch.' After the Cape Town debacle, the England team paid a visit to Robben Island, where Nelson Mandela was incarcerated for eighteen years. 'Although Nasser Hussain's men are only on a sightseeing visit to Nelson Mandela's former jail, the Barmy Army will be wishing the players could be left there to rot,' wrote Chris Lander in the *Mirror*. Clearly, Lander was unaware of one of the Barmy Army's central tenets: 'We will support the

England cricket team always, through thick and through thin.'

The final Test of that series took place in the Afrikaner stronghold of Pretoria, where the Barmy Army were forced to dodge showers of both rain and abuse up in the stands. 'Before the start of that game Paul [Burnham] had asked for a fence to be set up between the two sets of fans,' recalls 'Big John' Geagan, 'because they were just chucking so much abuse our way. They turned up with a white picket fence that a four-year-old could have climbed over. I'm not sure if they were taking the piss or not, but I'd say not, because the Afrikaners don't really do irony. It was real aggressive abuse, not like the Aussies. All they wanted to do was fight, even if it meant fighting each other – they'd spend all day rolling around on the floor and wrestling. I remember Vic putting this huge Afro wig on that made him about eight feet tall, which didn't really help his cause. Me and Vic were walking round the ground at one stage and two massive Afrikaners came over and said, "What are you, some kind of Kaffir lover?" They had a right go at both of us, so we called over a couple of security guards and the blokes told us they were going to kill us outside. To be fair, when we returned to Pretoria in 2005, it had calmed down a lot.'

Burnham, meanwhile, had thrown petrol on the flames with a disastrous appearance on South African television. 'He was due to appear on a show called *Extra Cover* with a famous South African cricket commentator called Mike

Haysman,' recalls Dave Turton. 'I said to Paul, "'Leafy', go easy, mate, if you're not careful this could be disastrous." Haysman was renowned for his posing questions and "Leafy" was well tanked up after a full day on the Castle lager. I remember we were all sat around the TV watching and Haysman says to him, "So, Paul, how are you finding the hospitality that's being shown towards the Barmy Army at all the Test venues?" And "Leafy" came back with, "It's great they have given us our own area – so we don't have to sit with all those bloody Dutchmen." "Leafy" had committed a cardinal sin, never call an Afrikaner a Dutchman! "Leafy", I thought, what have you done? On live TV, in front of millions. Forget the burning of a cardboard Allan Donald on the previous tour, now these boys are going to burn you! And chief of Barmy Army security, "Big John", is going to have to earn his corn now if you are going to get to the ground. In typical "Leafy" style he tried to blame it all on me, by saying "but you call them Dutchmen". Fortunately, I don't do much live TV. It was considered that he should probably go the next day in disguise and that "Big John" should not leave his side. The big Surrey lad "Leafy" is, I seem to remember he took ill and only appeared after tea the following day.'

The mood of the local population was not improved by what transpired on the pitch. Only forty-five overs were allowed by the weather on day one before the next three days were washed out entirely. Then, on day five, South

Africa's ill-fated captain Hansie Cronje decided to make a game of it, meeting with Hussain and agreeing to forfeit an innings before setting England 249 to win from seventy overs. It seemed like an extremely generous gesture, and so it proved, with England reaching the target with two wickets in hand and five balls remaining. 'We turned up to Centurion on the final day but we'd all given up on the game,' says Burnham. 'We ended up winning but there was a feeling at the time that Cronje had given us too much of a chance and the atmosphere, which had already been bad, got even worse. There were Barmy Army members getting beaten up because South Africa had lost, and the Afrikaners really hated the English and didn't need much of an excuse. I remember some bloke coming up to me and saying, "Are you the leader of the Barmy Army? Do you want to come outside for a scrap?" And I said to him, "I'll get back to you on that one."'

Adds Vic Sowunmi: 'That was the only place I've ever been in the world where I didn't feel safe inside a ground, even when I had "Big John" by my side.' It would later emerge that Cronje accepted money and a leather jacket from an Indian bookmaker in return for making an early declaration. One of the few high points on a largely miserable tour for Nasser Hussain's men had been the result of a gift. And while the Barmy Army did not know this at the time, they still could not get out of Centurion fast enough: it had been a rough, tough end to one of the roughest, toughest Barmy Army campaigns to date. Yet attitudes have apparently changed.

'I think it is a fair reflection of the way the Barmy Army has endeared itself to the South African public that outside St George's Park in Port Elizabeth, they opened a pub called the Barmy Army,' says Dave Turton. 'The walls are draped with Barmy Army shirts from their tours and pictures of "Jimmy Savile" sampling some local fare with the landlord. Could you imagine that happening outside the MCG or SCG? Or how about on the doorstep of Headingley, a pub called "The Springbok Supporters' Bar"? I think not.

'Any England tour to South Africa is met with great hype, but I often wonder where the real excitement is: in the minds of South African supporters, is it the actual cricket that gets them going or is it the thousands of English supporters, with their songs and chants and general good cheer? In truth, it's all about the Army. The carnival atmosphere they bring to a day's play is special for all. Test cricket in South Africa is very poorly attended as a rule, but not when the Army is in town. Everyone wants a piece of it, everyone wants their picture taken with "Jimmy", everyone (even locals) wants to have a singalong after tea. You can feel the buzz of anticipation: "Let the games begin!"'

5

The captain's blessing ... Australia 2002–03

By the time of the 2002–03 Ashes series down under, Steve Waugh's Australia had attained all-time-great status. Waugh was arguably his country's finest post-war captain and among his ranks were several players who would be in the mix for a greatest ever Test XI. In Matthew Hayden and Justin Langer Australia had the most potent opening partnership in world cricket; Ricky Ponting had matured into a rock-solid number three and a captain-in-waiting; Adam Gilchrist was undoubtedly the most destructive wicket-keeper-batsman the game had ever seen; fast bowler Glenn McGrath was almost unplayable on his day; and in leg-spinner Shane Warne Australia had perhaps the finest cricketer of the modern game. In short, England would have to be firing on all cylinders even to make it interesting. Inevitably, they rocked up in Brisbane for the first Test a couple of cylinders short.

There were probably only two English players the Aussies

truly respected, and neither of them played any part in that series. England's best bowler and Barmy Army lightning rod, Darren Gough, at least made the plane, but soon succumbed to a knee injury. England's best batsman, Graham Thorpe, cited personal reasons, umming and ahhing over whether to tour before eventually deciding against it. Andy Thompson, a retired policeman for whom that tour was his first, was particularly unimpressed. 'I wrote him a letter saying "What are you doing, you're a professional cricketer and people are spending a lot of money to go out and support the team, you are the one person the Aussies respect and you've made runs against them,"' says Thompson. 'It probably never got to him, but he pulled out, Gough got injured, so we went with a depleted squad. We'd gone from original positivity to "let's suck it and see, let's hope we do all right".'

Still, even without Gough and Thorpe, there were grounds for optimism. Nasser Hussain had instilled discipline, steel and pride in his side, taking a pathetic outfit by the scruff of the neck and hauling it from ninth in the Test rankings to third courtesy of three undefeated series in a row in 2002 and other improved performances. Hussain's England had defeated the West Indies in a series for the first time in thirty-one years in 2000, and nicked a rare series win in Pakistan later that year. And even without Thorpe, it was a side capable of making runs, with Marcus Trescothick, Mark Butcher and a young Yorkshire dasher called Michael Vaughan who had made two sublime hundreds against India at Trent

Bridge and The Oval, all in good form going into that Ashes series. Then came the Brisbane toss.

'On the morning of the first Test, I had a chat with Marcus Trescothick,' recalls Hussain. 'Marcus said: "It was doing a bit in the nets, the wicket looks the same, I think we should bowl first." To be honest, I should have had a good look at the wicket and then had a chat with [coach] Duncan Fletcher, but because it was the first morning of an Ashes series, with lots of other stuff going on, I got sidetracked. I found out later that Steve Waugh would have inserted us, so I didn't exactly make the most surprising decision in the world. The ball swung a bit at first and I thought, "Maybe this is going to work out." But by the fifth or sixth over nothing was happening and the world was closing in on me. I thought to myself: "Oh God, Nass, what have you done?"' The following day, the Melbourne *Herald Sun* went with the headline: 'NASSER INSANE'.

The sky above the Gabba having been partially cloudy when play began, Hayden and Langer were soon making hay under brilliant sunshine. 'I remember Andy Caddick actually bowled quite well on that first morning,' says Thompson. 'He had them hopping around a bit, and Matthew Hoggard was getting a hint of swing. But once the cloud broke, that was pretty much it, things were desperate from then on – and I don't just mean in that game, I mean for the rest of the series.' Glamorgan paceman Simon Jones, playing in only his second Test, having made his debut against India at Lord's, removed Langer for 32 before lunch, but his England career soon took a turn for the worse. Sliding in an attempt to save four, Jones's studs caught in the turf and he had to be stretchered off. It later transpired that he had ruptured his anterior ligament and he would not play for his country again until 2004. 'He had scared the shit out of Justin Langer as well,' says Thompson. 'And, to add insult to injury, when he was lying on the ground, waiting to be stretchered off, some Aussies were laughing at him and giving him abuse. I remember someone chucking a can of Coke in his direction and someone else shouting "Get up, you Pommie bastard." They say revenge is a dish best served cold, and he got the bastards back in 2005.'

'You could see it was horrible, it was so obvious he was badly hurt,' says Barmy Army co-founder Paul Burnham. 'That was the most disappointing moment on all of my tours abroad. Forget all the negative comments in the press or the crowds swearing at us or the Aussies pissing on the Union flag, the behaviour of the Queensland crowd that day was an utter disgrace.'

Aided by some desperate fielding – Hayden was dropped three times – the hosts finished the first day on 364 for two. Hayden was unbeaten on 186, while Ponting, with whom he put on 272 for the second wicket, made 123. England were not so much on the back foot as covering up in the corner, praying for the bell to sound. If there was a plus point for the Barmies, at least they had a new hate figure to hound.

'Hayden really didn't endear himself to us, not just because of his runs, but because that night he told the press that he was going to get a double-hundred the next day,' says Thompson. 'So we were giving him loads, and then it emerged in the press that he had piles. So we ripped into him even more: "You've got one grape up your arse, you've got two grapes up your arse . . ." Or: "He's gotta sit on a cushion, sit on a cushion . . ." And he didn't get his double the next day [Hayden was dismissed for 197], which was great.'

Nicky Bowes, who was making her Barmy Army debut on that tour, recalls: 'I seem to remember some stories flying about with regard to him off the field as well: you know you get those small children who go out as mascots at the beginning of matches? There was a rumour that he'd been not so nice to a couple of them, and this cemented his position as a hate figure with the Barmy Army. He just looks scary – those hooded eyelids, and he's built like a gorilla, he's just a big scary man. Although if he was English he'd be fine.'

That first day's play prompted the classic headline in the Sydney *Daily Telegraph*: 'IS THERE ANYONE IN ENGLAND WHO CAN PLAY CRICKET?' The Aussie media had written England off already. 'England, to no one's surprise, made another dreadful start to another seemingly ill-fated Ashes campaign,' wrote Robert Craddock. 'People want to know why Nasser Hussain sent Australia in to bat on a perfect wicket, why England could misfield 15 times, why they could drop four catches, why they are simply terrified by the prospect of playing Australia. The greatest worry for England is that they didn't bowl that badly. What we saw yesterday was about what they have got. And that isn't enough to beat Australia anytime this summer.'

Meanwhile, tour virgin Bowes remembers being unprepared for the sheer brutal one-sidedness of that opening day. 'I had only really got into watching England a couple of years beforehand, so it hadn't really occurred to me quite how bad it was going to be,' says Bowes. 'We were definitely underdogs, but there's always an optimism of sorts before the first day of any tour. It's a new series and you never know what's going to happen. But the Simon Jones injury was hideous, and of course Nasser made that monumentally stupid decision to field, which has dogged him for many years since. There was a feeling after that first day that it wasn't going to get any better from here.'

For Paul Burnham, however, the defeatism of the England fans and media on that first day left a bitter taste. 'The problem I had was that everybody decided, as soon as Nasser made that decision to bowl, that he'd screwed up,' says Burnham. 'There was uproar, especially in the press box: "What the hell has Nasser done? You can't do this at Brisbane. What a stupid decision." I remember at drinks I had an argument with [British cricket writer] Michael Henderson. I said, "What are you doing out here?" And he said, "The story's already written for tomorrow, what the hell has Nasser done?" And I said, "We're going to give him the three sessions, aren't we, before we get on his back?" But he replied, "You can't do this at Brisbane, we've got no chance." That sort of attitude got round the whole ground, so even the Barmy Army were starting to think like that. But my attitude is always that we're just there to give the team one hundred per cent support and we expect to get a hundred per cent back – but we didn't give a hundred per cent that day because too many people thought they knew better than Nasser Hussain. I noticed the players didn't seem to believe in themselves that day, they weren't going after the ball full-on, because they could almost sense that the will had gone from everyone, including the Barmy Army. People have got every right to question decisions down the pub after the close of play, but not before we've got to the pub. Our job is to give our full support to the team and that's the only time we haven't – and I don't think it's any coincidence that it ended up with such a poor result. On that first day people were already singing songs abusing the Aussies, "backs against the wall" songs, it was almost as if we'd lost the Test series already.'

England actually staged something of a fightback on day two, dismissing Australia for 492 before Trescothick and Butcher led them to 158 for one by the close of play. However, McGrath removed both early on day three, his 100th and 101st Ashes wickets, as Australia opened up a gaping 278-run lead by the end of the day. The following day, Hayden bludgeoned another ton before the tourists were skittled for a humiliating 79. For Hussain's team and their travelling fans, the writing was on the wall: it was going to be a long, hot winter. As for that toss, it was something Hussain would never be allowed to forget.

'When I went to South Africa in 2004–05,' says Thompson, 'Nasser was working as a commentator for Sky. Through my police contacts I'd managed to get an "access all areas" pass and I went into the media centre at Port Elizabeth. I wound up next to the Sky box and I asked Nasser to sign my book. He was as good as gold and signed: "Everyone knows my name, it's Nasser Hussain." He posed for a photo and everything. When we were leaving, we started getting a barracking from former South Africa batsman Daryll Cullinan, who was leaning over the balcony telling us we weren't supposed to be in there. So I thought, I'm not having that, I'll give him some back. South Africa had gone for loads the day before, Trescothick and Strauss had got runs, and skipper Graeme Smith had been doing the old teapot, with hands on hips, looking round for what to do. So I started giving out, "You're shit, mate, you're going to get hammered in this Test match, Smith hasn't got a bloody clue, doesn't know where to put his fielders, standing there with his hands on his hips – you know what he reminded me of? He reminded me of Nasser Hussain at Brisbane in 2002." And as I said it, Nasser appeared over Cullinan's shoulder, looked down and went "Thanks, mate", and looked at me as if to say "you two-faced bastard, I sign your book, pose for a photo, and this is how you repay me".'

However, Hussain remains grateful for the unstinting support of the Barmy Army to this day. 'At first I probably thought, "Is this just a bunch of inebriated oiks out for a good time?",' says Hussain. 'But the more it happened – the singing, the chanting, the getting behind the team – I realised these were people who would support you through thick and thin. I soon realised they weren't fickle, they weren't there to support us when things were going well and then go quiet and moody when they weren't – and we used to have a lot more bad days than good days back then. In any sort of sport, usually a team's fans go quiet when they're not doing well, but that just wasn't the case with the Barmy Army. You could set your watch by them, you didn't need a clock in the ground, you just knew that after lunch at some stage they would kick off with the usual tunes and you'd turn round to the rest of the lads and say, "The Barmy Army are awake, let's get going boys." It became a regular part of our day.'

In truth, England's boys never really got going at all on that tour. Things just kept getting worse – before getting even worse. John Crawley, who had made a nuggety unbeaten 69 to hold England's first innings together in Brisbane, was injured for the second Test in Adelaide, as was spinner Ashley Giles, who took six wickets at the Gabba. In came Kent's Rob Key and green Yorkshire spinner Richard Dawson, along with Durham paceman Steve Harmison, who replaced the stricken Jones.

Between Brisbane and Adelaide, the Barmy Army took to

the field themselves, playing Gold Coast outfit Helensvale. Predictably, they lost. Almost as predictably, they revelled in their defeat. 'We anticipate losing now,' Barmy Army member Neil Morris was quoted as saying in the *Gold Coast Bulletin,* 'so this was nothing new.'

Day one at the Adelaide Oval saw an innings of rare class from Vaughan, who took advantage of a pristine batting deck to compile a sublime 177. 'Vaughan was imperious in that series,' says Thompson. 'He was free of injuries and in his pomp. He could just plonk Glenn McGrath into the stands with a flick off his hip, he was a joy to watch, the player of the series on both sides. But song-wise, we never really got beyond "Michael Vaughan, my Lord" [to the tune of 'Kumbaya']. Let's face it, he wasn't the most exciting geezer, was he? He'd come out and have a drink and a chat with the fans, but he wasn't "Freddie" Flintoff, know what I mean? On his day, though, he was some player.'

From 294 for four overnight, England collapsed to 342 all out inside twenty-seven overs on day two. Australia racked up 552 for nine declared in their first innings, Ponting scoring 154, before McGrath was to the fore as England fell to an innings defeat on day four. 'I remember Vaughan was batting well on the fourth day,' comments Thompson, 'and McGrath went and took that bloody catch on the boundary, full stretch, on the run. You know you haven't got much of a chance when the opposition's pace bowlers are taking catches like that.'

Remarkably, England's players were hoisting the white flag after only two Tests, with Mark Butcher using his column in the *Sunday Express* to announce that 'Australia have a psychological hold over us'. The Surrey opener continued: 'We are getting slaughtered. There's no point hiding behind fancy phrases, the facts speak for themselves and we have to accept that Australia are playing a different game to us.' Meanwhile, former Australia fast bowler Merv Hughes, never backward in coming forward, accused Hussain of 'giving up'. 'The England selectors would do well to think of a new captain for Perth. In my mind, he just gave up (in Adelaide). His field placings were as if he had a complete lack of interest in what was going on. They had no plan formulated to get wickets and the Australia batsmen could do what they liked.'

In Perth, the Ashes were lost inside three days. On becoming captain, Vaughan would say the Barmy Army were England's twelfth man. During that third Test, the Barmy Army was playing for the other team. 'Brett Lee was left out for the first two Tests but replaced Andy Bichel in Perth,' says Thompson. 'I'd seen him in the nets at Adelaide having blagged my way into the members' area. He was doing boxing training and I thought "Christ, this bloke's fit", and he looked seriously slippery with the ball as well. Anyway, we made the mistake of no-balling him from the stands every time he sent down a delivery, but instead of putting him off, he thrived on it, just getting quicker and quicker and quicker. No one could handle him and Mark Butcher told us later that he was deliberately over-stepping by a couple of yards, trying to kill anyone who was English. Poor old Alex Tudor wore one towards the end of that Test, straight in the face, so we didn't actually do the England team any favours. That wasn't our greatest moment in terms of team relations.' Surrey paceman Tudor was reported as saying: 'We had a bit of duel during the Test, it was one fast bowler trying to get rid of the other fast bowler, but he's a lot quicker than I am and I've come off worse.' It was a microcosm of the tour as a whole, with the Australia side a juggernaut and most of England's players like so many splattered flies on the windscreen.

'That match was a low point, a little bit embarrassing to be honest,' concedes Thompson. 'There was Tudor getting ironed out and I remember Harmison losing his run-up at one point, which shouldn't really happen to a professional cricketer. A load of Barmies ended up watching the England women's hockey team play Australia after day one at the WACA, in the hope they'd see a win. We lost 2–1. But whatever's happening on the field you've got to keep the spirits of the players up, that's our job, we'll never get on any players' backs, that's the Barmy Army code. You all pull together, and it's kind of an unwritten rule that whatever you might say among yourselves in a small group – "He needs to sort his game out," or "He needs to get back to the nets" – when you're up in the stands you get behind them. Nobody goes out to deliberately play badly, do they? At the end of the day the Aussies were a tremendous side – Warne, McGrath,

Hayden, Langer, Steve Waugh as captain – and it was always going to be a struggle to try and compete.'

'That's the whole point,' says Cooke, 'that's what we do: we support the underdogs, we support our team through thick and thin – and when they're losing we support them even louder. And that's a very British thing. It's about digging in, British people get off on that and there are people out there who say Australia 2002–03 is the best tour they've been on. So there was no danger of people sodding off to the beach. That would never happen.'

'It's the press's job, if they want to, to start pulling people apart,' continues Thompson. 'That's for people like [former England fast bowler and Sky Sports summariser] Bob Willis, who's our anti-hero, to start slagging the team off, that's not what we do.' According to the *Daily Mail*'s Ian Wooldridge, who had been so scathing in his criticism of England's fans during the 1994–95 Ashes series, Willis was not a fan of the Barmy Army either. Wooldridge reported an exchange between Willis and a Kiwi commentator during England's visit to New Zealand the previous winter: 'Wonderful fun, aren't they?' said the commentator. 'I don't know about that,' replied Willis. 'I reckon there might be a few people who've paid good money to come in here and watch the game in peace.'

Paul Burnham reckons he knows the reason for Willis's distaste: 'Back in the summer of 1995, I spent the first two days of the Test match versus the West Indies at Lord's trying to flog a Barmy Army T-shirt to a very good friend of mine, an Old Rutlishian called Lance Keen. I bumped into him at the Lord's Tavern at the end of day two and offered him one for a fiver, and he finally caved in. Anyway, he stuck it on and within two minutes Bob Willis had walked in. What I didn't realise was that Lance, for whatever reason, had his own opinions about Bob Willis and he proceeded to give vent to them. Not surprisingly, Willis walked out of the pub with the hump, before his beer had even been poured, and ever since then he's seemed to us to be negative about the Barmy Army. And people occasionally ask me: "What has someone done to make Bob like that?" The irony is I loved Bob Willis to death, he was one of the heroes of that 1981 Ashes series, along with Ian Botham.' Hero or not, the Barmy Army, as ever, responded to his ire in song (to the tune of 'Daydream Believer'):

Cheer up Bob Willis,
Oh what can it mean,
To be the worst cricket pundit,
On the Sky commentary team ...

England had been so comprehensively outclassed in the first three Tests that flak was flying from the most unexpected quarters. 'My mate rocked up for the Melbourne and Sydney Tests and the immigration bloke said: "What's the purpose of your visit then, mate?" And my mate went: "To watch the cricket?" And the immigration bloke went: "No fucking point, why don't you turn round and get the next flight home? You've lost the Ashes." That was the pervading attitude, the Aussies were insufferable.' The British press were also wading in with sharpened pens. 'It was midway through the torrid afternoon at the WACA,' wrote Patrick Collins in the *Mail on Sunday*. 'Flabby acres of Britwhite flesh were turning an indecent pink and the footsoldiers of the Barmy Army were in loud and tedious voice. "We are England," they bellowed, "mighty, mighty England." At that moment, England's mighty, mighty first innings total stood at 156 for eight. It is difficult to isolate the moment at which this Ashes series became absurd beyond words but that depressing juncture would be my nomination.' Collins even mused that future Ashes series should be cancelled.

While the party line is that the Barmy Army never surrenders, a trawl through the newspaper archive reveals that the regular beatings were beginning to take their toll. The *People's* Nick Harris, embedded with the Barmy Army, wrote: 'Now I know why we are called the Barmy Army. Anyone who is prepared to pay their own money to come over here and watch this humiliation has to be a ball short of an over. Losing is acceptable. Losing without a fight is something I never expected from Nasser and his team. It's painful, I can tell you.' The Australian newspapers, meanwhile, were reporting with some relish that the Barmy Army roar had been reduced to a whimper by day three in Perth. As for the

Aussie fans, contempt for the England cricket team had given way to pity. 'They've seen it all before,' wrote Oliver Holt in the *Mirror*. 'The false starts. The promise of resistance. The potential. Followed by the collapses. And the crushings. It's all too familiar. They're inured to it. The visceral joy of beating England disappeared a long time ago for most of them. Now they just pity our cricketers. And wish they could give Australia a game.' Patrick Collins concurred: 'In the course of my tour [of the WACA], England lost three wickets for a trivial splutter of runs. And nobody was remotely surprised. But, by and large, there was little derision. This was England, you see.'

Even the England players were starting to question the sanity of their fans. 'Yeh, I guess we thought they were a bit mad,' admits Hussain, whose side had won their first match of the tour on 17 December – a one-dayer against Sri Lanka. 'We keep letting you down, but you keep coming back, keep spending their money, keep cheering us on. But we enjoyed it immensely. The real amusement came when the songs started up. Test match cricket, however exciting it can be, can also be very tedious and dull at times. All of us are out in the middle for six or seven hours, the over rate might be poor, and you need some moments of hilarity to lighten the mood. So every new tour brought different songs about different cricketers. Obviously they had loads of songs about Shane Warne, and I remember everyone calling Langer a gnome down on the boundary at the MCG after he'd criticised the

Barmy Army in the press. That sort of stuff used to make me smile, it was good fun. There were times when we were standing there listening to the Barmy Army rather than the other way round.'

Langer had invited the ire of the Barmy Army by calling its members 'a disgrace' during the Boxing Day Test in Melbourne, a reaction to the continued 'no-balling' of Lee, who even Aussie pace legend Dennis Lillee conceded had a questionable bowling action, from up in the stands. 'These people stand behind a fence drinking beer, with most of them fifty kilos overweight, making ridiculous comments,' added the diminutive opener. 'They pay their money and that sort of stuff but there's still some integrity in life, I think.' Merv Hughes, one of the game's most formidable sledgers, gave Langer his backing, saying without a hint of irony: 'They [the Barmy Army] are just complete meatheads.' Even some Barmy Army members thought Langer had understated his case. 'To be fair he had a point,' says 'Norfolk' Graham Barber, who was on his second tour down under. 'In fact, he was being quite kind to some of us, who were miles more than fifty kilos overweight.'

'Justin Langer described the Barmy Army's chanting as a disgrace, doubtless trying to protect his team-mate,' says England opener Marcus Trescothick. 'But I had to disagree. As far as I was concerned, Lee was not upset and did not seem to be trying to bowl any faster than he has done all series. He was rapid all the way through. As for the question of the Barmy Army and whether their chanting has any place at Test matches, in my mind it is not even an issue. There is not a player who has toured with England who has not appreciated their presence. England are fortunate. We are the only country among the Test-playing nations that has such a large group of supporters prepared to follow us wherever we go around the globe. They bring so much colour and atmosphere to our games.'

But one unexpected result of Langer's outburst was the reaction of sections of the British media, who rallied behind the Barmies. 'Never mind that the fans have spent thousands travelling to Australia,' wrote David Lloyd in the *Evening Standard*, 'in many case giving up their jobs in support of a team that, in their heart of hearts, they knew had only a slender chance (or, to be realistic, no chance) of victory. No matter that their enthusiasm and vocal support has remained undimmed in the face of three – and maybe four – of the heaviest defeats in our rich cricket history. Whatever happened to magnanimity in victory? Where is Langer's sense of humour? If there has been a bright spot on England's tour (and let's face it, there hasn't) it is the vociferous support given to the team by the Barmy Army.' Miracle of miracles, Ian Wooldridge was even beginning to come round. '... England's Barmy Army spectators, whose once dirgeful chanting from the terraces has been marginally enlivened by a ditty reminding the Australians that the current exchange rate is an advantageous three Australian

142

dollars to the pound sterling. It is the only thing we have to crow about.'

Meanwhile, the love-in between the Barmy Army and the Aussie media showed no signs of waning. When Christopher Bantick wrote in Brisbane's *Courier Mail* that the Barmy Army 'are not funny, witty or even clever', he was quickly slapped into line by fellow Aussie hacks. 'Hats off to the Barmy Army, they've enlivened our summer,' wrote Bernie Pramberg, in the same *Courier Mail* pages. 'Well, those of us with a sense of humour. But not Christopher Bantick, who sanctimoniously savaged the army as lager louts, a disgrace, an unwelcome distraction, unfunny, not witty or clever. It would never happen at Lord's, opined an outraged Bantick. That's too bad, because for the past two months between 2500 and 3000 troops of the Barmy Army have rescued many a dull day's cricket around Australia with their good-humoured antics. Significantly, there were no incidents of violence involving the Barmy Army. We saw no television pictures of sporadic fights among spectators and police dragging offenders away. We've witnessed enough of that in past years, when the yobbos were all Aussies.'

'The last day at Melbourne was the best day of that tour,' says Cooke. 'All players have certain songs about them – Muralitharan used to have a no-ball song we used to sing about him – but they just have to man up and deal with it. And because Lee never really got used to it, we never stopped doing it. In the end we were singing: "Brett Lee, give us a wave, Brett Lee, Brett Lee, give us a wave" and he'd give us a wave, and when he responded, we'd come back with "Keep your arm straight when you wave". So because Langer came out to bat on his behalf and protect his integrity, he had only made things worse. The next time Langer was fielding we all piped up with "hi-ho, hi-ho", and from then on he never stopped being a dwarf to us. And we had the song:

'Langer is an Aussie,
He wears the gold and green;
He is the biggest whinger,
That we have ever seen.
He wasn't very happy,
When we called Brett Lee's no-ball;
He's got a very big mouth,
And he's only five feet tall.

'To his credit, Langer did apologise for his comments, coming over to us at the end of the game to shake grateful Barmy hands and sign sunburnt Barmy bellies.' However, despite his attempts to build bridges at the end of the Melbourne Test, Langer still might have cringed when he read about the Barmy Army's plans for a charity cricket match on Coogee Beach in Sydney on New Year's Day. Hardly the behaviour of 'meatheads', and the event raised thousands for Leukaemia Research.

'We ended up losing [Langer scored 250 in his side's first

innings and Australia won by five wickets to take a 4–0 lead],' adds Cooke. 'But we had them five down on the last day, there were 10,000 of us in the MCG and one Aussie and his dog. It was a fantastic example of the Barmy Army doing its job well.' But it was symptomatic of that series that even when the Barmy Army was doing its job well, it was having a negative effect on the team. 'We had them four down in the second innings, they were chasing a small total, and there was a caught-behind chance,' says Thompson. 'If you talk to James Foster, who was the wicket-keeper in that match, he will blame the Barmy Army for Steve Waugh not being given out. We were all in one block, all getting fired up because we'd taken early wickets, and Steve Waugh got an edge behind off Steve Harmison, but nobody appealed until it was replayed on the big screen, and by that time it was too late. Because we'd all been jumping up and down and making a racket, all chanting "Barmy Army, Barmy Army", it was echoing across the ground, hitting the empty stand and echoing back, so nobody heard the nick.'

While Cooke was heartened by the performance of the Barmy Army at the MCG, she was less impressed that its ranks had been infiltrated by a more unruly type of England fan. 'My lasting memory of that tour was that by the time we got to Melbourne, there were a load of idiots along for the ride,' she says. 'Melbourne, Sydney, Barbados and Cape Town all attract a certain type of supporter. I'd happily never go to a Test match in any of those places again. You kind of get overwhelmed by an idiot football fan mentality, and, in the case of Sydney and Melbourne, lots of expats turn up and try to join up with their compatriots. They think that because there are 25,000 Barmy Army in town they can start fights and abuse people and everyone will back them up. It all becomes too much like football terraces and that's when you need to start managing crowds.'

And while Cooke believes that most of the Barmy Army ditties on that tour were by and large acceptable, she admits there were times when things got out of hand. 'There were a few naughty songs on that tour that went beyond the pale,' she admits. 'Obviously we had stacks of songs about Shane Warne, and most of it was fair game. But there was a song that started up about Warne being a paedophile – "Shane Warne is a paedophile", to the tune of "Go West", not that intelligent, to be honest – and obviously he wasn't very happy about that, he kept mentioning it whenever he was interviewed. And that was probably the result of some of these idiots who had been added to the ranks.'

Cooke, who enlisted with the Barmy Army on the tour of South Africa in 1999–00, was one of only eleven women among the ranks at the start of the tour down under, but the numbers swelled as the weeks ticked over: the female of the English species, it seemed, was every bit as masochistic as the male. 'It was a very laddish environment when I first joined,' says Cooke, who has worked for the Barmy Army for ten years, 'but they were very kind, and not in a lecherous way, they took me on as a mate. I'm very much a tomboy, and I suppose you have to be a bit laddish as a woman to fit into that environment. Most of us are. There are some very girly girls in the Barmy Army, but they all love their cricket and they can also drink and hold their own in the banter stakes. Saying that, we're all a bit odd. Liking cricket itself isn't really a typical female thing to do.'

Nicky Bowes remembers that while the boys were happy to have some girls around, she had to overcome a degree of suspicion. 'I was welcomed with open arms, totally,' says Bowes, who has played cricket since she was thirteen and now plays for and coaches Epsom Ladies. 'They were quite keen to have females on board, strangely. There's a certain type of woman who goes on a Barmy Army tour – it's a very masculine environment so you have to be able to deal with that level of humour and drinking and if you don't really know much about cricket there's a bit of scepticism as to why you're there. More than fifty per cent think that because you are a woman you don't know anything about cricket.'

However, Cooke is adamant the feminisation of the Barmy Army smoothed off some of the rougher corners (although perhaps we should gloss over the Barmy Army's foray into the recording industry on that tour: thousands of copies of 'Professional Boozer', cut in aid of the Red Cross's Bali Appeal, were destroyed because the B-side offended the said charity. The offending track? 'Semi-Flaccid Gun'). 'I think the laddish edge has been taken off the Barmy Army and that's partly my fault, or to my credit, whichever way you want to look at it. I used to try to stamp my authority on things and in particular make sure that we were looking after everyone and being inclusive, that we weren't doing things that would alienate people. I see the Barmy Army as a family brand, and in the cricket community you have to do things in a certain way. So by the end of the Ashes tour in 2002–03, there were definitely more women involved. Husbands had persuaded their wives or girlfriends or daughters to come along, and a lot of the core group had started to get older, so they wanted it to be a more family affair.' That Cooke was able to keep the men in line might say more about the type of men they were than any ball-breaking powers of persuasion: the Barmy Army had never resembled the Chelsea Headhunters, and by 2002–03 they were, according to Brisbane's *Sunday Courier Mail,* 'a mob of up-market yobs from the professions, here for fun and not infamy'.

'Large groups that came on that Ashes series as their first tour were typically in their gap year,' says Cooke. 'So there were big groups of young lads of twenty-one and they're very cliquey because they'd come over as a group from their university hall or whatever and have their own jokes and seemed weird to outsiders. They were young and fit and came straight to the game from nightclubs and casinos each day. But then they didn't come on another tour for two or three years, when they'd got a job and settled down and made some money, and then they came on tour with their girlfriends. Then they'll come regularly for a bit, get married, have children and then you might not see them again until the children were old enough. The touring party is an amalgamation of those three groups, and misses out certain age groups. As for occupations, you're talking lots of shift-workers, people who can save their shifts up: supermarket workers, lots of Post Office workers, lots of police, builders, ambulance workers, firemen. I always know where a doctor is, or a pilot, or indeed a trolley dolly.'

The fifth and final Test kicked off at the Sydney Cricket Ground the day after New Year's Day, and the fight England had shown on the final day in Melbourne had instilled in its fans renewed optimism. 'We hoped the momentum from Melbourne would carry into Sydney and the team would come together as well,' says Cooke. 'But whatever happened, they knew there would be 10,000 of us idiots cheering them on.' Adds Thompson: 'Hope always sprang. There was a guy on that tour called "Bullshit Jim", and I remember him saying as early as Brisbane, "Don't worry, we always win one," as we had done in '94–'95 and '98–'99.'

At the SCG, a group of Aussies decided to pitch idiot against idiot. 'Hamish Ogilvy took 250 friends and a Neanderthal named Gumby and called on Australians to sing,' wrote Peter Munro in the *Sydney Morning Herald*. 'It was the first sizeable challenge to the Barmy Army, the motley group of English cricket supporters whose voices have lorded it over Australian crowds during this summer's Ashes series.' Ogilvy's posse, it was reported, came dressed in bright yellow T-shirts and with a conductor dressed as a caveman. Close by, three hundred-odd 'Fanatics', Australia's 'official' answer to the Barmy Army, joined in the barracking. The Barmy Army were surrounded on all sides. Peter Munro's verdict? 'The Australians rivalled the English but it was perhaps our national Test team that deflated their voices. As a few wickets were lost, it seemed Australian cricket fans, unlike the English, can sing only when they are winning.'

While 'The Fanatics' might have come across as more than a little bit naff, there were signs during the Sydney Test that the Aussies' frustration at being constantly outgunned in the stands was beginning to boil over. A group calling itself Club 51 soured the good-natured mood on The Hill by handing out song sheets containing ditties that glorified the IRA. One excerpt read: 'I wish I was in London, I'd go down to Trafalgar Square and say to the old Lord Nelson there, "Get stuffed, get stuffed, you one-eyed Pommie bastard."' Understandably, the Barmy Army hierarchy was distinctly unimpressed.

Butcher broke free from Australia's psychological stranglehold on day one at the SCG, taking advantage of an attack shorn of McGrath and Warne to score his sixth Test century. No matter that he should have been out first ball, when seemingly plumb in front to a ball from Lee, or that he could have been out on at least three other occasions, the members of the Barmy Army went into raptures when he reached the milestone. All except one. 'There was one lad, Carl, who was selling Barmy Army sunglasses in the ground on the QT and the police dragged him out of the stands and into a detention room,' says Thompson. 'They confiscated his sunglasses and said, "Right, you're out." And he said, "Fair enough, but I've been to every day of every Test match on this tour, I'd like to keep my ticket stub." And the copper went, "You want your ticket stub?" And Carl said, "Yes please," and the copper ripped it up in front of him, like confetti. That was my introduction to the New South Wales police.'

It was a sign of the ruthless competitiveness of Australians that, even though they led the series 4–0, they still refused to give England an inch. 'On day two Steve Waugh reached his century,' says Cooke. 'For some reason, the next morning they had closed most of the ticket barriers and were refusing to let England fans in. The irony is that we were all desperate to get in to see Waugh's final Ashes innings, and he was batting for his place. It was all very frustrating, and at that time in the morning fighting would not have been very good publicity for the Barmy Army. I was trying to calm things down and I do think there was something going on with the Sydney authorities, presumably they thought we were going to try and ruin the moment.'

Australia's swashbuckling wicket-keeper Adam Gilchrist reached his century on day three before the hosts were dismissed for 363, a first-innings lead of one run. Then came another masterclass from Vaughan, who cemented his status as man of the series with a third magnificent ton. 'He was a big hero on that tour, he was phenomenal,' says Bowes. 'He had all the shots, a classic technique, and to see him play like that at Adelaide, at the MCG and the SCG, all these iconic grounds, just made it seem even better. That tour would have been over pretty quickly if he hadn't been there . . . well, even more quickly than it was.'

On day four, Vaughan was finally dismissed for 183 in an England total of 452. Before close of play, Somerset fast bowler Andy Caddick – a man who made Devon Malcolm look like a model of consistency – ripped out Langer and Ponting, while Matthew Hoggard dismissed Hayden, to leave the hosts reeling on 91 for three, still 360 behind. 'Caddick always tried his best, I think,' says Graham Barber, 'but when he was good he was very good, when he was poor he was bloody awful. Thankfully, that day he was good.' The upshot of Caddick's efforts was that after seventy-five days of one-way hurt, England were finally on top. 'I know people who have been to ten Test matches and never seen England win,' says Bowes. 'But that only makes a win so much more precious – you think, I've watched you so many times and now, finally, you're repaying us for all that pain. But there is always a feeling, even now when we're managing to win a lot more, that we could collapse to defeat at any point. Even when we had Australia on the ropes in that game, we turned up on the final day thinking we might lose, and that's a very British trait.'

The pessimism was unfounded. The same Caddick turned

up on day five who had done so much damage the day before, finishing with figures of seven for 92, for ten in the match, as Australia were skittled for 226. England had won by 225 runs. 'In those days any victory was a huge thing,' says Barber, 'and that's what you kept going back for, because you knew that if England put everything together on a given day they could pull something off. We were 4–0 down in the series and suddenly we've stuffed them by 225 runs – how does that work? But we knew a victory might be just around the corner, whatever had happened previously. And the result of that is, suddenly you're thinking, "yeh, I'm definitely coming on the next tour now, we'll be better next time", you forget about everything that's come before.'

'My abiding memory of that match will be that of the support the England side received,' wrote Angus Fraser, now behind glass in the press box with the *Independent*. 'As the match progressed, and the likelihood of an England victory increased, more and more fans seemed to make their way to this suburb of Sydney. The way they sang and cheered as England performed their lap of honour, which was more for the supporters than in celebration of their belated win, it looked as though you were at Highbury and Arsenal had just won the Premiership. [But] these supporters do not need police escorts ... they come to drink, sing, feel the sun on their backs and have some fun at the expense of their hosts but never is there even a slightest threat of violence. For them, and the England team, this was a day to be proud of.'

Others in the British media were asking if it was time for the Barmy Army to be invited through the gates of Lord's. 'Cricket's authorities used to fear the Barmy Army,' wrote Jim Holden in the *Sunday Express*. 'They were mistrusted and misunderstood, and for many years the ECB and Lord's have refused requests from the "generals" for blocks of seats to be reserved for the Barmy Army at home grounds. Surely that must change. The Barmy Army have proved themselves a force for good in English sport for many years now – and I believe that demands official recognition and respect.'

While the Aussie fans, or what was left of them, might have trooped from the SCG cursing that they missed out on a 5–0 whitewash, New South Wales tourism chiefs were rubbing their hands with glee: the Australian government estimated that Sydney businesses would collect more than $3.2 million from the Barmy Army, and minister for tourism Sandra Nori urged the success-deprived England fans to celebrate their one win with even more gusto than usual. 'Australia did not manage a 5–0 clean sweep but an English win is a small price to pay for the benefits the Barmy Army have delivered to Sydney,' said Nori.

'After that Sydney Test, a group of us hung around the SCG after most of the Barmy Army had headed back into town and managed to get ourselves into the members' area,' recalls Thompson. 'We found this empty bar and managed to get served when in walked two middle-aged Aussie birds. They looked us up and down and said: "Who are you guys?"

And without batting an eyelid, this guy Nigel Ryman says, in his broad Brummie accent, "I'm the England physio, these are a few of my mates." And they were like, "Really, you must know all the gossip about what goes on in the dressing room?" And Nigel goes, "Marcus Trescothick is a slave to his neck, I've had to send him to neck realignment classes." Anyway, before you know it, he's signing her programme, slapping his name right next to Nasser Hussain's: "Nigel Ryman – England physio". And the next thing you know he's sat this bird down and he's massaging her neck. Then suddenly, the doors swing open and in walks Michael Vaughan, and one of the lads falls to his knees and starts singing: "Michael Vaughan, my Lord ...". Of course, the penny dropped, and we got chased out of the SCG by security, like something out of *Benny Hill*.'

While for the Barmy Army an England tour is always a glorified holiday, with fun and mischief every bit as important as the cricket, for Hussain the tour as a whole had been a very public form of torture. But that only made the win in Sydney that much sweeter. 'That win was very special,' says Hussain. 'I remember going round to the Barmy Army and letting them know how appreciative we were. You're more appreciative of fans who stick with you, you feel that you owe them. They put a lot of money, time, effort, thought and emotion into their trips. Of course you're doing it for yourself, you're doing it for your country, you're doing it for your team, but you do feel that these people who have stood in this corner of the ground for five days and five Test matches deserve their moment. And we loved giving them a moment to be genuinely cheerful and happy about. We felt we owed them something.

'One of the saddest things in my career was when it went from being "Nasser Hussain's Barmy Army" to "Michael Vaughan's Barmy Army". I didn't mind losing the captaincy, that didn't hurt me too much, but the first time I heard "Michael Vaughan's Barmy Army", that's when it hit me, I knew I had gone. There was nothing better than hearing them singing that, it was very uplifting. I'm sure they had a few dodgy songs about me, but I enjoyed hearing that one best.'

6

Pirates of the Caribbean – the West Indies

Speak to any of the players who were part of the England side that toured the West Indies in 1993–94 and the chances are they will tell you the Barmy Army was born during that series. They would be wrong, of course – the Barmy Army did not officially come into existence until the following winter down under – but the scenes which followed England's victory over the home side in Barbados, the first West Indies defeat at the Kensington Oval since 1935, bore all the hallmarks of Barmy Army tours to come.

'When we beat the West Indies at the Kensington Oval, the first time in almost sixty years we'd beaten them in Barbados, it was like a home game, there was more English support there than West Indian support,' recalls Phil Tufnell. 'They kept us going all the way and by the end of the game everyone was on the side of the pitch, flags were flying everywhere, and when Chris Lewis bowled Curtly Ambrose to win the match the place just went mental, absolutely mental. Everyone came running on the pitch, we all went sprinting off, the players were held shoulder high to the dressing room, all wafted along on top of this mass bundle, and the party ensued from there. We were throwing out jumpers and hats and beers and everything over the balcony and it carried on in the evening. We knew where the England fans were going to have a drink and we had a little wash and brush up and went down and carried it on.'

'I was aware of a Barmy Army-type support before that Ashes series in '94–'95,' says Tufnell's Middlesex team-mate Angus Fraser, who took eight wickets in the hosts' first innings in the 208-run win in Barbados. 'In '93–'94 there was a huge contingent of England supporters when we won in Barbados. I got some wickets and Alec Stewart got a hundred in each innings, and the scenes at the end were unbelievable. All the England fans ran on the pitch and probably half the crowd, maybe eight thousand people, was English. We had a drink with them on the outfield and then in the pavilion after the match. So for me, that was the first time a major army of England support had become apparent on a winter tour. But it obviously became more organised on the Ashes tour the following winter and gradually became more and more recognisable.'

Darren Bailey is a pre-Barmy Army veteran, who remembers that the supporters on that '93 –'94 tour were not so much cricket fans, but transplanted football supporters, although a watered-down version. 'I was in Antigua in '94, when Brian Lara scored 375, which was the highest ever Test score at the time,' says Bailey. 'On the rest day we all ended up on the beach – I say "all", but in those days it was about ten of us – with "Tuffers" [Phil Tufnell] bowling at us, Robin Smith, Gus Fraser. That was old-school. That tour we won in Barbados, with back-to-back centuries for Stewart. I got a big band of us over there, all football types, and we all had the Union Jacks and it was all old-school football chants. Not too raucous, but that's the way it was back in those days, almost like singing on the terraces.

'I preferred it that way. It's great now, but it's huge, it's got even bigger. It became more orchestrated and all of a sudden there was a structure, with songs, charity matches, merchandise, and it had really got big by the 1998–99 Ashes tour. It used to be more unique and compact and more intimate, but I don't think it will ever go back to those early days.'

By the time of the next tour to the Caribbean in 1997–98, the Barmy Army had been in full swing for three years and thousands descended on Jamaica for the first Test at Sabina Park, with many England fans confident of a first series win in the West Indies for thirty years. On the eve of that Jamaica Test, former fast bowling great Colin Croft wrote: 'Almost everything is ready. Almost everyone is in place. The air is tight with expectancy, hope, tension and resolve. Sabina Park is a picture. Yet, the only question mark, the only unpredictable ingredient in this cauldron of tight bellies and straining sinews, is the actual playing strip, the 22 yards of a pitch. No one really knows how it will behave initially, much less how it is supposed to settle down over the next five days.' We were not to find out. After only fifty-six minutes and sixty-two balls on the first day, the match was abandoned, with the pitch deemed too dangerous for play. England had reached 17 for three before the sixth appearance of their physio, to treat batsmen for blows to the hand or arm, prompted an abandonment. Understandably, England's fans were fuming. 'It's a bit of history, I suppose,' Scotsman Eric Sanderson was quoted as saying by the *Jamaica Gleaner*. However, for some of the fans at least, the abandonment came with a silver lining.

'We turned up for the opening day of the first Test only to witness the first ever abandoned match after less than an hour,' says Gary Taylor. 'Before the game was abandoned we realised we were situated in the wrong place and that on the grass bank across the oval was the "Trini Posse" stand, a temporary set-up which provided free food and drinks, a DJ, a swimming pool – and semi-clad dancing ladies. It just had Barmy Army written all over it and we knew this is where we would be spending the rest of the series.

'The West Indies Tourist Board and government quickly sprang into action after the abandonment, realising that this was a public relations disaster, and within twenty-four hours we heard that a party had been laid on at the Prime Minister's house. The following evening all of the England fans were invited down to his place for a huge barbecue, and all of the players were in attendance, with a brief to spend as much time as possible mingling with the fans. The following day we were whisked off to an all-inclusive Jamaican beach resort, and obviously we made full use of the facilities. These resorts are normally frequented by couples and honeymooners. However, as luck would have it, an American bar chain had sent over a group of their best performing barmaids as part of a company incentive scheme. Which, as you can imagine, was nice.'

'The decision that was made was the correct one,' adds Paul Burnham. 'There was one funny story from Jamaica, though: in the nets, [Essex seamer] Ashley Cowan was bowling left-handed and hit the stumps with one delivery. David Lloyd, the coach, said, "I thought you bowled right-handed?" Cowan replied: "I do, but you haven't picked me, so I thought I'd try something else."'

When England returned to Jamaica in 2003–04, it was a very different West Indies team they faced. The 1990s had seen the slow disintegration of a once almost invincible team and by the time Michael Vaughan's men came knocking, the West Indies were borderline woeful. 'Sabina Park in 2004 was very special,' says James 'Beefy' Beare. 'That was the Test Steve Harmison bowled them all out for 47 in their second innings – that was a great day. There weren't many of us in the ground, both teams had got similar scores in the first innings and we'd been out somewhere late the night before and a lot of people didn't make it in. Then when West Indies were five or six wickets down, there was this late influx of people streaming in from all over Kingston trying to get into the ground, and even when we came out to bat again – we only needed about twenty – it was fever-pitch. After we won [by ten wickets inside four days, with Harmison taking seven for 12 in the second innings] they were playing "Three Little Birds" by Bob Marley and the whole England end were singing along. I remember them hanging out of the commentary box, pointing at us, laughing their heads off. In the end they shut the music off, but everyone carried on singing.'

'It's hard to escape the effects of the Barmy Army, with the lower ranks on duty in the Mound Stand and a crack squad on patrol in the Air Jamaica Stand,' wrote Freddie Auld in *Wisden*, 'both of which flank the drowned-out press box. Most days it comes as some relief to the journalists that the Barmies don't get into full voice until the afternoon, usually because they are still feeling the effects of one Red Stripe too many. But today Steve Harmison and Matthew Hoggard gave them an early wake-up call, startling them out of their hazy hangovers while the local supporters sat in stunned silence. For most of the morning, the hooters and whistles were put away. Chris Gayle, a Jamaican, failed again: the locals were not impressed.' The British pressmen were in raptures over the performance of the man former Australia captain Steve Waugh dubbed 'England's white West Indian' on the Ashes tour of 2002–03. 'During an unbelievable 132 minutes of cricket, the Durham paceman transformed an even contest into a stroll for his side with an awesome display of fast bowling,' wrote the *Independent*'s Angus Fraser, who knew all about awesome fast bowling in the Caribbean. 'The West Indies simply had no answer to Harmison's pace and bounce.'

The West Indies team was moved to issue an official press release, in which they 'sincerely apologised to the West Indies public for the shocking performance on the fourth day'. Immediately after the match, four of the West Indies squad were reportedly seen in one of the stands drinking and partying. 'How much lower can it get?' asked the Barbados *Nation*. 'How much more can Caribbean people take?' In the end, said *Nation* reporter Haydn Gill, 'enough was enough for West Indians. The quicker it finished, the better it seemed. The agony wasn't prolonged. The misery was over, the West Indies innings lasting only 25.3 overs. What next!'

Caribbean cricket was in meltdown, and even some of the England fans were wincing. 'Even though I'd seen them batter us for all those years there was some sadness to see a formerly great side being humiliated like that,' says Darren Bailey. 'They got a proper tonking, and have been taking tonkings ever since.' 'We used to go up and have a chat with some of the old boys and they were very knowledgeable,' says James 'Beefy' Beare. 'They'd been to every Test match at Sabina Park for God knows how long – I remember Simon Jones was bowling and this guy was saying what a good bowler he looked and how he'd seen his dad bowl there [in 1968], and he knew all his stats from that match [Jeff Jones took five wickets in that Sabina Park Test]. I felt a little bit for those guys after Harmison had steamed through them. But at the time they weren't that used to losing, so I didn't feel that sorry for them. Although there has been a sense of sadness since, because we all grew up with that unbelievable team in the 1980s, and it would be a real shame if cricket was lost over there.'

The Jamaica pitch debacle of 1998 caused there to be a hastily arranged match in Trinidad the following week, meaning the Queen's Park Oval would host back-to-back Tests. This meant a double dose of (good-natured) verbal warfare between the Barmy Army and the 'Trini Posse'. 'An unlikely fraternity are sitting cheek by jowl at the Queen's Park Oval,' wrote B.C. Pires in the *Guardian*, 'shouting one another down but getting drinks in for one another between overs. The Trini Posse fight an undeserved image at home of being a fair-skinned privileged band of dilettantes. The Barmy Army labour not to be condemned as cricket's version of England football's lager louts and hooligans.'

'We were looking forward to meeting up with the Trini Posse,' says Gary Taylor. 'For the first time we seemed to have found a group similar to us and the only difference was that rather than being shunned by their cricketing hierarchy, the West Indies Cricket Board had embraced their style of support and given them their own section of the ground, where they could sell tickets, run a bar with a DJ, along with a T-shirt operation which was sponsored by some of the top companies in the Caribbean. We arrived in Trinidad late in the evening and got cabs straight to the Pelican Pub, a real landmark in Port of Spain. On arrival we bumped into the Trini Posse's main generals and they took us to heart straightaway. A great night was had and we took them up on their invite to join them the following day for the first day of the Test. A ticket for the Trini Posse stand cost around £12, and for that we got breakfast, lunch and tea, a free T-shirt – and we could drink all day, whether it be beer, rum punch, or any kind of spirit and mixer we could think of, including a local delicacy of rum and chocolate milk. We tried to drink them dry, as we had done to many bars around the world, but to give them their credit, they never ran out – even though they admitted we ran them close!'

England also ran their hosts mightily close on the pitch. Despite mustering only 214 in their first innings, they still grabbed a lead of 23 thanks to eight for 53 from an inspired Angus Fraser. Curtly Ambrose took five for 52 as England made 258 in their second innings, which left the West Indies chasing a daunting target of 282. But despite three more wickets from Fraser, giving him eleven in the match, Carl Hooper played the innings of a lifetime – an unbeaten 94 – to guide his side home with three wickets to spare. 'England dominated that first Test and then managed to lose it on the final day,' says Gary Taylor. 'But because of the abandoned

Test in Jamaica, a second Test had been shoehorned in in Trinidad, which meant we would now be in Trinidad for the carnival – the second biggest in the world and one that we would never forget.

'At lunch in the second Trinidad Test, and at the end of each day's play, we would spend our time in the Cricket Wicket, an open-air pub opposite the ground. We'd stand outside, as most of the crowd spilled over on to the pavement, while the steel pan groups were practising for the carnival next door. That match followed a similar pattern to the first, but this time it was England who prevailed on the final day.'

Remarkably, Fraser took another nine wickets in what was now the third Test as Atherton's men hit back to square the series 1–1. Brian Scovell in the *Daily Mail* wrote that 'the Barmy Army's rendering of "Jerusalem" rang around the ground' as Fraser was steaming in on day one, taking five wickets to help reduce the hosts to 159 all out. Matthew Engel noted in the *Guardian* that on day four, with England chasing 225 for victory and openers Atherton and Stewart inching towards the target, 'even the Barmy Army seemed to have given up chanting, perhaps because on West Indian grounds they are normally no match for million-decibel sound systems'.

'It's different in the West Indies,' concedes Paul Burnham, 'for a start they play music at the grounds and it tends to drown out most of the singing. Anyway, winding up West

Indies bowlers in those days was not advisable. But we did have a couple of songs for the England bowlers – Gus Fraser was immense on that tour, and he had his own song which hopefully helped him to keep going in temperatures we were struggling to watch cricket in, let alone play in:

> My name is super Gus Fraser,
> I'm as sharp as a razor,
> I bowl right-arm fast for England;
> When I walk down the street,
> All the people I meet, they say
> "Oi, big man, what's your name?"
> My name is super Gus Fraser ...

Then there was one for Andy Caddick, who also took a five-fer in that Test:

> Andy Caddick, Andy Caddick,
> Must be worth 500 grand;
> He was too good to play for New Zealand,
> So he plays for Engerland.'

B.C. Pires, again in the *Guardian*, observed what many Barmy Army fans had already noted, that while England supporters would back their team through the dark times, as well as the good, their hosts melted into the background at the first sign of defeat. 'Although the Oval gates were thrown open early, there were precious few locals,' wrote Pires. 'Trinidadians will skive off work on the off-chance of witnessing a West Indies victory but they do not make time for losers. The crowd was almost entirely foreign, with the Barmy Army regulars chanting on the front line. "Where's the Trini Posse now then?" called out a Barmy Army infantryman at the presentation ceremony. It was a fair question. Even Anselm Douglas's hit Carnival song, "Who Let the Dogs Out?", was appropriated by the Barmy Army for the benefit of Jack Russell.'

'The game was finished by lunch on the final day,' adds Taylor, 'and after the post-match presentations and interviews we headed back to the Cricket Wicket. Everyone was so high as we had just witnessed a rare England Test match win in the Caribbean. At one point, one of the lads had just got a round of drinks from the bar and we were all standing outside when a mini-bus drove past with all the windows open. As it went past, we realised it was the England team bus and we instinctively ran towards it. The first player I recognised was Mark Butcher, who we had got to know during the Prime Minister's party. Mark liked a bit of banter and "Chopper" had nicknamed him "O.J.", because he thought he looked a bit like O.J. Simpson. As I got to the window of the bus I cheered and shouted: "Well done, O.J!". And as I did so, Butcher sprayed me full in the face with a can of Tango. Without a thought I took my finger off the end of my full beer bottle and sprayed it back in Butcher's face, and before

How it all began . . .

Paul Burnham (front) joins in the chanting at Sydney in January 1995, as the Barmy Army get into full cry.
Barmy Army Archive

Darren Gough, one of the Barmy Army's early heroes, holds court with the supporters on tour.
Barmy Army Archive

Dave 'The General' Peacock celebrates with Alec Stewart after the famous win in Adelaide during the 1994–95 series. Getty Images

Spreading our wings . . .

The Barmy Army CC pose for a photo before their game in Soweto. From the very early days, the Barmies have always looked to support a range of worthy causes. Barmy Army Archive

Jack Hyams, president of the Barmy Army CC, had so much energy when it came to the evening's entertainments – an extraordinary character. Barmy Army Archive

Mark 'Chopper' Randell (right) makes it up to Shaun Pollock during the 1995–96 tour of South Africa after he finally got his autograph.
Barmy Army Archive

Loyal supporters . . .

A few of the Barmy Army diehards wait for any action on the rainswept third day of the third Test in Durban during the 1995–96 tour.

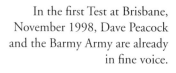

In the first Test at Brisbane, November 1998, Dave Peacock and the Barmy Army are already in fine voice.

The Barmy Army rises to salute the England team at the end of the fifth Test in Sydney, January 1999. Was this a famous win? No, England had just lost the series, but the Barmy Army always back their team. Getty Images

Barmy Army officers . . .

Eight years on from the start of it all, and a Barmy Army reunion gets under way as England take on Australia in 2002–03. Back row, left to right: Monty, Larry, Dave 'The General' Peacock, Colin 'The Eagle'; front row: Yorkshire Gav and Ian Golden. Barmy Army Archive

Vic Flowers, aka 'Jimmy Savile', makes sure that everyone will be in tune for the final Ashes Test of the summer of 2005 at The Oval. Getty Images

Graham Barber leads the choir in 'The Twelve Swanns of Christmas'. Barmy Army Archive

Katy Cooke restores order at pub-closing time with a message to the Barmies that allows for no comebacks. Barmy Army Archive

Having fun on tour . . .

The Barmy Army slip cordon was unlike any other she had ever seen.

Mike Prideaux (in fur bikini) discovers one of the problems that comes from a long session following England with the Barmy Army.

Getty Images

Fancy dress is a vital part of life on tour with the Barmy Army.

Barmy Army Archive

Whatever the weather, the Barmy Army want to enjoy their cricket (and their refreshments), as they demonstrate here during a tour match in Matara, Sri Lanka 2001.

Getty Images

Barmy Army heroes . . .

Patron Matthew Hoggard greets the Barmy Army in Perth during the 2002–03 Ashes series. Getty Images

'Freddie' Flintoff joins the celebrations after England had beaten the West Indies in Barbados in 2004. If he hadn't have been playing, perhaps he'd have joined the Barmy Army.
Getty Images

Paul Nixon dives into the Barmy Army after England's victory in the limited-overs series against Australia in 2006–07. Getty Images

. . . and villains

Justin Langer once accused the Barmy Army of all being seriously overweight – at least he did his research very thoroughly.
Getty Images

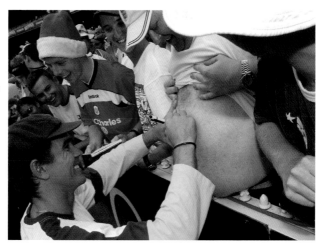

Shane Warne was more of a pantomime villain for the Barmies, and he was always happy to exchange some words with them, as here in 2002 after Australia had retained the Ashes by the third Test. Getty Images

Glenn McGrath tries to silence the Barmy Army during the 2006–07 Ashes series. Even though it was a whitewash, he couldn't do it.
Getty Images

Taking the urn home

Adelaide airport. Australia have just lost by an innings and they are flying out to Perth. Was 'Jimmy' the last person Ricky Ponting wanted to pose with for the cameras?
Barmy Army Archive

Mental disintegration. The Barmy Army do the Mitchell Johnson song in the Sydney Test match in January 2011. Getty Images

Graeme Swann celebrates Ashes victory with (back row) 'Jimmy Savile', 'Bill the Trumpet' and 'Deco', and 'Neil the Pilot' appearing here as the Queen.
Barmy Army Archive

we knew it we were diving through the windows of the bus, spraying every player in sight. We jumped back out of the windows in hysterics and the bus moved on. It was only when the bus drove off that we all looked at each other and said, "What the hell have we done? We've just trashed the England team bus." But within a few minutes the bus was back again, with "Bumble" [England coach David Lloyd] right at the front. All of the players had cameras in their hands and this time they were all hanging out of the windows taking photos of us. Later that night I met "Bumble" in a bar and apologised for drenching the team. "You're joking," said Bumble, "the players loved it so much we made the driver loop around the stadium and come back for more."'

Also in Trinidad in 1998 was journalist Victoria Coren, who concluded, after spending four days with the Barmy Army, that they were not as barmy as they claimed. 'A group of Barmy Army soldiers sit behind a Tadcaster flag. Nick from Sheffield explains their qualifications for the Barmy Army: "We follow football and cricket, drink beer and chat up women." Any success with the women? "None at all," says Nick. And what's the barmiest thing they've got up to out here? "Today we missed some of the cricket to watch a Sheffield United game on TV," says Mike. Compared to the West Indian fans, I suggest, this is not terribly barmy. "Well, no," admits Mike. "But they're completely insane."'

England also won in Port of Spain in 2004, with

Harmison taking six more wickets in West Indies' first innings in a seven-wicket victory. Even the old lions of West Indies cricket, it seemed, were in denial. 'We were on a plane with a lot of the Windies old guard before the Trinidad Test and I remember talking to Viv Richards,' says James 'Beefy' Beare. 'He was chairman of selectors, and he said, "We're gonna come back, you boys are going to get beaten in this Test match." But Graham Thorpe got a few runs [the Surrey left-hander scored 90 in England's first innings] and Harmison bowled well again and we ended up winning easily again early on the last day.

'Port of Spain was great. A friend of a friend who had a cousin out there, some Chinese guy who seemed to know everyone in the whole town, he took us to all these bars and clubs – although it's the sort of place you want to watch your back, you don't want to walk into the wrong place. We found this late-night drinking den. You went up the stairs and they shut this grilled, iron door behind you, and they'd serve us through a banister on the stairs. There was a gambling bit out the back and at far end of the room there were a load of people asleep. The owner just said, "Man, don't worry about them, they've just had a bit too much to drink . . ." We took a load of merchandise down there and they were happy as Larry, looked after us just great.

'The match itself was absolutely crazy. The Trini Posse were in the party stand and you'd get free drink in there all day. The music was pumping and all the promotions girls would come round and dance for you, rolling their arses in your face. Mick Jagger was in the ground on the final day, up in one of the boxes, and the whole ground was jumping up and down, singing "Satisfaction". He loved it, he was doing his walk, sticking his lip out and clapping his hands.'

England were crushed by 242 runs in the fourth Test in Guyana in 1998, Ambrose wrecking the tourists' second innings with four for 38, but the match did at least give the Barmy Army another opportunity to give Douglas's smash hit another airing. 'A dog walked on to the pitch in Georgetown and left an Australia-shaped mound on the square, so from then on "Who Let the Dogs Out?" was sung every night in bars all around the islands,' says Burnham.

As in 1994, the first day of the fifth Test in Barbados saw a mass invasion of England fans – but in 1998 it was on an unprecedented scale. 'Mike Atherton's men might have thought they were playing at the Kennington Oval, not Kensington Oval,' wrote Chris Lander in the *Mirror*. 'Never in 122 years of Test cricket has there been such overseas support for England. Out of a capacity crowd of 12,000, some 7,000 cricket fanatics had made the 10,000-mile round trip to the Caribbean for this one Test match. Paul Burnham, the long-standing organiser of the Barmy Army, said: "I've never seen anything like it." As Atherton and Stewart walked to the crease, the noise was more akin to the England soccer or rugby team running out at Wembley or Twickenham.'

England's victory charge in Bridgetown, set up by a

majestic 154 by Mark Ramprakash, his first for his country in thirty-eight innings, was ruined by the weather on the final day. Luckily, for England fans, Barbados is always about far more than just the cricket. 'Barbados is always a great Test, there's always a party,' says Ricky Ward. 'And there's always a bit of star-spotting that goes on, always a few famous faces. I remember we were staying on Rocky Beach and there was a hotel there where all the press and famous faces used to stay, and a great beach bar serving strawberry daiquiris. We played beach cricket there every evening, and one night we had Gladstone Small bowling to us and various celebrities in the field. One day I was bowling and I was driven straight back over my head, the ball went miles, and this old boy picked the ball up. And I thought, I won't embarrass him by trying to get him to throw it back to me, sprinted up to him, and it was Dickie Bird. He held up the ball and said, "I don't think you'll get much spin with that, lad." That will live with me for the rest of my life. I invited him to do some umpiring for us, but he had some books to sign. But that's why people love Barbados so much: you can be standing in a bar in The Gap and Brian Lara will sidle up beside you, it's that kind of tour.'

'I was having a bit of a romance with a young Swedish bird on the 1998 tour,' says Darren Bailey, 'and I took her to the Test in Barbados. On the last night of the match we ended up in this club and lo and behold, Mr Lara was there. He started dancing with her. And a few of my mates were saying to me, "Have a look, mate, you're in trouble." He was with her for a while. But I walked up and took her away from under his nose and said, "Come on, Brian, you can't get all the girls." His face was a picture. I said to him, "Any chance of a photo, mate?"'

'At the old Kensington Oval, they had the bar at the back of the stand selling rum and Banks beer,' adds Ward. 'In '98 there were always kids running around asking for your empty Banks bottles, and we soon realised there was a five- or ten-cent deposit on every bottle. In the end we'd be giving the money to the lads for ten new bottles and they'd go and buy them, bring them back with the correct change and everything, so we never missed an over of cricket and they were making some money out of us. Over the course of the five days we got to know them quite well and ended up paying for them to get in. They had a good little enterprise going. It's funny how the little things always stand out.'

Occasionally in Barbados, some cricket breaks out. 'We won the series in Barbados in 2004,' says James 'Beefy' Beare. 'We were in trouble at one point and Thorpe got a really important knock [Thorpe rescued England's first innings with a magnificent 119 not out]. Then Matthew Hoggard got a hat-trick on the third day [West Indies were all out for 94 in their second innings], but I overslept and missed it. I got in the ground afterwards and everyone was giving me stick, I'll never live that down. But I'd been on the lash for about three weeks by that stage and it was starting to take its toll. Everyone went mad when we wrapped it up [inside three days]. There was this group of nuns there, lads from Oldham, and when we won one of them got on the pitch and he was being chased by this security guard, he got right out into the middle, and by the time they were taking him off even the guard was laughing his head off. Then the team came round and one of the players started spraying champagne into the crowd and all of a sudden the fence collapsed and everyone spilled on to the pitch. Well, it was England's first series win in the Caribbean for thirty-six years.'

'I'd been going to the Caribbean for a good few years and we usually went to Barbados 3–0 down, so it was great to actually win after all that time having been battered by Marshall and Garner and Ambrose and Walsh for all those years,' says Darren Bailey. 'It was good to see. But even though that was my first big series win after almost twenty years of travelling with England, it was also a bit of a shame. They were my idols growing up in the 1980s, people like Viv Richards and Desmond Haynes. So there were mixed feelings.'

It was in Barbados in 2004 that the legend of Bill 'The Trumpet' Cooper was born. Almost. 'I saved up with a few mates to go on the Caribbean tour in 2003–04, that was always a dream of ours,' says Cooper. 'Five of us went over for Barbados and Antigua and I took a trumpet with me because that's what I do for a living and the day I was due to get home I had to do a big concert. I freelance as a classical trumpeter with various orchestras and opera companies and ballets and whatnot. I've played with the English National Ballet, the Royal Ballet, the London Philharmonic. But I've always been a cricket fan, unfortunately I was never any good at playing it.

'I got to Barbados, and of course I didn't do any practice at all. To make matters worse, I ended up losing the trumpet in the taxi on the way from the airport. I reported it stolen for the insurance and didn't really think anything more of it. Two weeks later in Antigua, the fourth Test when Lara got his 400, on day four of the game I could hear this noise on the other side of the ground which sounded a bit like a trumpet. So I went over, where the Barmy Army hardcore were, and said, "That's my trumpet." And the bloke said, "I found it in a taxi in Barbados". He had played the trumpet for six months when he was young and was trying to squeeze a few notes out of it for a bit of a laugh. So they said, "If it's your trumpet, prove it, give us a few tunes." I played "The Great Escape", which is what I always kick off with to this day, and we ended up having a bit of a singsong. I also remember playing "Rule, Britannia!" and it was commented upon in *Wisden Cricket Monthly*, about it not being particularly apt in a former colony. But it was just meant as a patriotic song, like "Jerusalem" and "Land of Hope and Glory". At the end of the day Paul Burnham came over and said, "I run the Barmy Army, that was brilliant, can you do the same tomorrow?" So I did the next day as well, the final day of the tour. After that Paul said, "I want you to do it at home Tests as

well, and I want you to come to South Africa next winter."
I didn't really believe him, to be honest, but he was true to
his word and it took off from there.'

Having suffered thirty-six years of heartbreak in the
Caribbean and been blitzed by an innings in Antigua in
1998, Vaughan's England were keen to secure a series whitewash at the Recreation Ground in 2004. They had not
bargained on an act of sporting genius from the very top
drawer from one B.C. Lara, who rewrote the record books
with a mind-boggling innings of 400. 'I didn't really take
much joy from Lara's knock,' admits Ricky Ward. 'The West
Indies desperately needed a win and I thought he played for
himself and they ended up with a draw. The track was so flat
and if it wasn't for Chickie's Disco and a few rums, a lot of
the boys would have stayed in the pub.

'Everyone was offering you rum all the time, you could buy
gallon bottles and bring it into the ground. Things are a bit
more sanitised now. But the old ground in St John's was the
best bit about Antigua. You were right in the middle of town
and there was that Double Decker stand with the wooden
benches, so you were right on top of the action. There was
"Gravy" dressed up as a woman – I saw him once arriving at
the ground, some middle-aged bloke wearing jeans and train-
ers. But when he reappeared he was in tights and a dress. But
it was Chickie's Disco that really made it. "Chickie" has been
there a long time, and had the whole ground wired up for
sound and these huge, skyscraper speakers. In between overs

he'd even delay the play because he'd be whacking on a new tune, he really got the place jumping. When Lara was racking up the runs, the stand was rammed with locals, and everyone was jumping up and down with the reggae beats. And not having been there before, we were all thinking, "Bloody hell, the whole thing's moving." And when Lara reached his 400, it felt like it was going to collapse, we were all hanging on to the railings. Put it this way, it wasn't Lord's.'

Nick Davies described the giddy clash of cultures in the *Guardian*: 'The Double Decker is madness on legs, a boiling mass of flesh, as the two tribes begin to merge – Rastamen, the Barmy Army, huge old ladies with children crawling over them like cats in a tree, a rather prim English couple (he adjusting his spectacles, she in her pink summer-fete hat with a scarf round the brim), all jigging and jogging and joining in the riot.'

'The West Indians all thought they were going to get whitewashed,' recalls James 'Beefy' Beare, 'and I remember after Lara got that score they were all walking around with these T-shirts, "Too Black for a Whitewash". The place just went wild when he went past Matthew Hayden's previous record [of 380]; all the England fans were singing his name in the end. A lot of us were staying at this resort called the Jolly Beach, an all-inclusive place, and both the teams were staying there as well. And I remember the locals used to call it Cell Block H: all the rooms were in this concrete block, the beer was terrible, so we used to go to this casino and on the last day a lot of the players joined us and they were all up singing karaoke, "Freddie" [Flintoff] was standing on the bar singing "Suspicious Minds". It was awesome.'

'I was asked by their local media after the match if we had any sympathy with what was happening to West Indies cricket,' says Ricky Ward. 'Ultimately, the players still saw themselves as superstars, and I remember saying, although England didn't have any superstars in their squad, what they put together were workmanlike performances and they played for each other. All their players were swanning around as if it was going to be easy and they came a cropper. They thought they'd just have to turn up – "England haven't won here for years, we've got Lara, of course we'll win the series." So I didn't feel for them at all really. Obviously I didn't realise how far they would fall, but at the time I thought it was great. You had poor sods like "Bails" [Darren Bailey] who hadn't seen England win a major series on the road for twenty years. There was a long time there, in the nineties in particular, when there was not a lot of success, and that's what the Barmy Army prided itself on, we would still cheer and still have a lot of fun. But while much is made of the Barmy Army thriving as the underdog, most of us will say we prefer to see England winning, which is why that series win in the Caribbean in 2004 was such a legendary one. To win in the Caribbean for the first time in thirty-six years was sensational. Although it's all a bit blurry, what with the rum.'

7

Barmy Army special forces – Asia

England's tours to Pakistan, Sri Lanka and Bangladesh are chances for the Barmy Army to prove to the British media that it is more than a glorified Club18–30-style booze crew: no clubbing in Karachi, no daiquiris in Dhaka and no lap-dancing in Lahore. The tours are evidence the Barmy Army was a shifting entity, altering its make-up depending on which country it happened to be in at any given time. So while the fair-weather fans seek out more hedonistic desti-nations, Pakistan, Sri Lanka and Bangladesh play host to the hardcore.

'I did Bangladesh from start to finish in 2010 and that was probably my favourite ever tour,' says Barmy Army veteran Katy Cooke. 'It felt as if we were the Barmy Army's crack squad. Me and Nicky [Bowes] were there from the very first day of the first warm-up match at the Bangladesh Institute of Sports in Fatullah. What I remember about that match was that there was no seating, we were all sat on grass banks and at one point there was a huge commotion over the other side of the ground. Someone had snapped a chair from the concrete and it looked like he was hitting someone with it, which seemed weird, because that tour was pretty much alcohol-free. It turned out it was a snake that had snuck on to the outfield. You don't get that at the MCG.

'You could have a drink in Bangladesh, there was a British club, but if you want a drinking holiday, you don't go to a Muslim country. We wouldn't really have to tone down the behaviour in Bangladesh, that naturally happened, because of the lack of alcohol. The boozers save up their money for Barbados, Sydney or Cape Town. But you'd be surprised how many were on that tour. We did a hundred and seventy-five shirts that we were going to give away for free for anyone who turned up, and we ran out and had to do another batch. But the Barmies that end up in a place like Bangladesh are there for two things: cricket and culture.'

Nasser Hussain was skipper when England pulled off their famous win in Karachi in 2000. As he and Graham Thorpe guided England home in near darkness, it may have seemed like they were on their own. But there were England fans out there amid the gloom, albeit a happy few. 'I think it says a great deal about the commitment of the Barmy Army that they make it to places like Pakistan,' says Hussain. 'You look at some of these Test matches abroad, in places like Karachi or Lahore, they don't always sell very well. But the England fans make the crowd, make it an interesting arena, an interesting place to be. There's nothing worse than playing a Test match in front of one man and his dog. So I used to be very appreciative of the Barmy Army members who made trips like that.

'But aside from what it says about their commitment, it also says a lot about the type of people they are. They don't just go to Pakistan or Bangladesh or India because they want to show their commitment to the England cricket team. That's part of it, but they also go there to show they are deep, thoughtful people who want to sample different cultures of the world. They don't just want to do posh hotels in rich parts of the world, they want to visit places that are off the beaten track. It says something about a person, whether they be a member of the Barmy Army or not, that they want to come and follow England in these places.

'It was something we had to remind our team of all the time. Pakistan used to get a bad name [Sir Ian Botham once quipped 'Pakistan is the sort of place every man should send his mother-in-law to, for a month, all expenses paid'], but we had some great tours of Pakistan. We used to enjoy going out, mixing with the locals, and that sort of mentality led to the series success in 2000 [England won the three-Test series 1–0]. The Barmy Army have a similar mentality: they go to a country and sample the culture, enjoy the culture and take it on board.'

'Michael Vaughan has always said that if England were playing in a place like Faisalabad and they had even fifty people up in the stands, it made a hell of a difference,' says Graham

Barber, who has toured Pakistan twice, the last time in 2005. 'I was there in Faisalabad in 2005, when a gas canister exploded on the boundary and Shahid Afridi did his dance on the wicket and was subsequently banned. It was the first time we'd been back there since the "Shakoor Rana affair" in 1987, and, to be fair, that's probably a good thing, it is a bloody awful place. There is a sense that we're the Barmy Army's crack platoon, the only ones mad enough to go. I thought I was paying six pounds a night for a hotel room in Faisalabad, but, when it came to paying up at the end of the Test, it turned out I was paying six pounds for the week. There was no blanket, just an animal skin on the bed, and every room came with its own cat, because the cat ate everything else that lived in the room. Mention Faisalabad to Matthew Hoggard and he'll just start talking about his rat that was eating all his fruit. Not sure where his cat went, probably got eaten by the rat. Bit different from the Radisson in Sydney, know what I mean? But you know what, it's stuff like that which makes those smaller tours far more memorable, and bloody good fun.

'They've got their own cheerleader up in the stands, the bloke who wanders about with the green outfit on, and the ones who turn up are all nuts about cricket. And a lot of them are just fascinated by the fact that you're in their country, they all want your email address and your autograph. You've got to do those places as well because you learn so much more. Some of the places you visit are just wonderful – the Gardens in Lahore, for example, and the changing of the guard ceremony on the Waga Border between Pakistan and India. People can't believe I go and watch England play in Pakistan. But I say, "Why not? It's a lovely country." If you go there with an open mind you're never going to have a problem.'

'There weren't many fans out there in 2005 because of the earthquake and everything else, it wasn't easy at times,' says David 'Speaky' Speak. 'You used to wake up in the morning and the place was just full of smog, it was hot and humid. The first day of the Test match in Lahore the bus turned up to take us to the ground and the motorcycle cop said, "We're not going to give you an escort because you'll become a target for the suicide bombers," and I thought, "You're having a laugh aren't you?" When we arrived in Pakistan we had the television cameras all round us, and if you have a television camera with you in Pakistan it's like a bee to honey, loads of kids around you grabbing your hands, it's quite intimidating. We all got in there before the start of play on the first day, Michael Vaughan was walking out to open the batting with Marcus Trescothick, and they heard Billy ['The Trumpet'] pipe up with "God Save the Queen". And Vaughan told us later that he turned round to Trescothick and said, "Come on, let's do it for them," and they put on a hundred for the first wicket.'

England lost that three-match Test series in 2005 2–0, and, watching Mohammad Yousuf score a double hundred in dusty Lahore, the glorious Ashes victory of the previous summer must have seemed a dim and distant memory for even the hardiest of Barmies. But every Pakistan century, every England wicket, every night spent under an animal skin with only a cat – or a rat – for company only ramped up the kudos for those who were able to say 'we were there'.

'There's a hell of a lot of snobbery,' says 'Surrey' Mark Jacobs, 'and there's also snobbery in the way you do it. There are those who say you should do everything as cheap as possible, preferably without a roof over your head. But I'm always about the best hotels and restaurants – me and Graham [Barber] have been called the "BCBs" in the past – the "Business Class Boys".'

'There are people on these tours who will choose to pay fifty-five pence a night for a room, sleep on a piece of sack and travel everywhere by bus,' says Andy Thompson. 'Those sorts of people you won't see in Australia or Cape Town or Barbados. There is a bit of a Barmy Army hierarchy, a bit of snobbery that goes on: sometimes you'll be in a bar and some people will walk in that the hardcore might not know and you'll start hearing stuff like "when I was in Karachi in 2000", or "remember that time in Chittagong in 2003". I call it Barmy Army Top Trumps. There are people who make snidey comments about people who only come out for the "glamour" tours. I just want to watch England play cricket, I don't care where they're playing. But there are people who think, "I fancy Australia, there are nice birds there, or South Africa, where the women are even better looking," and to be honest, each to their own, you can't really argue with that.'

'Paul [Burnham] calls them his "Category A" members,' says Nicky Bowes, who was in Bangladesh in 2010. 'Other people might call them "the clique" – people who have been around forever, who go on all the smaller tours, almost like the Barmy Army's special forces. People who go on tours like Bangladesh tend to be people who are ultra-keen on their cricket. It's not a glory tour, it's hard work. I know that sounds really crap, because you're on holiday and all you're doing most of the time is sitting in the sunshine watching cricket, but it's a very poor country and your luxuries are completely taken away from you. And you know when you go to Bangladesh you might get dysentery and, even worse, you're not going to be able to drink in the ground, and some people get put off by that. A lot of people think, "Barmy Army, it's all about drinking, isn't it?" But actually some of us can go along and spend the whole day watching the cricket without having a drink. Admittedly, not that often, but we can do it. It's what travelling is supposed to be, about experiencing new things and different cultures. And the fact you can combine that with cricket and close friends is fantastic.'

Andy Thompson, however, is keen to point out that even in deepest, darkest Lahore, there is plenty of drinking to be had. 'In the Barmy Army we've got something called "Neil's Rules", named after one of our members, Neil Stentiford: when the opposition are batting, you go to lunch and you stay in the pub until a wicket falls. That Test match in Lahore in 2005, we went to the American Club and Yousuf had just been joined in the middle by Kamran Akmal – they put on 269 for the sixth wicket and we got absolutely spangled.'

'There was about fifty of us in Lahore and it was amazing, because we didn't really know what to expect,' says 'Surrey' Mark Jacobs. 'They were friendly people and there was a bar just across the road from the cricket ground, which was excellent, because we had feared the whole week would pass without getting drunk, and you can't do that. We all signed up as members and they took more in that week than they usually take in the whole year. But I went because I wanted to see Pakistan, you really want to see every country, complete the set.'

Tours to poverty-stricken countries such as Pakistan and Bangladesh also provide the Barmy Army with the opportunity to show off its altruistic side. 'We try to arrange it now that we get one charity game in before every Test match, people just want to play against the Barmy Army,' explains David 'Speaky' Speak. 'We even had a streaker on the last tour of Australia. We played a Geoff Lawson XI at Sydney University Cricket Club, which is a beautiful place. [Australian wicket-keeper] Tim Paine was playing, and let's just say "Speaky" cleaned him up; that was another big "Speaky" scalp. We all went to Pakistan in 2005, played two or three games during a stop-off in Bahrain, then on to Lahore to raise money for the earthquake victims. The game in Lahore raised £2000–£3000, people came from everywhere to watch it. We won and I got the first wicket – lbw, their opener. In fact, I'm probably the number one wicket-taker in the Barmy Army.'

'The Barmy Army does a hell of a lot of charitable events and raises a lot of money,' says Barmy Army diehard George Summerside, from Sunderland. 'Most of it is very well organised by the Barmy Army hierarchy, but on that tour of Bangladesh in 2010, something happened that was a lot more off the cuff. There were about forty Barmies in the crowd for the first Test in Chittagong and after the usual opening hymn of "Jerusalem" we started to make some noise, going through our usual repertoire. The Bangladeshi kids were fascinated and swarmed round where we were sitting, looked at us in amazement. This was frowned upon by the local constabulary, who tried to move them on with big sticks. Obviously, we never felt uncomfortable at all, but the police insisted.

'After lunch they started to sing some of their songs. It was then that myself, Giles Wellington and his wife Hayley noticed Bilal: he was in the middle of their crowd and was singing away like an angel. So, at tea, when it was a little calmer, I kidnapped him and smuggled him in with the Army. Giles decked him out in a uniform, a Barmy Army T-shirt, which he wore with pride, and a Barmy Army flag, which he waved in the breeze. He was a fantastic kid, eloquent, very polite and very, very cheerful. But it was his singing voice which stood out most. I remember he sang a ballad about his country, which was beautiful to the ear, almost made us cry.

'After tea, we were swamped by kids again. We were fine, but the "Bangladeshi Old Bill" (BOB, as we got the locals to call them) tried to move them off. I had been to Bangladesh in 2003 and had learnt the native lingo for "no problem" and "OK". What this sounded like in a Sunderland accent I have no idea, but "BOB" moved back and let the kids mix freely. We soon had them singing Barmy Army songs, which was great, and even the players acknowledged it. Bilal wouldn't take anything off us – ice lollies, water, nothing – until we absolutely insisted. And then at the end of play we had a whip-round. It wasn't much to us, but it was obviously a lot to Bilal. Myself, Kevin Adams and Phil Knaggs put Bilal in a tuk-tuk and told him to give the money to his mother, but also to buy a ticket for the next day's play and meet us in the stadium. I gave him my phone number and his mother phoned me on his immediate return home to thank us all.

'The next day, bright and early, there was Bilal, in his Barmy Army shirt, knotted at the waist to take up the length, waving his Barmy Army flag. He was glowing with pride. After "Jerusalem", Hayley suggested he start the chants off. He duly obliged with a rousing rendition of "We are the Army ..." He was a star. His favourite chant was "Swanny Supernova in Chennai", and he even got to sing this to "Swanny" himself.

'Play finished early and we ended up at the players' hotel, a good group of us and Bilal. He was fascinated and had pictures taken with most of the players (we later had the pictures developed in Dhaka and mailed them to Bilal). And when the players had to leave it was time to put Bilal in a tuk-tuk, as it was early evening by now, and we were all standing there in tears – none more so than me! A fifty-one-year-old ex-fireman, sobbing, like a child. I told him to phone me when he got home. He did, and this time he got his dad and his mam on the phone. And his sister, his two brothers, the next-door neighbour ... in fact, I think, pretty much the whole village. It was a very emotional side of tour-ing that one wouldn't expect.'

'Everyone hankers after the old days, it's just about getting old, I suppose,' says Ricky Ward. 'There are a lot of younger guys on tour now, which has to be a good thing as far as the Barmy Army is concerned. But I class the period between 1998 and 2003, when England visited Pakistan, Sri Lanka and Bangladesh, and there was the coming together of a real hardcore group who went on pretty much every tour, as the Golden Age of the Barmy Army. It was all so intimate and we really got to know each other. With success, people want to get involved and it's become a bit more structured, if you like. I wasn't out there when we won the Ashes in 2010–11, and although I wished I was, I actually prefer the smaller tours. If England were going to play Pakistan in Abu Dhabi, I'd rather do that than go back to Australia. I've done all that, I'll leave it to the younger guys now.'

For Cooke, the more intimate tours have provided her

with the chance to prove to a still suspicious media that, not only did the Barmy Army have a heart, but that its members were as into the intricacies of cricket as they were. 'We'd bump into the *Test Match Special* guys all the time on those tours,' says Cooke, 'and because I was a girl, they'd want to chat to me, stuff like "what's a nice girl like you doing in a place like Lahore?" So when [*TMS* scorer the late] Bill Frindall went home after the Tests, I ended up scoring for *TMS* in the one-day series. I had to spend the entire Test series learning Bill's linear scoring system, which was quite traumatic. At the end of each session I'd have to go up to the box and have my work marked, to see if I was up to it. I was, so I travelled with the BBC for the rest of the tour.'

Bill 'The Trumpet' Cooper, too, finds time to hobnob with the doyens of the commentary box on the so-called 'smaller' tours. 'I sometimes bump into "Bumble" [David Lloyd] on tour and have a drink with him and when I was out in Australia I ended up talking at a few functions he was talking at as well,' says Cooper. 'And I always say to him, "Have you got any requests?" Back in Pakistan a few years ago he asked for "Now Is the Hour" which I didn't know, so I had to ring my mum and get her to sing it down the phone to me. And on the last tour of Sri Lanka he asked for "Lord Hereford's Knob", by Half Man Half Biscuit [who also wrote the seminal cricket pop song 'Fuckin' 'Ell It's Fred Titmus']. It's not the sort of thing I'd expect to know, to be honest.'

You might think spending an entire Test series in Pakistan

learning Bill Frindall's linear scoring system is a little bit geeky. And you would be right. 'We're all nerds, that's a given,' Cooke happily admits. 'We all like cricket – what's more nerdy than that? I have sat in a ground as a spectator and scored a Test match, for Christ's sake. The Barmy Army decided early on to be as inclusive as possible and it's a very strange club from that point of view. You will meet certain members and think, "Oh my goodness, how does this man have any friends?" And sometimes they don't. There's one Mancunian nerd, he's very special. He writes amazingly well, really funny pieces, and every year he writes a spoof cricket journal which everyone can't wait to read. He's a comedy genius, and then you meet him. Even the ones who look quite cool and sound quite cool, the ones who are season-ticket holders at football clubs and Essex CCC, they might look and sound the part, but you'll find out they collect Toby Jugs or something. But the Barmy Army doesn't turn anyone away. If you want to support England playing cricket, come along, there's a place for you.'

By the time of England's three-Test tour of Sri Lanka in 2001, Cooke was working for the Barmy Army one night a week, and being at the heart of the operation gave her an even greater sense of achievement when her troops performed manoeuvres well. 'I went on my own completely,' says Cooke. 'I didn't book any accommodation, I just thought "I'll meet them all when I go out there". I'd been working for them one night a week since the South Africa tour, typing emails and generally helping out with their admin, helping them be more organised. I only made it to the last Test in Colombo, and we won it to claim an historic series win [it was the first time England had won four successive series since Mike Brearley's side in 1978–79].

'There was quite a lot of controversy on and off the pitch on that tour. It was Graeme Hick's last series, Graham Thorpe was reported to have marriage problems and there were all sorts of niggles in the press about the team. So we were desperately trying to get behind them, there was a huge rallying of the troops to try to deflect all the negativity coming from elsewhere. That was a big pat on the back for us, you always feel you've been a part of it when something like the win at Colombo happens [twenty-two wickets fell on the third day as England won by four wickets, with Thorpe making 113 not out and 32 not out], it becomes quite personal because you feel the players have reacted to you as a group. When we do it well – there are times when we do it drunkenly and badly – the hairs on the back of my neck have stood on end, you can feel the love.'

However, despite their obvious passion, the Barmy Army still had a long way to go to win over everybody in the press box: 'For those of us who endured the Barmy Army's limited repertoire on last winter's tour to Bangladesh,' wrote David Hopps in the *Guardian*, referring to England's visit in 2010, 'a contest that did not noticeably cause the nation to miss a heartbeat, the collapse of sterling is even more disconcerting.

Nobody sung in Dhaka or Chittagong about the fact that there were about 111 Taka to the pound. And even the dimmest Barmy Army foot soldier knows that it is not the done thing to boast about the exchange rate in a poor third-world country. Nobody has done that since colonialism was universally regarded as a jolly good idea.

'All that the Barmy Army – more a platoon than an army actually – sang in Bangladesh was endless renditions of "Jerusalem", most discordantly just as the morning mist began to clear before start of play. The England players loyally waved their thanks as they walked out to field and in the media box we all grumbled at the noise, both of us – players and press – playing our parts to perfection.'

For many Barmy Army members, Sri Lanka is Shangri-la, a beguiling mix of cricket, culture and all-important hedonism. 'Sri Lanka is my favourite,' says David 'Speaky' Speak. 'The first time I went there in 2003, I just felt at home. People have said to me, "What do you want to go to Sri Lanka for?" But it's great, the locals want to talk to you, they want you to play cricket with them in the street, sometimes they want to feed you at their house. Then you've got access to the players at the practice games, when you can walk round the pitch and have a craic with them.'

Adds Andy Thompson: 'I love Sri Lanka. Australia is great, but it is hard work. You can't go for a quiet beer in a Barmy Army shirt in Australia, you just end up getting hammered wherever you go. In Sri Lanka, the food's brilliant, the people are brilliant, that's my favourite tour. On my first trip to Sri Lanka I stood on the hill for a week and it cost me less than a quid – twelve and a half pence a day. Fantastic. In Pakistan they were letting people in for free. The smaller tours are better because you get to know people better, you get to bond. And in Sri Lanka, they just don't understand why you're there, they don't get it. But they welcome you, they'd give you anything. Also, I like trying to blag my way into places, press boxes, things like that, and that's always easier on those smaller tours. I managed to blag my way into the old pavilion at Kandy and ended up sitting there with all the players' families having a meal. It's bit of a challenge, when there's a bit of a lull in play, "Where can we get into? What can we try and do?" You can usually get past security, but it's when you get into the press box that they all start har-rumphing. None of the journos has got the guts to stand up and say, "Excuse me, he's not supposed to be here," but you can tell they're not happy, they're all looking round in despair.'

'The first Test in 2003 was in Galle and then we went down to Kandy and back up to Colombo,' adds Speak. 'From Galle to Kandy is "the road of death", as anyone who has ever done that trip will tell you – it's like *Wacky Races*. Before I left Galle I got gastroenteritis – which is something you don't want. So I said, "There's no way I'm getting the bus all the way from Galle to Kandy, not a chance." So I got a cab back to Colombo and hired myself a driver. The next day the Barmy Army hardcore were going up to the elephant orphanage on the way to Kandy. I got the bloke to drop me off at the orphanage and waited for the Barmy Army to turn up and when they got there I was in the middle of the river with the elephants, I just had to bung one of the fellas a quid and a fag. I always remember them all walking down and people saying, "What the fuck are you doing in there?!"

'Then, on the last tour of Sri Lanka, on the streets there were all these big dropdown posters of "Murali" [Muttiah Muralitharan], who was on the verge of reaching some milestone or other, on every street light. There were only about four left by the end of the day because my little bloke who was driving me around was climbing up and we were flogging them to the Barmy Army. I brought mine home and this year I'm going to try to get "Murali" to sign it. But I always like to get a bit of culture in as well as the cricket. When I was in Sri Lanka it was the elephants, in Barbados I swam with the dolphins, in South Africa I got in a cage with some lion cubs, which was interesting: if it wasn't for the chap who was sweeping up I might not be here because he ended up hitting one of them with a brush as he was digging his claws into my back.

'When we finally got to Colombo, which is just a mad city of shantytowns and Lion beer, we ended up in the Cricket Club Café playing *A Question of Sport* with three members of the press and three England players – Michael Vaughan,

Robert Croft and Paul Collingwood. All the England players turned up for that, because everything we do we try
to raise as much money as we can for charity, there's no
personal gain for anyone. After that several of the players said
they were going back to the Hilton for karaoke. "Freddie"
Flintoff, myself and my wife were in one tuk-tuk, the other
players were in their tuk-tuks, and there were other Barmy
Army members in a few more tuk-tuks, all steaming through
the streets of Colombo. It probably took fifteen to twenty
minutes, the tuk-tuks bobbing and weaving through the
cars and on and off the pavements, and as soon as I walked
in the club I started singing "Suspicious Minds" with a few
of the England players as support. "Freddie"s' got a big Elvis
voice – but he's not as good as me.

'As an out and out cricket hero, you'd have to look at
"Freddie", but Michael Vaughan, too, the Barmy Army love
Michael Vaughan. But to be honest, not everyone is always
as clued up on the cricket as everyone else. Collingwood,
Croft and Rikki Clarke always used to be the three subs on
that 2003 tour and I can remember one of the Barmy Army
members' wives said to Robert Croft that night at the
Hilton, "I recognise you, what do you do?" And he said,
"I'm the window cleaner on the aeroplane, that's why I'm
drinking water now, because we've got a Jumbo coming in
tomorrow."'

However, even in Shangri-la there are hidden dangers
lurking beneath the surface. 'I was on the beach before the

Galle Test in 2007 and I swam out about half a mile to this rock and trod on all these sea urchins,' says James 'Beefy' Beare. 'When I got back to the beach my feet were covered in blood and I had all these needles hanging out of my feet. I was asking around for tweezers and I ended up getting carted off to the hospital by this crazy Sri Lankan doctor. I had twenty-five holes in one foot and fifteen in the other. He put forty needles in them – as if I needed any more needles – it was horrific. He bandaged them all up and said I'll give you a lift back to your hotel if you want. So I asked how I was supposed to get to his car, I couldn't feel my feet, and he grabbed these two patients who were waiting to see him and told them to carry me to his car – I'm six foot four and built like a brick shithouse and they were about five foot tall. All of a sudden I'm in his car and blood starts pouring out of my feet, and this doctor's got the only brand new car in the whole of Sri Lanka, a gleaming new BMW. He took one look and said, "I'll call you a taxi."

'If it wasn't for two nurses who were staying in the resort I would have been in a lot of trouble because I had to have these dressings changed every day. It didn't stop me watching the cricket, though. One of the lads managed to hunt down some crutches and a wheelchair from somewhere and I was being wheeled in every day. And because in a wheelchair you can get in everywhere I ended up in the sports minister's box. They stuck a tie on me, even though I was wearing a T-shirt and shorts, and all the dignitaries were looking at me like I was scum. I got flown back first class, because I had to lie flat, and I had about three weeks off work. I couldn't walk for a month after that, I couldn't feel my feet.' That, my friends, is what you call commitment to the England cause.

8

The home guard . . . Australia in England 2005

If you were to measure the greatness of a sporting event by 'I was there when . . .' moments, the 2005 Ashes series would eclipse anything that came before or since: 'I was there when Harmison hit Ponting at Lord's'; 'I was there when Flintoff shook Lee's hand at Edgbaston'; 'I was there when Ponting held firm at Old Trafford'; 'I was there when Giles hit the winning runs in Nottingham'; 'I was there when Warne dropped Pietersen at The Oval'. It was the summer when everyone in Britain 'was there', whether they were actually 'there' or not. In short, it was the greatest sporting summer of all.

For nine weeks, the nation could not avert its gaze. It was unifying, electrifying, excruciating, invigorating, frustrating, stifling, side-splitting, gut-wrenching and utterly discombobulating. The 2005 Ashes series was an anachronism, a throwback to a time when cricket was in the hearts of every English man, woman and child. But it was also very much of its time, confrontational cricket celebrated in an uproarious style. It was the summer when everyone went barmy for cricket: 'Say it loud and say it proud, we're all Barmy Army now.'

Back in the summer of 1995, Paul Burnham had attempted to reheat what he had created on the Ashes tour of 1994–95 on home soil, but to no avail. The English Test grounds, deeply suspicious of this new brand of raucous support, simply would not play ball, refusing to allow the Barmy Army to block-book tickets, while the TCCB was also dismissive. In addition, cricket fans in England simply watched cricket in a different way, pitching up for the odd day here and there throughout the summer rather than bedding in for an entire series, as was the case on tours abroad.

Indeed, Burnham did not even attend the first Test of 2005, and while there may have been off-duty foot soldiers in attendance, the Barmy Army was keeping its powder dry. 'The Barmy Army didn't get into Lord's, so I watched that Test match on TV and with various Barmy Army members at various venues at various times,' says Burnham. 'I can kind of understand why we've never been welcome at Lord's. For one, it's already got its own Barmy Army, namely the Marylebone Cricket Club. Plus, they don't really like that noise.

'The irony is that my first experience of watching cricket was at Lord's in 1976, when Middlesex were playing

Somerset: the old Lord's Tavern was pretty fiery that day and I remember there being quite a lot of very drunk people, drinking cider, all of them singing West Country songs. But Lord's has got its own atmosphere and, actually, during the Ashes series in 2009, they did a very good job in inspiring England, particularly Alastair Cook and Andrew Strauss in that first session. So I don't really object to it, I think it's quite nice to have a Test match where there's a different type of intimidating atmosphere for the opposition. Having said that, apart from 2009, we're normally pretty poor at Lord's, especially against Australia. So the jury's out as far as I'm concerned.'

As ever, Australia turned up in England with a formidable outfit. The side that had pummelled Nasser Hussain's team in 2002–03 was pretty much intact, with Langer, Hayden, Ponting, Gilchrist, Warne and McGrath still forming the spine. But for England, things had changed. The honourable but beleaguered Hussain was replaced by Michael Vaughan following the 4–1 defeat down under, and under his astute stewardship England had blossomed into a highly competitive outfit. Going into the Ashes series of 2005, Vaughan's men had won fourteen and drawn three of their previous eighteen Tests and won five successive series. In Marcus Trescothick and Andrew Strauss, England had an opening partnership to rival Langer and Hayden; Vaughan, although injuries had blunted him, was still a first-class number three; in Steve Harmison and Simon Jones, England had two of the most fearsome quicks in world cricket; and in all-rounder Andrew Flintoff, who was finally realising his huge potential, England had a game changer to rival Shane Warne. The stage was set for a play of monumental proportions. Exactly how many acts this play would run to, and the fervour contained within each one, no one could possibly have imagined.

Vaughan had an inkling that something was afoot, but even he could not have predicted how epic that summer would be. 'I remember the Twenty20 game at Hampshire [England crushed Australia by 100 runs],' says Vaughan. 'There was a sense in the crowd that we really did have a chance, even though that Australia side were among the top three or four sides that ever played the game. As for the team, we knew we had something with us when we were out in the middle. And that first morning at Lord's, there was just something different about the place, a real sense of belief among the fans.'

For Robert Frumkin, whose parents live in one of the houses on the ground, Lord's has always been a second home, so he is well placed to compare and contrast the atmosphere on the morning of the first Test. 'The thing that always lives with me from that game was the feeling of deep intensity and deep anticipation on that first morning,' says Frumkin. 'After the two one-day series [England and Australia had shared the triangular NatWest Series after a thrilling tie at Lord's; Australia had won the NatWest Challenge 2–1] and England's win in the Twenty20, there was a real feeling that we might finally have a chance to win the Ashes for the first time in, well, far too long.

'I've been going to games at Lord's since I was born, and we would always sit in the same area, at the front of the bottom tier of the Tavern in the members' area. I remember I arrived at my parents' at about eight o'clock, and normally at about 8.30 the members' queue is just about reaching Grove End Road – even the members start queuing early, to get the prime seats. But this time the queue was past my parents' house on Grove End Road and round into Elm Tree Road. For the members to be that excited – some might argue they don't get excited about much – suggested this was all going to be rather special. We went in fifteen minutes before the start and the buzz was just incredible – never before or since at Lord's have I felt anything like that, England's win in 2009 didn't even come close. In fact, the only time I've experienced anything like that in any cricket ground was at Melbourne in 2010–11, when there were ninety thousand in the MCG and the Aussies thought they had us on the ropes.'

Nick Hughes, too, remembers that there was a very different vibe swirling around Lord's that day. 'It was a very special day for me because it was the first Ashes Test I'd attended as an MCC member. I joined the queue at six in the morning and, although I was about seventieth in line, as a thirty-eight-year-old I quite fancied my chances of getting a decent seat when the gates opened at eight o'clock because a hundred-yard dash against sixty-nine octogenarians, even giving them a head start, should have been a breeze. Bloody hell, how wrong was I. These old boys were past the Grace Gates and through the turnstiles before you could say "Egg and Bacon blazer". They'd seen it all before – and more – but even they knew this series was going to be something special.

'Using wide-load picnic hampers as effectively as a Miami Dolphins blocking guard, I made very little impression on the grey peloton until I reached the steps of the pavilion. But then age caught up with my older colleagues because many of them could not remember where they'd put their membership books [mandatory to get into the pavilion]. So while many of them were emptying pockets full of Handy Andies, Werther's Originals, Warfarin tablets and return train tickets from Worthing, I flashed mine as quickly and nonchalantly as a commuter swiping an Oyster card on the Jubilee Line and strolled straight in. A minute later I was past the Long Room, through the players' gates, down the steps and bagging a seat in Row 1, four to the left as you looked at the pavilion. I was there on my own, deliberately: I just had this feeling I was about to witness the first act of something special, and I wanted to savour it, to enjoy the whole experience without the distraction of friends.

'I had been in the Long Room before when the England players had walked out to field on the first morning of a Test and the relationship between the players and the members can be, at times, strained. Some members do have a "this is my club and you're bloody lucky to play here" attitude and, in return, some of the England players didn't appear to have the highest respect for the members. But all domestic hostilities cease when the common enemy, the bastard Aussies, are in town.

'So at ten fifty-five, I heard a roar go up, emanating from the Long Room, that genuinely made the hairs on the back of my neck stand on end. I've been the token Englishman on the terraces at the old Cardiff Arms Park and I've seen the odd heavyweight bout, so I've heard some sporting "noise" and experienced a fair amount of sporting "passion". But the escalating noise from the Long Room that day was unlike anything I'd heard before: it was visceral, it was intense, it was from the heart and it came from the mouths of an august body of men whose average age must have been sixty-five. It was also a bit weird. There were no discernible words you could make out, it was just a roar – very English, very public school, but blimey it really was intense.'

Most great boxing matches have great opening rounds. They set the scene, provide a tantalising glimpse of the drama to come. Arguably the greatest opening round in history came in the fight between Marvin Hagler and Thomas Hearns in 1985: 'It's like walking into a minefield,' said legendary commentator Reg Gutteridge during the opening stanza, 'no scouting reports with these two ...' The first morning at Lord's was much the same. Harmison was at the head of England's charge, giving Australia's top order fits with a barrage of bouncers. Langer, hopping around at the crease and swatting wildly, like a man being attacked by a hornet, was hit by the second ball of the innings. Ponting was next to wear one, a nasty, rising delivery from Harmison smashing into the grille of his helmet and drawing blood. Softened, Australia's skipper was dismissed by Harmison, who finished with five for 43, in the next over. Flintoff's first over in Ashes cricket was a wicket maiden, Langer holing out to Harmison at deep square-leg, and the tourists were all out for 190 before tea. In boxing terms, it was England's round, with a couple of knockdowns thrown in.

'The roar when the players came out was just incredible,' says Frumkin. 'There was a real frisson around the place and you could see the players react to it, they were as pumped as we were. As I recall Harmy's first ball wasn't too great, but when he smacked Langer with his second it was very much game on. Every England fan knows Langer's a hard nut, but that hurt, and you could see the England players grow because of it. When Ponting got hit a few overs later you really could sense this was an England team who wanted to fight – and for England fans, that was a whole new experience. This England team weren't going to roll over, they were going to fight tooth and nail. They just kept taking wickets throughout those first two sessions and looked for all the world like a proper cricket team.'

'That first morning at Lord's was feverish,' recalls Martin Clarke, who had driven through the night from Manchester to make sure he would be in his seat for the first ball of the series. 'It was as close to being a contact sport cricket can get – England's bowlers out for blood, the Australia batsmen looking to counter-attack. I had been to Lord's on a number of occasions before, but I had never seen support as fervent as that. People talk about there being electricity at sporting events, but there rarely is in reality. But that day there was: you could feel it, almost hear it crackling.'

'Given that "Vaughany" and team were hugely in the ascendancy in world cricket at that time, there was high expectation that we would draw Aussie blood on that first morning,' says Nick Hughes. 'And we didn't have too long to wait, with "Harmy" really steaming into them. The Aussies, five down at lunch, on the first day of an Ashes series. Just unbelievable. I remember walking round the ground during the interval and most people were a little shocked – sure we were good under "Vaughany" but, bloody hell, this was beyond our wildest dreams. And it continued after lunch – Australia 190 all out. At Lord's. On the first day of an Ashes series. For the "text speak" generation, that's a big OMG. So the next bit was supposed to be easy: "Banger" [Trescothick] and "Straussy" bat out the thirty or so overs left in the day and we all come back tomorrow and watch England build an unassailable 300-run lead. Or not.'

Inevitably, Australia's bowlers hit back. And hit back harder. Glenn McGrath, always a lover of Lord's, tore through England's top order, removing Trescothick, Strauss,

Vaughan, Ian Bell and Flintoff for only 21 runs. 'I was directly, absolutely directly, behind Glenn Donald McGrath's arm that day,' says Nick Hughes. 'I could see everything that was unleashed from his gangling frame, every nuance in pace, line and length. And, bloody hell, what a privilege it was to watch that man bowl. I know this is a cliché, but it was as if he'd cast a spell on the England batsmen. It was the greatest and most mesmerising spell of bowling I'd seen. Bastard. Still we had a bit of hope – that young, cocky South African lad with a raccoon on his head was still in. Surely he'd bash us to safety in the end? In the end . . .'

Amid the carnage, a new England hero was indeed born. 'What I remember most about that second day at Lord's was the innings by Kevin Pietersen,' recalls John Nolan, who was attending his first Ashes Test. 'I'd never really heard of him before and as far as I was concerned he was just this South African bloke with a stupid haircut in England's middle order where Graham Thorpe should have been [Pietersen had been involved in a selection shoot-out with Thorpe, not Bell, as is often thought]. But he absolutely piled into McGrath, smacking him all over the park as if he was a club bowler, and even got stuck into Warne. I thought, "This bloke has got some big old bollocks on him, and he's going at them bollocks out." That series was all about big bollocks, and Pietersen's were bigger than most.'

Nolan's recall is correct. Under an ashen sky, in three

deliveries Pietersen slog-swept McGrath into the railings, lofted him into the stands and drove him through the covers for four. He took Hampshire team-mate Warne for one huge six into the Grand Stand, and almost repeated the trick, only for Damien Martyn to take a fine catch sprinting in from the deep. Harmison and Jones put on 33 for the final wicket but England were dismissed for 155, a deficit of 35. Thereafter, Australia assumed full control of the match. Michael Clarke, dropped by Pietersen on 21, and Martyn raised 155 for the fourth wicket as the tourists posted a second innings total of 384 for an imposing lead of 420. Having dragged England out to sea in the middle rounds, Australia's bowlers were poised to drown them.

'After that great start, by the end of day one it was same old bloody England,' says Frumkin. 'Don't get me wrong, McGrath's one of the greats, but it just needed one batsman in England's first innings to get his head down and graft and we might have won the day, even the match. There was just this sense of resignation all around the ground. Were we really surprised? Nope, even after convincing ourselves on day one that things were going to be different, that this England team was going to give as good as it got, it was all depressingly inevitable. And I, for one, thought the rest of the series would be the same.'

By the end of day three, England had been reduced to 156 for five, with Warne and Lee destroyers-in-chief. On day four, England's lower-order surrender was pitiful, their last four batsmen all falling for ducks as McGrath finished with figures of four for 29. Only Pietersen glowed in the furnace of battle as his team-mates melted around him, making an unbeaten 64. 'It was just all so inevitable,' says Evan Bartlett, who was only two when England last held the Ashes. 'And with McGrath, who had that gentle run-up and mechanical action, it was always such a slow and painful death, even when he was wreaking havoc. I just remember the Aussie fans being cock-a-hoop, they revelled in it. It's what Australians are good at, they do winning well. If anyone says they thought England was going to win the series after that day, they'd be lying.'

But despite the 239-run rout and the inevitable soul-searching that followed, for Frumkin, at least, it was a bitter-sweet ending. 'My parents had a barbecue on the Saturday night and a few of the Aussie players came in for a quick drink, including Adam Gilchrist,' says Frumkin. 'He ended up staying for a few drinks (no booze though!). One of my mates asked him if there was a sex ban for the team during the Test, and as we'd been talking about Gilchrist's parents just beforehand, this was a slightly odd deviation. I remember him making his excuses and leaving the room pretty sharpish after that. He missed the team bus back to their hotel. So I ended up being volunteered to give him a lift to a restaurant in Marylebone, where he was meeting his mum and dad. As a thanks, he sent me a signed bat the next day. It almost pains me to say this, but most of those Aussie players were tremendous blokes.'

While the prevailing mood was one of doom and gloom, there were some wise old heads who saw reasons for optimism. 'McGrath killed us in the second innings,' says Burnham. 'And he was pretty good in our first innings as well. But McGrath always pulled out the stops at Lord's, that was almost a given. Obviously everyone wrote us off after that, but all our bowlers bowled well at Lord's and you could see we had something over the Aussie batsmen, which was a real rarity. I was lucky enough to play nine holes of golf with "Freddie" before that series and he was predicting England would win it. His two mates were telling him to shut up and that he was deluded, but "Freddie" was waxing lyrical about the bowling unit they had, about the plans they had for Australia's batsmen. I believed him, he was convincing. That's why when I was interviewed by the Aussie media after that defeat at Lord's I was very confident we'd hit back, and I was almost using the exact words "Freddie" had given me to back up my argument. Obviously, they just called me barmy.'

Then came the morning before the first session of the second Test at Edgbaston, and perhaps the defining moment of the series. 'I'll never forget when the news came in that McGrath had stepped on a cricket ball during the warm-up,' says Burnham. 'The rumour went round outside the ground that he was out, and it was like a wicket had gone down before the game had even started. People were punching the air, forming congas. I remember a double-decker bus going around promoting some Mexican restaurant or other. The bus had got hold of the news and all these blokes dressed as Mexicans, with moustaches and stuff, were shouting it from the top deck. It was like a goal had just been scored in a cup final. The atmosphere was unbelievable. And obviously it wasn't a case of "poor old Glenn", it was "let's get stuck into them while they're down".' To that point, the thirty-five-year-old McGrath had taken 126 Ashes wickets at an average of under twenty. While revisionist historians – usually English men and women – will line up to tell you England beat a full-strength Australia that series, they are being somewhat economical with the truth.

England also benefited from the generosity of Australia skipper Ponting, who won the toss and asked England to bat. 'Ponting put us in, even though he didn't have McGrath in his line-up, and Strauss and Trescothick went berserk and got plenty of runs on the board in that first session,' recalls Burnham. 'It was a major mistake. We're usually the ones who make mistakes and have the bad luck with injuries, so there was a real sense that the tables had turned.'

'The Ricky Ponting decision at the toss was a bona fide "did that really just happen" moment,' says Gary Foster. 'Vaughan's glance at the sky immediately after Ponting had made it will stay with me forever. It turned out to be a magnificent day, full of runs, wickets and some of the finest "stick it in the stands" shots I've ever witnessed.'

Says Australia fast bowler Jason Gillespie: 'Glenn went down with that injury in the warm-up, then all of a sudden we'd won the toss and bowled. It took me by surprise. However, Ricky would have been totally justified had we held our catches. Then England smacked 407 in a day.'

England's openers came flying out of the traps, climbing into anything loose from the Australia bowlers – and anything else besides. Trescothick took a particular liking to Brett Lee, taking him for nine boundaries. And with Gillespie and Michael Kasprowicz struggling to replicate McGrath's metronomic line and length, the ball was flying to all parts. England scored 132 before lunch, for the loss of only Strauss. After the break, Trescothick and Vaughan brought up their 50 partnership in 5.3 overs, but the tourists refused to wilt. Three wickets fell in twenty-seven balls, with Bell, playing on his home ground, posting his third single-figure score of the series – before England launched a thrilling counter-attack of their own.

Pietersen had launched himself into the public consciousness with his ballsy assault on McGrath at Lord's, and that performance had raised the tantalising prospect that one day during the summer he would cut loose in tandem with England's other powerhouse hitter, "Freddie" Flintoff. That moment came after lunch, when the dynamic duo put on 103 in 105 balls, with Lee in particular taking a fearful clattering. 'The "KP" and "Freddie" partnership was unbelievable to watch,' says Ben Coley. The fact they put on a hundred going at a run a ball was unheard of for English cricket, especially against Australia, and I specifically remember the spell Brett Lee bowled at them that day: he was bowling at the speed of light, but "Freddie" kept taking him on. It was as good a "mini-contest" in Test cricket as I've seen.'

His duel with Flintoff was reminiscent of Botham v Lillee at Old Trafford in 1981 – Lee kept on bouncing him and, instead of ducking, Flintoff kept pulling out the hook, clearing the square-leg boundary on three occasions. Flintoff fell for 68 from 62 balls just after tea, while Pietersen, who hit ten fours and a six, fell not long after, having made 71 from 76. It had been spine-tingling stuff, and the Eric Hollies Stand, never a place for shrinking violets, was rocking.

'That Edgbaston Test in 2005 wasn't strictly the first time the Barmy Army had worked at home,' says Burnham. 'In the Ashes Test in 1997, we had a Barmy Army reunion and we had three hundred of us in the middle of the Eric Hollies Stand. Mike Atherton and Alec Stewart chased down a small total and I remember vividly Atherton was hitting the ball over the top, scoring at a quicker rate than Stewart – he was definitely turbo-charged by the Barmy Army effect that day. Edgbaston has always had a very unique atmosphere, but in 2005, I have to admit, it was cranked up several notches. There were three hundred of us in the ground again, but everyone seemed to be Barmy Army that day.'

'Edgbaston always had a peculiar atmosphere, a more patriotic atmosphere than some of the other grounds,' says

Atherton. 'The Eric Hollies Stand was always quite lively. Compare Edgbaston to Lord's, for example, which is quite serene, there's a hum about the place, people sit quietly and watch the cricket. But Edgbaston was always a bit more raucous. Thinking of 1997, I'm not sure I was playing how I did because of the crowd or if it was just because I wanted to get the game over with as quickly as possible. But the combination of all that probably led to me playing shots I perhaps wouldn't have normally played, and the same thing probably applied to England's batsmen on day one in 2005.'

However, rather than being cowed by the muscularity of England's stroke play, there were signs Australia were revelling in the novelty of being involved in a punch-up. 'My main memory from the day was the stick Justin Langer was getting in front of the Hollies Stand,' recalls Richard Anderson. 'He was diving everywhere, really straining every sinew, but the ball kept going for four. Eventually he made a terrific diving stop and got a standing ovation from the crowd, to which he pulled up his sleeves and flexed his biceps. It showed us that while they were tough players, the Aussies were still good sports. Not only that, the impression was that after sixteen years of one-sided series, they were as thrilled to be in a fight as we were. Our respect for Langer, who had had a big falling out with the England fans on England's previous tour down under after he called the Barmy Army a disgrace, grew very much after that day.'

While Warne finished with four wickets, he had been

taken for 116 runs, but even he appeared invigorated by England's spirit. 'I do remember Warne getting a standing ovation when he got hit for his hundredth run of the day,' says Ben Coley. 'And how did he react? He doffed his cap and bowed. You wanted to hate him, but you just couldn't bring yourself to do it.'

However, Michael Vaughan reckons Langer, at least, was bluffing. 'I've spoken to Justin Langer, and he said for the first time he felt under pressure fielding as an Australian,' says Vaughan. 'And there were two reasons for that: one, because we had the Barmy Army up in the stands; two, because we were playing good, pressurising cricket. I think you need to be playing the good cricket first and foremost and then, if you've got the added advantage of the crowd behind you, it turns into a double bonus.'

England were eventually dismissed for 407 just before stumps and it was the first time since 1938 that any side had amassed 400-plus on a first day of a Test against Australia. However – and this particular series was littered with 'howevers' – while it had been thrilling fare, the general consensus was that England had let the tourists off the hook and that if even one England batsman had applied himself, England's total could have been nearer 500. 'Although we scored four hundred in just shy of eighty overs that day, I can still remember leaving the ground and the feeling being we hadn't got enough,' says Ben Coley. 'Given that we had just spent the day watching the Aussies chase leather, that was a mark of just how much we feared them.'

Such thoughts were banished before lunch on day two, with Australia losing three wickets, including Hayden for his first golden duck in Tests. Langer made a typically gritty 82, but Australia's lower order was undone by the England seam attack's mastery of reverse swing, two words that would become part of Britain's everyday lexicon by summer's end. But it was Warne's leg-spin that had the final say on day two, England's arch nemesis ripping one through Strauss's defences to become the first overseas player to take one hundred Test wickets in England. But to Warne, milestones were not milestones at all, rather signposts pointing him down the road to more greatness.

If on days one and two Australia had been way off England's pace, on day three they moved up on England's shoulder and put themselves in an ideal position for the finishing straight. Having seemingly been cruising to victory, England were reduced to 75 for six after 26.5 overs, Warne and Lee sharing out the scalps between them. 'Warne was getting a lot of stick from the crowd that day because he was going through some troubles with his missus at the time and it was all over the tabloids,' recalls Jon Moreby, who had driven up with a couple of mates from Leamington Spa on a whim and managed to score tickets for the third and fourth days. 'But he stood there, he took it and he waved. And then when he started taking his wickets, he waved to us again and smiled, as if to say: "Give me all the grief you want, boys, I'll keep on taking your wickets."'

'A real bond grew between Warne and the England fans during that series,' says Burnham. 'That was the series we started singing "We wish you were English" and bowing to him. We'd thrown everything at him, and it hadn't worked, so now we were trying to soften him up with love. He would applaud the Barmy Army when we sang that song, but once he had that ball in his hands, he'd be giving it his all. He had reason to be pissed off with England fans in the past, when they were calling him a paedophile back in '02–'03, when they were singing those songs about bookies and drugs. But he was great on that tour, in every respect he was absolutely spot-on.'

Then, in the twenty-ninth over, came the moment every England fan had feared. Flintoff, a shire horse in stature, but delicate as a thoroughbred, crumpled to the floor having heaved Warne through point. If the Edgbaston faithful had been subdued before, things were now funereal. 'It was just one of those gut-wrenching moments,' says Gary Foster. 'Australia had really come back at us hard, which you couldn't really argue with, but then it looked like we were going to lose our talisman as well, which would have just been devastating beyond words. I was on the point of tears at various stages during that series, but that was the first time.' There followed a lengthy stoppage in play as England physio Kirk Russell wrestled with Flintoff on the ground. A nation held its breath. And then, like some fallen stone colossus, Flintoff was hauled back on to his feet. A nation exhaled.

As wickets continued to fall at the other end (Warne finished with six for 46, for ten wickets in the match), the wounded Flintoff stood firm, and he found a worthy ally in number 11 Simon Jones. Together, they put on 51 runs for the final wicket, with Flintoff taking Lee for 33 off 28 balls. At one point, Ponting had nine men on the boundary, but Flintoff was undeterred, smashing four sixes in all, including one steepler off Lee that landed up on the TV gantry. Says Jon Moreby: 'I found myself repeating that famous Richie Benaud line from the Headingley Test in 1981: "Don't even bother looking for that one ..." It looked to us as if he was almost batting one-handed. But not just batting: smashing sixes. When he was on the deck being treated, it was looking pretty grim. We were six down, the cloud cover had come in and the feeling in the stands was "here we go again". We thought it was going to be all right, now it's all gone a bit wrong, and then, when "Freddie" started smashing it to all parts, everything was all right again.'

Burnham adds: 'Flintoff would play a big shot, you'd think he'd be out, and then you'd realise it had gone for six – it was all very Botham at Headingley 1981, and on another day everyone might have been saying, "'Freddie's given his wicket away again." He was just going for it, and he became a hero that game. Like Botham in Leeds in '81, it wasn't the best innings he ever played, but he hit some very telling shots, they took their toll on the Aussie bowlers and they carried those scars into the coming games.'

Set a target of 282, Langer and Hayden set about it in positive fashion, and by the twelfth over Australia were 42 without loss. Time for another superhuman intervention from Flintoff. 'The Aussies were looking pretty comfortable and there was a real sense that 282 might not be enough,' says John Nolan. 'And then "Freddie" rocked up and bowled "that" over: Langer was cleaned up by a leg-cutter, and then he softened "Punter" [Ponting] up before getting one to nip away and take the edge of his bat. Wallop! England on top again. And don't forget that slower ball from Harmison that got rid of Clarke: so badly disguised, it might as well have been festooned in neon bulbs spelling out "slower ball".' At the close, the tourists were 175 for eight, still 107 short of the victory target and looking doomed.

'Everyone walked away thinking, "That's it, game over,"' says Jon Moreby. 'We went out that night, got absolutely lashed, thinking, "We've cracked it." We were even considering not bothering to turn up the next day: "What's the point? We'll have terrible hangovers, if we get on the road by eleven, we'll be back home in Leamington Spa half an hour later." But we went along, just in case anything exciting happened . . .' While most England fans were in raptures at the end of day three, the beard-stroking Barmy Army elders, who had been hurt so many times before, were preaching caution. 'After the first three days there were people partying down Long Street and out in the pubs and clubs of Birmingham,' says Burnham. 'But it was us wise men, who had seen it all go wrong time and time again, who kept saying, "it's not done yet, we need to be there for them tomorrow".'

As Warne strode to the middle on that fourth morning, he may or may not have turned to Lee and uttered the phrase: ''Tis but a scratch.' But like the Black Knight in *Monty Python and the Holy Grail*, Warne was utterly convinced of his invincibility. 'My overriding memory is being sat beside a load of very confident and vocal Aussies,' says Jon Jackson. 'They wanted 107 at start of play, and the chant went up, "107 to go, ee-ai-adio ... 107 to go ...". And on and on it went, painfully edging downwards. Wickets wouldn't stop it. Distractions from the Barmy Army, enquiring after Jason Gillespie's caravan, wouldn't stop it either.'

'The tension when Warne and Lee started knocking the runs off was unbelievable,' says Jon Moreby. 'It didn't take too long for the expectant buzz to give way to complete silence.' Warne played confidently, freeing his arms and finding the boundary with frequency. Lee, too, looked untroubled. 'When they got to within seventy or eighty, the feeling was "surely not?"' adds Moreby. Then, having scored 42 and with his side still needing 62, Warne shuffled back to a Flintoff delivery which was speared down leg and trod on his stumps. Game over. Surely?

Kasprowicz played with the same assurance as Lee, piling into spinner Ashley Giles (one of his overs went for 13) and taking advantage of some too-short bowling from England's seamers. And the scoreboard just kept on ticking towards the target. 'I couldn't liken that atmosphere to anything I'd experienced before or since,' says Jon Moreby. 'It was just a horrible feeling of absolute dread. Not only that, but a feeling I'd been made a fool of. England were supposed to knock them over and then it was party time. Credit to the Aussie fans sat behind me, they weren't celebrating either. It was a unique situation: both sets of fans felt hoodwinked, a feeling of "it wasn't supposed to be like this".'

'I actually left the stand, I'd just lost the plot,' says Burnham. 'Everyone had gone quiet, they were all biting their nails. I thought we should all be making a noise but everyone kept telling me to shut up. But when Simon Jones put that catch down at third man [Kasprowicz was the batsman, Flintoff the bowler] I went and hid in the Edgbaston shop, it was just too nerve-wracking to even watch. I was thinking, "We've thrown this away, we've thrown this away," and it meant so much.'

Even Bill 'The Trumpet' Cooper, who had been tooting his horn with abandon for the first three days, fell silent. In hindsight, a mournful 'Last Post' might have been appropriate. 'Sometimes the cricket is so gripping you almost don't want to be playing the trumpet,' says Cooper. 'I remember the last morning at Edgbaston, I didn't play because it was such gripping drama that it just didn't seem right to pipe up with some stupid tune. A couple of people afterwards, writing on blogs, said: "Where were the Barmy Army today? You were rubbish." But it just didn't seem the right time. It was much better just to let the cricket talk for itself, it was just so tense.'

Lee and Kasprowicz had put on 58 in 12.1 overs and were only four short of their target when Harmison served up an attempted yorker, which ended up being a full toss. Lee, however, could only find the fielder on the boundary. 'It went straight to the fielder,' recalls Jon Moreby, 'but a foot either side and it was game over.' The batsmen crossed for a single and, with the tourists three short of their target, Kasprowicz was the man on strike, Harmison the bowler at the other end.

'I'll be honest with you, I wasn't looking when that final ball was bowled,' says Moreby, 'which is a huge regret now. I looked up to see the ball ballooning off Kasprowicz's glove and Geraint Jones flying through the air. He took a great catch low down to his left, and the place just went absolutely crazy: it was two days of tension and sixteen years of hurt uncorked. It was one of those really cheesy, corny moments when you'd just hug the nearest person next to you; there were fully grown blokes crying all around me – big, ugly, meathead blokes, there was just a feeling of relief. I'm a huge Manchester United fan, but only one football match I've attended would even get close, and that was the 1999 European Cup final, when Teddy Sheringham and Ole Gunnar Solskjaer both scored in injury time to win it. But I couldn't separate the two moments, I couldn't tell you which was better – and that's quite something coming from a Man United supporter. It was an "I was there when moment", you never forget a sporting moment like that. And you know that in twenty years' time there will be at least a hundred thousand people claiming they were at Edgbaston that day.'

'Generally people ask, "Did you hit it?",' says Kasprowicz. 'There was an Indian guy who came up to me and said, "Thank you so much, thank you for saving Test cricket. If you had got the runs the series would have been dead and Test cricket would have been dead. You single-handedly changed cricket." I thanked him nicely and said that the single hand was actually off the bat at the time.'

Famously, Flintoff did not immediately join in with the England team's delirious celebrations. Instead, he walked over to a crestfallen Lee and offered him his hand. It chimed with the feeling of some England fans up in the stands. 'My feeling certainly was that we got away with it,' says Moreby. 'And I think that's what that gesture from Flintoff demonstrated. It was his way of saying, "Unlucky, mate, that was some performance, you deserved to win it." And there was even some sympathy towards the Aussies among the England supporters, which is a grim feeling in itself. But that didn't last long, we were ribbing them again as we made our way out. You might have expected us to have carried on the party, but we all kind of drifted off in different directions in this sort of dream-like state. We were exhausted, and there was a feeling that, while the battle had been won, the war wasn't over yet, we better get home to rest for when hostilities recommence.'

England's series-squaring victory in Birmingham was

watched by 4.1 million people, taking Channel 4's audience share for the whole day to 15.1 per cent of viewers, the best Saturday for the broadcaster since it was established twenty-two years earlier. Live Test cricket has not appeared on a terrestrial channel since that 2005 series, and the fact that anyone was able to plumb into the drama that unfolded that summer gave the series a distinctly old-school feel. 'That series was watched by tens of millions rather than hundreds of thousands and that was a key reason it became so big,' says Burnham. 'I remember hearing about people running into pubs when "KP" and "Freddie" were batting, gathering in front of the windows of TV shops. It was like a throwback to the 1970s. Cricket missed a trick there because, while Sky does a good job, that was the only time in my sixteen years with the Barmy Army that people who knew what I did, but didn't like cricket, were ringing me up to ask my opinion on it.'

From Birmingham, the Test series clattered on to Manchester like a runaway train, new twists and turns arising all the time. Before the match at Edgbaston had even finished, McGrath declared he would 'need a miracle' to play at Old Trafford. Of course, he was visited by one. Lee, too, passed a late fitness test and so, on paper at least, Australia were at full strength. The reality was rather different. Vaughan won the toss and chose to bat and, aided by some butter-fingered fielding from the tourists, who spilled four catches, England assumed control on day one. Trescothick made 63 and Vaughan, who had until then been struggling for form, a majestic 166 as England reached 341 for five at stumps. Even Ian Bell, whose first four knocks in the series were 6, 8, 6 and 21, joined the party, making an unbeaten 59. But perhaps the biggest story of the day was Warne's 600th Test wicket, that of Trescothick, caught behind by Gilchrist from a mistimed sweep. The *Yorkshire Post* reported: 'The crowd cheered the leg-spinner for several minutes and he doffed his sun-hat to all corners. Vaughan was one of the first to shake the maestro's hand.' It was the sporting equivalent of the 1914 Christmas truce.

The two sides were at each other's throats again the following morning. England's first innings was finished off either side of lunch, with Flintoff (46) and Geraint Jones (42) combining for 87 in England's total of 444. McGrath finished with his worst ever Test figures of nought for 86, a woefully out-of-form Jason Gillespie was given a mauling, but again there was a nagging feeling among the England fans that England should have scored more.

In reply, Australia were 214 for seven at stumps and staring down the barrel. Spinner Ashley Giles ripped out Langer, Hayden and Martyn, while Glamorgan's Simon Jones, reversing the ball round corners, did for Ponting, Gilchrist and Clarke. 'People were talking about getting rid of Giles after the first Test, but that Edgbaston Test brought the team together,' says Burnham, 'forged that team unity, that team spirit. They stuck by the team and they had a bowling unit that picked itself. That was when we started singing our version of "Men of Harlech", the old Welsh anthem from the film *Zulu*, every time Simon Jones bowled:

'Men of England do not fear,
We have brought a bowler here,
Who has batsmen far and near
Shaken to the bones;
Ricky Ponting stop your dreaming,
We can see the new ball gleaming,
See it swinging, see it seaming,
Bring on Simon Jones;
Aussie wickets falling,
Makes them look appalling,
Bring on Simon Jones,
You hear the Barmy Army calling;
He has pace and he has power,
See the Aussie batsmen cower,
Ninety-nine miles per hour,
Bring on Simon Jones.

'I know for a fact it was really inspiring him and he ended up with six wickets in that innings.'

'Paul Burnham could be right, in that the batsman has got something else to concentrate on other than the ball when the crowd's going nuts,' says Michael Vaughan. 'And it might give a bowler a psychological advantage over some players.

But what the Barmy Army certainly gave the team was an element of invincibility at times in that series. You knew they would always be singing, being jovial, all in the right spirit, but at times when we needed a lift and a bit of extra energy, I would send a message or give a little bit of indication to "Jimmy Savile" and away we'd go. It pretty much always coincided with us producing better cricket for a while and would often result in a wicket.'

Only fourteen overs were possible on day three because of rain, but that was long enough for England to spurn several chances to put Australia out of the game. Warne, who had been 45 overnight, had two lives courtesy of wicket-keeper Geraint Jones and at the close the tourists were 264 for seven, when they could quite easily have been ten men down. The next morning, Warne made the most of his mistakes, falling just short of his maiden Test hundred as Australia were bowled out for 302, 142 behind.

The England batsmen then set about the Australian bowling, Strauss finally finding his mojo with a sometimes brutal knock of 106 and Bell making his second half-century of the match, including a straight six off an out-of-sorts McGrath. Perhaps most worrying for Australia was the quality of their fielding: Gilchrist missed two stumping chances, while misfields abounded. For Australia skipper Ponting, these were worrying signs. Ponting later said: 'I must admit at different times in the last two Tests I've been scratching my head. Where are we going to go? What are we going to do here?'

'Old Trafford was going mental that day,' says Essex fan James Anthony, who had made the trip up to Manchester with an Aussie mate. 'It was a mixture of utter euphoria and disbelief, there was just this feeling that Australia were on their knees and England had the whip hand raised. Early in Strauss's innings, he got an edge and Ponting and Warne just looked at each other as it flew between them and away to the fence. And at that moment there was also this sense that the Aussie team spirit was disintegrating. That never happened to Australia, and for my Aussie mate that was the most shocking thing to behold.'

Twenty thousand found themselves locked out on day five as England fans flocked from all corners of the United Kingdom to see England's rabid pack of bowlers deliver the *coup de grâce*. 'If you saw two Supermen, three nuns and a Fred Flintstone in Manchester yesterday you knew they were among the unlucky ones,' wrote John Etheridge in the *Sun* the following day.

'The afternoon before, Channel 4 announced there would be £10 tickets on the last day,' says Sarah Ayub. 'I'd just got back from a wedding, but thought it would be a really good idea to jump straight in the car and bomb back up to Manchester from High Wycombe. So my little brother and I loaded up on provisions and we set off on Sunday night. We arrived at Old Trafford at about midnight and dumped the car down a back street. There were already thirty or forty people in the queue and it had swelled to about a hundred strong by four o'clock. By seven, it was snaking about half a mile down the road.'

'Me and my Aussie mate Scott were there on the Sunday and thought, "Let's cry off work on Monday and watch the final day,"' says James Anthony. 'My thinking was, I could get on the smash in Manchester on Sunday night, get the booze out of my system for the first two sessions while England were bowling Australia out, before celebrating another England win all the way home. I'm not sure what Scott's thinking was, but I remember him being grimly determined as we walked to the ground that morning.'

Langer and Hayden had survived a nasty ten overs the evening before and Australia required a further 399 for an unlikely victory on the final day. Hoggard made an early breakthrough, Langer feathering an edge behind, and Flintoff worked Hayden over before bowling him behind his legs. Martyn, having hit the cover off a ball from Harmison, was the recipient of a dreadful lbw decision by umpire Steve Bucknor, before Flintoff ripped out Simon Katich and Gilchrist in quick succession. But when Clarke, whose back injury appeared to be in remission, started playing some shots, the England fans suddenly started eyeing the scoreboard nervously.

'Clarke was meant to be injured, that's why he came in at number seven,' recalls James Anthony. 'But he was stroking the ball to all parts. And with Ponting standing firm at the other end, there was a period of an hour or so where I was thinking, "Hang on a minute, they might actually win this."

Not that my Aussie mate was saying much: in fact, I'm not sure he said anything from the time he went through the turnstile to when stumps were pulled. He just sat there staring at the middle for eight hours, fist propping up his head, looking a lot like Rodin's *Thinker*.'

Clarke scored 39 before he was out shouldering arms to an absolute crackerjack of a delivery from Simon Jones. And when Hoggard accounted for Gillespie, England needed three wickets from twenty-nine overs. But Ponting remained an immovable object, more a sphinx than the wounded lion you might have expected him to be. 'That was Ricky Ponting's moment,' says Burnham. 'That was an unbelievable innings. You knew you had to get him out – getting other people out wasn't good enough – otherwise he'd save the game. He got a lot of stick that day. Because of the free-for-all for tickets, there were a lot of people in the ground who weren't really traditional cricket fans, it was almost like a football crowd. Ponting was really getting it, it was like an old-fashioned Aussie crowd. But it just showed the courage of the man. I think that was his greatest knock.'

Adds Sarah Ayub: 'It was an afternoon of Mexican waves and rubbish being chucked up in the air which told you they weren't necessarily cricket fans and had got a bit bored. They wanted something to be happening every over, probably because of the previous two Tests, but for real cricket fans this was compelling in a different way. I was into every ball, into every little nuance. I don't remember seeing that kind of atmosphere at a cricket ground before, and I don't think I've seen it since. Most fifth days, you kind of know it's going to be a draw from a certain point in the day, but this was on a knife edge from start to finish, there was this sense that anything could happen. Ponting was getting plenty of grief, that was the series he almost turned into a pantomime villain for the Barmy Army. But he got a big standing ovation when he reached his century, which was great, it kind of summed up the spirit of that series.'

The immovable object was now joined in the middle by the irresistible force, Shane Keith Warne. Warne batted positively and, aided by another simple dropped catch by Pietersen, stuck around for almost twenty-two overs before Geraint Jones atoned for his shoddy display on Saturday, snaffling a sharp chance off the thigh of Strauss in the slips. Five overs later, England finally toppled Ponting. 'If I remember, it wasn't that great a delivery from "Freddie", a touch leg-side, but "Punter" just tickled it off his glove to [Geraint] Jones behind the stumps,' says James Anthony. 'And I absolutely lost it, was just roaring in my Aussie mate's face, veins bulging, fists clenched. "Ding-dong, the witch was dead!"'

'I had all sorts of different emotions and feelings going through me. I thought the game had slipped away from us,' Ponting later admitted. 'It was difficult enough for me batting out there against Flintoff and Harmison at the end, and having Glenn [McGrath] and Brett [Lee] subjected to it for four overs – I didn't have a lot of faith in them.'

For twenty-four balls, England's pace attack, shorn of the injured Simon Jones, battered away at Australia's final line of defence, but to no avail. McGrath and Lee held firm, and when Lee eased Harmison's final ball through the on-side for four, it was the Australia team which was celebrating. 'The Australians were obviously happier with a draw than we were,' says Sarah Ayub. 'And there was this immediate sense the pendulum had swung back towards them, that we had let them off the hook. We just didn't know what was going to happen in the coming Tests, so at the time it was gnawing away at you: what if there hadn't been the rain delays, what if we hadn't missed those stumpings and catches, what if Simon Jones had come on earlier. So many "what ifs?".'

Burnham adds: 'You felt we had thrown it away again: "We had our chance, we won't have the chance to do it again, Shane Warne will be turning it sideways on a spinners' track at Trent Bridge." There was a feeling almost that the chance of winning back the Ashes had gone at Old Trafford. You definitely thought it had swung back to the Aussies.'

Despite the draw, despite the pessimism, for lovers of cricket the final day of the third Test had been another 'I was there' moment. 'It had all been worth it, says Sarah Ayub. Obviously, we were expecting to see an England win – you don't really drive all that way if you know it's going to be a draw. But even the draws were classics in that series. It was a great draw. That summer, everything just came together, there was a perfect alignment of the stars: two great teams, packed with great personalities, the whole series on terrestrial TV, everything just clicked. And I was part of it.'

However, for James Anthony, who along with his Aussie mate had been transfixed for seven hours, it was the day friend turned against friend. 'Because we hadn't been saying much to each other, we were ploughing through the beers at a faster than normal rate,' says Anthony. 'By stumps, we were slaughtered. He had barely said a word all day, but when Lee hit that final ball for four, he just went berserk, it was like someone had been shaking him up all day and had suddenly popped his cork. That night, we headed into Manchester and ended up in some terrible dive. The only thing I remember about that night is some massive bouncer breaking the toilet door down, dragging me out of the place and drop-kicking me on to the pavement.

'The next morning, he still hadn't turned up at the hotel and my phone started ringing. It was his wife, informing me he'd received a kicking and was in hospital. Obviously, this was a bit of an unexpected sting in the tail. Then, about five minutes later, I got another call. "Hello, is this Mr Anthony?" "Yep." "It's Lloyds TSB." "OK." "We wanted to check it was you that took £2000 out of your account last night and early this morning?" "Oh God . . ." Someone, somewhere along the line, had wiped me out, and because of the types of establishments we had been attending, and the fact we couldn't remember where they were, I had no chance of getting it back. The really funny part, looking back now, is that my bonus had cleared that day – £2000 exactly, and I never got bonuses. My mate was off work for a week, and we never really spoke about that evening, or really saw eye to eye again. But that was that series all over, it affected people's lives in the weirdest and most unexpected ways.'

An unprecedented 7.7 million people watched the denouement of the Old Trafford Test on Channel 4, and word in the British newspapers was that cricket was 'the new football'.

'Interest in the game, which for much of the past decade has been as unfashionable as John Major, is starting to eclipse even that of football,' waxed *The Times* in its editorial. The *Sun*'s Steven Howard added: 'Even people who thought they didn't like cricket are suddenly talking about googlies, sliders and reverse swing.'

If Australia fans (excluding James Anthony's battered and bruised mate) left Manchester on something of a high, they were brought down a peg or two by the news that McGrath would miss the fourth Test at Trent Bridge with an elbow injury. As for England's fans, who spent nine days fretting over which side the draw in Manchester had benefited most, it was the perfect pre-match tonic. Meanwhile, the malfunctioning Gillespie was dropped, leaving him to take his frustrations out on the England fans. 'Some of the crowd behaviour is appalling, the insulting things people say,' he told the *Mirror*. 'People pay their money to come in and they think it is their right to question your parentage and have a crack at your mother. It's always these guys that abuse you, call you "effing this" and "effing that" and ten seconds later they are asking for an autograph for their kids. You say, "Look, mate, I'm not going to sign it for you," and all of a sudden you are the worst bloke in the history of the world, so you can't win.'

His complaints cut no ice with the Barmy Army. Spokesman Katy Cooke told BBC Radio 5 Live: 'I think he's been a bit pathetic really. I hope he's been misquoted because the Australians give the English more stick than any other country in the world. Us lot questioning his parentage or saying he lives in a caravan – and let's face it, he looks like it – is not bad compared to what the Australian public give the English players over there. Hopefully, we're squaring it up now.'

Former England spinner Phil Tufnell also had no sympathy for Gillespie. 'Every time the ball came to me at Melbourne or Sydney I used to be petrified,' he said. 'It was a case of get it in your hands or get it away, otherwise the flak you got was awful.'

Once again, Vaughan won the toss and elected to bat and once again Trescothick and Strauss got the hosts off to a flyer. Trescothick moved to 50 from only 77 balls as England steamed through the 100 barrier at their now customary four runs an over, before Warne interjected, removing Strauss courtesy of a bottom edge off his boot. Rain swept in after lunch, before debutant Shaun Tait removed Trescothick and Bell after tea. Vaughan and Pietersen having wrested the momentum back England's way under gathering clouds, Ponting introduced himself into the attack and had the England captain caught behind. Remarkably, Ponting bowled the same number of overs – six – as Warne on that opening day. England were 229 for four at stumps; the consensus was that honours were even.

The next morning, Pietersen fell early before Flintoff and Geraint Jones came out swinging. Together they added 103 before lunch, after which Flintoff slipped up a gear, unleashing an array of punishing strokes – whipcracked cover drives, coruscating pull shots – against an increasingly desolate Australia attack. 'We'd been on tours and, to be honest, while "Freddie" was a good craic to have a drink with and all the rest, he did have a lot of critics,' says Burnham. 'People spent a lot of money to go and see the England team play away and some people felt he wasn't really delivering in the early part of his career. I think he felt that as well, felt he needed to pull out a string of fine performances in a row, and that series was when everyone started loving "Freddie", he became a Barmy Army folk hero. He needed that inner confidence, as well as the outer confidence, and I think that game at Edgbaston had given him that, provided the foundation for his performances to come. I don't think it was "Flintoff's Ashes", not like Botham in '81, but it was the series in which his performances were most notable. And his ton set us up nicely at

Trent Bridge, you could almost see the Aussie players unravelling before your eyes.'

Flintoff eventually fell to Tait for 102, his first Ashes century, and Geraint Jones fell not long after for 85. Warne cleaned up the tail, but England had passed 400 for the third successive innings. Enter Matthew Hoggard, the one England bowler who had yet to have a major say in the series. Swinging the ball prodigiously below grey skies, the Yorkshireman dismissed Hayden, Martyn (who was unlucky, again) and Langer, while Simon Jones did for Ponting, Harmison trapped Clarke leg before with the final ball of the day, leaving the tourists' innings hanging like a tattered windsock on 99 for five, still 378 runs behind.

Given the seesaw nature of the previous Tests, some might have expected an Aussie backlash on day three, but it never really materialised. Simon Jones tore through what remained of Australia's batting line-up, finishing with figures of five for 44, as the tourists were dismissed for 218, a deficit of 259. 'The Aussies were in total disarray,' says Tim Sorrell. 'As a long-suffering England supporter, witness to all too many batting collapses and miserable innings' defeats, it felt both sweet and like the end of an era to see the Aussies humbled like this. It was spine-tingling.'

Nick Toovey and his mate Davey, two Aussies in the lion's den, could not quite believe what they were seeing. Says Toovey: 'Resplendent in shirts especially made for the occasion – the recently single Shane Warne's headshot above the words "Call Me ..." – we squeezed past an already rowdy crowd to several catcalls and plenty of "Bowling Shane's" in poor Aussie accents. Davey shot back something in his thick drawl and a few hundred pairs of eyes lit up as they realised they had some real live prey for the rest of the day. I wasn't singing any more, apparently. I reminded them that they hadn't sung since 1987. Or they certainly shouldn't have been. "Hey, Aussie," someone shot back, "when was the last time your lot followed on?" "I don't know, mate, I don't think it's been in my lifetime." Davey and I repaired to the bar and vowed to give as good as we got in the banter. This is where the day really picked up: the joviality in the crowd that day was a real highlight, particularly for somebody brought up on the draconian behavioural laws and watered-down beer of the SCG. Back and forth all day, all in good spirits, on the convict heritage of my grandparents, and the heritage of Geraint Jones and KP.'

'Simon Jones's spell that day was as devastating as I have seen,' says James McNeilly. 'He was fielding down in front of us during the spell and the reaction from him and the crowd – there was a collective sense that he had the Aussies in his pocket, he was so dialled in. Then there was Strauss's one-handed catch in the slips to remove Gilchrist, who had started playing some shots. That's still the best catch I have ever seen live, he seemed to find an extra stretch right at the last minute. Not bad for a fella who isn't exactly the best athlete in the side. But there were still signs of life in the Aussie line-up: Brett Lee's knock was absolutely savage [Lee hit five fours and three sixes in an innings of 47], and included a six that went through the bonnet of the Notts' chairman's car at the back of the stand!'

'We had tickets for both the Saturday and the Sunday, and as always the plan was fancy dress and beer in the cheaper seats on the first day, then some serious cricket watching from the posh seats on the Sunday,' says Tim Sorrell. 'Our theme that year was "Spanish Cardinals", and the six of us were dressed in matching red robes, with white gloves, jewelled rings and ridiculous stick-on facial hair. We were sat in the front of the upper tier of the Parr Stand, had a banner hung over the side: "Nobody Expects the King of Spain!" We thought it a fairly obvious reference to Monty Python's Spanish Inquisition [sketch] and to England's very own "Wheelie Bin", Ashley Giles, but Henry Blofeld on *TMS* seemed to be very confused by it, even when a very patient Victor Marks tried explaining it to him.'

Giles had been lumbered with the moniker 'King of Spain' in 2004 after the Warwickshire souvenir shop had commissioned some mugs to celebrate their favourite son. They had requested that the mugs should bear the legend: 'Ashley Giles, King of Spin'. But somewhere along the line, the message got garbled. It was an easy mistake to make...

'After Katich and Gilchrist added fifty-odd runs in the morning, I was sent out for bacon sandwiches,' adds Sorrell. Wearing fancy dress always attracts a fair bit of attention, so

I found myself chatting away with people dressed up as cowboys or nuns or queuing at cashpoints with a murder (surely that's the only appropriate collective noun) of Hannibal Lecters. I was away from my seat for less than five overs, and in that time no fewer than four wickets fell. The one that I really missed was Andrew Strauss's sensational, stretching catch to remove Adam Gilchrist. Every single time I see that catch on TV, as Strauss tumbles, reaching for the ball with both hands before finally, impossibly, stretching out and snaffling it with one hand, it makes me feel just a little bit sick. It was a pretty average bacon sandwich too. Gutted.'

Vaughan decided to gamble and send Australia in to bat again – the first time they had been forced to follow on for seventeen years. Hayden and Langer put together a gritty opening stand of 50, only their second half-century partnership of the series, before Hayden slashed Flintoff to Giles in the gully. But if running through Australia's first innings had been like taking sweets from children for England's attack, this was rather like chiselling away at granite. Langer was finally prised away by Giles for a gutsy 61, before Ponting dug in. Then came the moment England's fans had been waiting for all series: Ponting finally cracked. Martyn pushed to cover and called his skipper through for a quick single. Ponting came down the pitch hard, but substitute fielder Gary Pratt – on for the injured Simon Jones, who had been taken to hospital – ran him out with a direct hit from cover. Ponting, who saw England's frequent employment of subs as gamesmanship, was fuming. He chuntered all the way to the dressing room, before directing a few choice words to England coach Duncan Fletcher. Ironically, Simon Jones was genuinely crocked, and has not played for England since.

'I had absolutely no idea of the storm brewing over the English use of substitute fielders to allegedly rest their bowlers,' says Tim Sorrell. 'I did, however, have a grandstand view from my seat alongside the pavilion as Ponting let loose a torrent of abuse at Duncan Fletcher. I think I even saw Duncan smirking as he realised the extent to which Ponting (and the whole Australia team) had lost the plot. They were rattled now and no mistake.'

Adds James McNeilly: 'I was to the side of the pavilion so was pretty close to "Punter" as he walked off after the run-out to chants of "Cheerio! Cheerio!" from the crowd. I couldn't hear exactly what was said, but you could see the anger in him – those eyes could have turned you to stone. It was the moment the Ashes turned bad. All the talk before then had been about the great spirit between the teams and the fans, but as it became clearer that England might, just might, win the Ashes back after all those years, things got a little bit nasty. It was as hostile as an England cricket crowd is ever likely to get.'

'In the end, steady batting from Clarke and Katich took them to stumps at 222 for four. What an amazing day. The most intense session of Test cricket I have ever seen was Allan Donald bowling full throttle at Michael Atherton at Trent

Bridge in 1998. But this was the most intense full day's play. Although, to be honest, I'm not sure I remember much of what happened once Ponting was gone and the Australia innings began to consolidate. But I do remember that the Dame Edna Everages won the fancy dress competition at tea and got to meet Mike Gatting to pick up their prize. But it was hard to feel too disappointed as they were both excellent and – as a between-overs fancy dress summit between the Hound and Fox Road Stands revealed – it was the correct decision.'

Australia resumed on day four still 37 runs behind England, with only six second innings wickets in hand. 'We got to Trent Bridge quite early and were having a wander around when we bumped into umpire Steve Bucknor,' says Richard Sharpe. 'So I said to him, "Would you mind raising your finger for me for a photo?" And the guy next to me said, "He's only got to do that six more times and we're out of here ..." We were all thinking, "We're good to go."'

Clarke and Katich provided stubborn resistance until Hoggard had Clarke caught behind ten minutes before lunch for 56. Hoggard then had Gilchrist lbw for 11 and Katich got a stinker of a leg-before decision to leave his side 314 for seven, only 55 ahead.

'The tail wagged around "Warney", and my memory of that game is all about Shane Warne,' adds Sharpe. 'Whatever his faults as a human being, what an unbelievable cricketer, the guy was just never beaten. And if ever there was an example of that, that day at Trent Bridge was it. Warne only got forty-odd in that second innings, but his whole persona would extend beyond the boundary. He was in charge – "You guys have come to watch me, and this is what I'm going to do." He played with an abandon that lifted the rest of his team, and he never expected second best from any of them. When Brett Lee came in or Michael Kasprowicz, his attitude was "You're gonna get fifty as well, mate."'

Australia were finally dismissed for 387, leaving England with a seemingly paltry winning target of 129. Trent Bridge had been the ground where Australia had celebrated their previous two Ashes triumphs in England, but this had to be England's day. 'They got a lead, but the prevailing attitude was, "This should be no problem from here,"' says Richard Sharpe. 'Trescothick went out like a train, smashing them to all parts. And then Ponting tossed the ball to Warne. And even him standing there spinning the ball to himself, pointing out field placings – "You're going there, you're going there, and we're going to take ten wickets" – I just remember thinking, "He's going to do something," because he always did.'

Tim Sorrell takes up the story: 'What followed is the most tense passage of play I have ever seen. We were cruising until Warne took the ball. He got rid of Trescothick with his very first ball, Ponting snaffling a sharp one at silly point, and then he cleaned up Vaughan with the first ball of his second over. Then, when he had Strauss caught in the slips, well, I nearly shat myself.'

Adds Sharpe: 'When Bell was out attempting to hook Lee, I remember my dad turning to me and saying, "I'm not going to the bloody Oval, because it will be a bloody morgue." The mindset after only a few wickets was that we were going to snatch defeat from the jaws of victory, and that would have been the Ashes gone.'

'I remember we were sitting quite high up and there was a group of lads in front of us giving it the absolute large one, baiting Warne at every opportunity, giving him so much stick about his wife, about bookies, about drugs, anything they could think of,' recalls Ben Crisp. 'And I remember thinking, "Don't make him mad – why are you making him mad?" There were England fans actually telling them to shut up and sit down. Half of the crowd saw it as witnessing the greatest spin bowler ever in his absolute pomp, the rest were ridiculing him. But it wasn't actually going down that well, to the extent that there was almost some satisfaction when he started running through us.'

Pietersen and Flintoff played watchfully to reduce the runs required to twenty-six, with every single cheered to the rafters. 'I had been to Trent Bridge to watch England play New Zealand the year before and it was all very polite, like a cricket crowd was meant to be,' says Crisp. 'But it was almost more like a football crowd in 2005. Everyone was on edge, everyone was buzzing, and every run was effectively like a last-minute winner in a World Cup final, it was that kind of experience. Then, when Pietersen and Flintoff went, it was like the life just got sucked out of the place. I remember Brett Lee [who accounted for both of them] celebrating wildly in the middle as if they were going to go on and win it.'

Adds Richard Sharpe: 'There was a sense of unbelieving and it was just getting quieter and quieter. We were all of that defeatist attitude by the time six wickets had gone down, and I think that only made it even worse for the England players. Pietersen came in and you just thought, "For God's sake, man, we only need thirty-odd runs, you've got a day and a half to do it, just nurdle the runs." But he can only play one way and he got out to some flashy drive. Geraint Jones came in, who was apparently in the side because he was a good batsman, and played a similar shot off Warne to get out for three, and I was just head in hands, thinking, "I can't believe you've thrown this away." Three wickets left, Giles and Hoggard in the middle, Warne with the ball in his hand, and he not only had this mental stranglehold over the players, but over the crowd as well.'

'I've never been tenser in my life,' says Tim Sorrell. 'And my friend, who had been present on the last day at Edgbaston, was religiously clinging on to his lucky hat and rocking gently, muttering, "Not again, not again ..." But never have I been more pleased to have Ashley Giles in the side. I never rated the "King of Spain" as a bowler, although he clearly did a job, but England were not blessed with bowlers who could bat, and the solidity he added to the order – as demonstrated here, but again at The Oval in the fifth Test – was priceless.'

'It was when Hoggard hit his four [a textbook cover drive off Lee] that everyone knew it had turned back to England again,' says Ben Crisp. 'It cut through the tension like a knife. I've never seen a cricket ball move so slowly, it crept towards the boundary and hobbled over the rope. And everything just went berserk.'

Adds Richard Sharpe: 'I remember we were right underneath the England balcony and when Hoggard hit that four, I looked up and "Vaughany" was sitting there with a big grin on his face as if to say, "Never in doubt, never in doubt." But even then I couldn't agree, because as far as I was concerned, we were only three Warne deliveries away from losing the Test.'

Sharpe need not have worried. Giles finished the job, later admitting, 'I don't think I'll score more important runs in my career and I don't think "Hoggy" will hit a better extra cover drive.' For many of the England fans who were lucky enough to be in attendance, the duo made it a day they will never want to forget. 'I'm a big Chelsea fan but that day at Trent Bridge was my favourite sporting moment,' says Ben Crisp. 'The relief, the surprise, the release, it was like nothing I've ever experienced, before or since.'

Says Sharpe: 'Every session of that series, every ball, was unmissable. It wasn't the most enjoyable day's sport I've ever had, but, looking back, it was one of the greatest days of sport I've ever attended. It was mayhem, everybody was just bouncing around, the nature of the victory meant everyone was a lot more relieved and ecstatic than if we'd just knocked off the runs. It was just incredible to be there. Suddenly cricket was on everybody's lips again. Previously you had to be a real connoisseur to enjoy Test cricket, but in that series there was something for everyone.'

'I nearly didn't get there at all,' says Tim Sorrell. 'I had bought the tickets for the game roughly a year in advance, but as summer approached my girlfriend informed me that her brother was getting married. In Italy. On Saturday 27 August. Bang in the middle of the Test match. I'd had the tickets longer than this guy had been going out with his fiancée. Noooooo! How could this be happening to ME? I mentioned this fact to my girlfriend, and in a fit of pique she promptly rang her father to discuss the situation. "... Well, it *is* the Ashes" was his reply. I love that man. Oh, how glad was I that I wasn't in Italy when this game was played. Can you imagine? I still wake up in a cold sweat just thinking about what I might have missed.'

With England 2–1 up going into the final Test at The Oval, some more jingoistic sections of the press already thought Vaughan's boys had it in the bag. 'The Ashes are coming home,' roared the *Mirror*. Meanwhile, even with one Test to play, the consensus seemed to be that this was already the greatest series ever. 'For spectacle and sheer unrelenting excitement, if not for the quality of the cricket,' said Christopher Martin-Jenkins in *The Times*, 'this really must be accounted the greatest of all Test series.' Simon Barnes, also of *The Times*, feared for the nation's sanity: 'Just when Wimbledon was safely over, the England cricket team have set to outdo Tim Henman as a cause of national neurosis. One unbearable climax has followed another as England have repeatedly outplayed Australia and have repeatedly found it hard, if not impossible, to make the killing stroke. The finger freezes on the trigger. England simply cannot believe in their own superiority over the old enemy.' Looking ahead to The Oval, the *Telegraph's* Paul Hayward wrote: 'There will be a five-day hole in the English economy, a flooding back to the sport that dominated our childhood summers before football rolled its tanks on to the village green and the local rec. Thumb through the catalogue of great sporting events on English soil since the honeyed summer of '66 and few reach the magnitude of the Oval Test.'

Ponting's outburst at Trent Bridge turned out to be an aberration rather than a prevailing trend: the Aussies took defeat well, were generous with their handshakes and good relations were restored. It was as if they were determined that nothing would besmirch the almost perfect aesthetics of the series. McGrath was recalled for The Oval, in place of Kasprowicz, while England plumped for batting all-rounder Paul Collingwood, instead of fast bowler James Anderson, in place of Simon Jones. It was seen by some as a rather conservative decision and perhaps a sign England were losing their nerve with the finishing line in sight.

Day one ended as day one had begun, with the war for the

Ashes urn still on a knife edge. Vaughan won his third toss of the series and again elected to bat, before Trescothick and Strauss came flying out of the traps once more. Even the most unpredictable Test series in history had its recurring motifs, none more prominent than the greatness of Warne. With his seamers being taken for more than four an over, Ponting was again forced to wheel Warne into the front line inside the opening hour. In the space of sixteen overs, Trescothick, Vaughan, Bell and Pietersen were gone, all victims of the bogeyman who refused to die. However, Flintoff (72) combined with Strauss (129) for an invaluable partnership of 143 as England wrested back control of the game, before the Aussies came roaring back with three wickets before the close of play. With England 319 for seven, the tourists could claim to have had the better of the day.

On day two, Australia were frustrated by a thorny last-wicket stand of 28 between Giles and Harmison, before eventually closing the innings for 373. Langer and Hayden having posted their first century stand of the series, Australia were then frustrated by bad light and rain. The following day only 45.4 overs were possible, but it was enough time for the Australian openers to advance their side into a position of strength: both men posted three figures for the first time in the series, Hayden's century his first in Tests for more than a year. While England remained disciplined, a number of decisions went against them and they badly missed the reverse swing of Simon Jones. When Australia accepted the offer of bad light, they were 277 for two, a deficit of only 96 runs.

Before the final Test had even begun, a contributor to the *Guardian*'s ball-by-ball coverage had asked: 'Is it cowardly to pray for rain?' The answer was probably yes, but that evening thousands of English men, women and children would have been kneeling by their beds. 'We were waving our umbrellas about and the Aussies came out at one point with sunglasses on as if there was nothing wrong,' recalls Adam 'Streaky' Carroll. 'It's the only game I've been to where the supporters have cheered when players have gone off for bad light or rain. We just wanted the Ashes back, it had been too long. If I'd paid £500 for five days' cricket and didn't see a ball bowled, that would have been fine by me. There are times when the result is all.'

All series Warne and Flintoff had been vying for the spotlight, and day four was the Englishman's turn to shine. Australia's openers having laid a platform for a healthy first innings lead, Flintoff dredged up one more Herculean effort, running through the Australia line-up and finishing with figures of five for 78 as the visitors were bundled out for 367, six behind. Warne removed Strauss before bad light intervened again, but, with another fifty-six overs lost, it seemed like advantage England heading into the final day. But for some of those sporting the scars of a thousand Aussie drubbings, it did not look that way.

'We turned up thinking we might scrape a draw, although

it was going to be close, that was the general consensus,' adds Carroll, who was there at the birth of the Barmy Army, on the Ashes tour down under in 1994–95. 'There was a huge buzz on the Tube on the way there, massive expectation, but it was also unbelievably tense. Those tickets were going for an awful lot of money if you wanted them too, but my mate "Wooders" sold one at face value to a guy he recognised from a Barmy tour back in the day, which was an incredible thing to do when all those touts were sharking about the place.

'Previously we'd always said, "We just want to be competitive." But in reality that was a load of crap: we wanted to win, being competitive was not enough. We'd witnessed absolute canings for sixteen years, live and on the telly, and when we were being trounced, winning the odd game seemed like a bonus. But on this occasion we had to win, being competitive was no longer part of the equation as far as I was concerned. They'd inflicted so much pain on us – those actual players, not just the Australian team.'

Trescothick and Vaughan began that final day in confident fashion, the England skipper looking particularly unruffled as McGrath and Warne howled at his door. However, having stroked six fours on his way to 45 runs, the door finally flew off the hinges. McGrath produced a sweet away-swinger which Vaughan edged behind, before repeating the dose next ball to get rid of Bell. Enter Kevin Pietersen, on hat-trick ball. McGrath sent down a snorter, the ball rearing up off a length and squaring Pietersen up. The Aussies went wild, but umpire Billy Bowden adjudged, correctly, that the ball had flown into Ponting's hands via Pietersen's shoulder. Pietersen grinned, McGrath grinned back, but there weren't too many people grinning up in the stands.

'I don't think I spoke to my mate "Wooders" or my brother-in-law for about an hour and a half when things were looking really ropey,' says Adam Carroll. 'I was just sat there, looking at the cricket through my fingers, thinking, "Where is this going, surely we can't get this close and lose it?" It was very scary stuff – in fact, it was awful, almost painful, one of those "why do I watch sport?" moments.'

Pietersen was still not off the mark when he lunged forward to Hampshire team-mate Warne and got an edge, only for Gilchrist to deflect the ball to Hayden at slip, who was unable to complete the catch. Then, with Pietersen on 15, came another one of those moments where England fans thought they must have been dreaming: Lee served up a juicy half-volley, Pietersen was unable to resist, the ball took the edge of his bat, and Warne put down a head-high lollipop at slip.

'It's become a bit of a cliché now, but Warne really did drop the Ashes,' says Adam Carroll. 'That was a regulation chance – he just didn't drop those catches. And if he'd have caught that, that was game over, no one else would have saved us. It was wonderful, the cheering went on for I don't know how long.'

Two overs later, an emboldened Pietersen slog-swept

Warne for two sixes to bring up the England 100, but Warne, who bowled thirty-two consecutive overs from the Vauxhall End, was still swinging back with haymakers. First he produced a fizzing leg-break to dismiss Trescothick, before removing Flintoff, caught and bowled. At lunch, England were 133 ahead with only five wickets remaining.

'Then, after lunch, it slowly turned,' recalls Carroll. 'You could hear the volume of the crowd being turned up ever so slightly every couple of overs, as if someone had their fingers on the volume knob. Lee almost got him with a bouncer, but after that it was one-way traffic, Pietersen just took Brett Lee apart and the crowd was going berserk. It was an awesome innings, with a hint of insanity about it. Before that series he was just some bloke people had vaguely heard of, playing for so and so, who could hit a ball a long way and had a daft haircut, that's all anyone really knew about him. But he was just so assured that day, he looked cool – "I'm where I should be, I'm good enough to play at this level, and this is how I play."'

Pietersen hooked Lee for two massive sixes before playing what might have been the shot of the day, a flat-batted baseball shot straight down the ground for four. 'Matthew Hayden was a bully, and he was one of many Australians we'd watched over the years who had bullied us like that,' says Paul Burnham. 'But Pietersen played the game the same way, and you could see it on the Australian faces that day, they looked slightly baffled when the boot was on the other foot.

That was all about him stamping his charisma on the Aussies and taking it to them the way they had always taken it to us.'

Collingwood contributed 10 to a crucial sixth-wicket stand of 60 before Giles weighed in with another vital knock of 59. Pietersen struck seven sixes in all, but it was the last one, a hook over square-leg off Lee, that hammered the final nail in the Australian coffin, taking England past the 250 mark with only thirty-nine overs left in the day. By the time he was bowled by McGrath, England were 314 ahead with fewer than nineteen overs remaining. 'The denouement might not have made great telly, but in the ground it was brilliant,' insists Carroll. 'No one knew what was going on, but by then no one cared, the party had been going on since about four o'clock. Once Pietersen had got past a hundred and it had started to look safe, nothing mattered any more.'

Harmison bowled four balls at Langer before the Australian openers were offered the light, which they accepted. After a period of confusion, the umpires eventually re-emerged, made their way to the middle and it was left to Rudi Koertzen to remove the stumps. And so ended the greatest Test series in history, the series when everyone in England went barmy for cricket.

'If you're an England cricket supporter now,' says Carroll, '"Barmy Army" is a label you will be given. Whether you're out there on your own or with Gullivers Tours or whoever, you're seen to be Barmy Army – and there's nothing wrong with that. Because for the most part, the Barmy Army are a force for good. It had taken a lot of years, but finally in 2005 we were being seen as just a group of lads who wanted to watch cricket and enjoy life while we were watching it. When it was necessary, we'd make a bit of noise, have a singsong, take the mickey a bit, but it would never degenerate into anything more than that. And that summer, the whole nation came along for the ride. No doubt about it, we were all Barmy Army now.'

'When the Barmy Army are revved up it becomes a tough environment for the opposition to play in and the Barmy Army certainly played a huge part in England beating Australia in 2005,' says BBC cricket correspondent Jonathan Agnew. 'It was a very hostile environment, albeit in a nice cricketing way. For the first time you really felt an English crowd were fully behind their team in a home series. They played a huge part in Gillespie and Kasprowicz having poor series, Gillespie in particular. There is no doubt the English players appreciate them, the Barmy Army is a twelfth man.'

'The crowds were loud and raucous that summer, but they did what they did in the Barmy Army way,' says Burnham, 'with lots of humour and charisma. They played a massive part in creating these new heroes – Flintoff, Pietersen, Simon Jones, even a lesser talent like "Gilo", we were all behind. And that must have been recognised in the corridors of power, because Mike Soper, vice-chairman at the ECB at the time, and a really top guy, invited us along to the celebrations in Trafalgar Square. He was adamant the Barmy Army should be there. The night we won the Ashes I spent on the phone, rounding up the Barmy Army hardcore. We had a cordoned-off area right at the front of the stage for two hundred Barmy Army fans and halfway through the ceremony "KP" and "Vaughany" asked Bill "The Trumpet" Cooper and "Jimmy" to come up on stage to lead the Barmy Army song, with all the players joining in.'

Says Cooper: 'It was just bizarre. I was crouched behind Marcus Trescothick and he was like, "No, don't worry about it, wait until they do the interview and we'll get a proper singsong going." I remember security running over and Duncan Fletcher turning round and saying, "No, he's all right, he's with us." It was nice to know they knew you and accepted you.'

'When the England players were doing their parade on the double-decker bus, I got asked to go on BBC Radio 5 Live to commentate,' adds Burnham, 'which was their way of recognising we'd played a central role in the drama. There was this feeling that finally we were being appreciated in England. It wasn't so much that we'd become part of the establishment, more that the establishment had realised if they harnessed this right, as they did in '05, the crowd could be a vital weapon for the England cricket team, at home as well as away.'

'I remember on the 2002–03 tour down under, even though I had a wonderful time individually, I noticed the Barmy Army would make more noise when England were doing badly,' recalls Michael Vaughan. 'They kept coming back louder and with more people, which was the most amazing part about it. Ask Nasser Hussain and Michael Atherton and they'll tell you they were wonderful times for England players. They didn't win a lot but they always felt they had a huge amount of support behind them, which was important. But in 2005, that was the first time we had experienced that kind of support at home, and it was a tremendous boost. I always felt in the field they were like the twelfth man, and sometimes a thirteenth man, particularly against Australia, and they definitely upped the level in '05. In '05 they were absolutely outstanding, gave us a real advantage at home, as home fans are supposed to do. I think the Barmy Army have transformed and built up Test match cricket in the last ten years in terms of a spectacle – without them it would be a very boring scene.'

9

Keeping the faith ... Australia 2006–07

Talk to enough Barmy Army members and you will soon learn that however badly England perform on the field, however easily they get beaten, however humiliating the results appear on the scorecards, there never has been – and never will be – a 'Tour of Hell'. Too much sun, too much beer, too much partying to be had. But the Ashes series of 2006–07 would come close to breaking the resolve of the most stoic of Barmy veterans. If not exactly hell, for some it was tantamount to six weeks' singing in the stands of purgatory.

On paper, the two sides did not look much different from those that had contested the greatest, most tightly fought Test series in history in England in 2005. But it did not take the sagest of cricket followers to realise things would be different this time around. The tourists were without injured captain Michael Vaughan, who had proved so key to England regaining the Ashes in 2005. In his place, coach Duncan Fletcher chose Andrew Flintoff over Andrew Strauss. While Flintoff had led England competently in India in 2006, it was an added burden England's talismanic all-rounder could have done without, given the extra pressure of an Ashes series down under. Also missing from the touring party was paceman Simon Jones, who had arguably been England's most effective bowler in 2005. And while England had rather coasted through their engagements over the previous fourteen months, seemingly still hungover from the mother of all Ashes-winning parties at Number 10, Australia had regrouped and galvanised themselves, winning eleven and drawing one of their subsequent twelve Tests. The press knew a heavy reverse could be on the cards, the fans knew it, and the bookies knew it, too, with some installing Australia as 1–3 favourites.

'There was a bit of a hangover from the Ashes,' says Andy Thompson, whose first tour following England was down under in 2002–03. 'They thought, "We're the best team in the world now, we beat the Aussies." And I don't think they appreciated how much it hurt the Australians, losing in 2005, and they were ready for them. We also knew it was going to be "Warnie's" swansong, McGrath, Langer, too, and obviously Ponting was hurting. And I think the biggest mistake England made was appointing "Freddie" captain. I think Fletcher just went with the flow, there was a bit of pressure from sections of the media. That said, I went in with optimism, because they were virtually the same sides, and I at least thought we'd make a fist of it.'

England hit the ground stumbling. In their first warm-up match they were crushed by a Prime Minister's XI and things took a turn for the worse when experienced opener Marcus Trescothick left the squad nine days before the start of the first Test in Brisbane because of a stress-related illness. 'Send in McGrath and Warne and then all the Poms will be going home depressed,' noted former Australia fast bowler Jeff Thomson. For the Barmy Army, too, it had been an unusually difficult build-up. 'A huge number of England fans were ticketless on arrival in Australia,' says Paul Burnham. 'These were people who had been planning the trip for years. Cricket Australia clearly had a policy of breaking up the massed ranks of England supporters, whose passion and influence clearly unsettled several of Australia's players in 2005 and on previous tours. I've heard Shane Warne went back after the 2005 series, spoke to the authorities and Cricket Australia compiled a list of ten reasons why they had lost the Ashes, and on the list was the English fans. Basically Warne had said, "They were giving us a hell of a time out there, we need to do something about it." The Barmy Army did such a good job in '05 that they didn't want us sat together in '06–'07; they didn't want us having that positive effect on the England team and perhaps be laying into the Aussies. It just wasn't cricket in '06–'07.'

With the pound still relatively strong against the Aussie dollar and with many England supporters still on a high after

England's Ashes series win in 2005, the invasion was huge. Most of Brisbane's hotels were booked out for the five days of the Test two weeks before it started, while the Pig 'N' Whistle, traditional Brisbane hangout of the Barmy Army, had five English ales on tap, including Thwaites, one of Flintoff's personal sponsors. It even installed a hand pump on the bar, allegedly the only one in Australia. The Aussie fans, too, announced themselves ready for their Barmy adversaries in the stands, with 'The Fanatics' giving the press a sneak preview of their series songbook, including one ditty called 'Ode to a British Girlfriend' (to the tune of 'Living Doll'):

> Got myself a yawning, boring, pasty, nagging,
>   whingeing Pom;
> Got to do my best to leave her, just 'cos she's a
>   whingeing Pom;
> She's got a lazy eye and big fat thighs from all those
>   chips and pies;
> She's not the only boring, pasty, nagging, whingeing
>   Pom.

Not that the Barmy Army hierarchy seemed fazed. 'When I first came to Australia one of the best quotes I heard was that the Barmy Army would outsing, outdrink and outshag the Aussies,' Dave 'The General' Peacock was quoted as saying in Sydney's *Sun Herald*, 'and nothing has changed since.'

In truth, it was not the first time a posse had been raised in an attempt to scare off the invading Army. On England's 2002 tour of New Zealand, the New Zealand Cricket Board, faced with the arrival of up to five thousand England supporters, decided to fight fire with fire. It recruited fifty people to form the Mad Caps, who were then groomed to take on the Barmy Army during the one-day internationals which preceded the Test series. 'They held auditions and had dance routines and everything,' says Paul Burnham. 'Any time we sang a song or anything, we'd get abused by these Mad Caps. During the one-day series, before most of the Barmy Army old guard had arrived, these Mad Caps were throwing stuff at these young uni kids from England, who were giving it back. And because they were getting abuse, they started singing a dodgy song about [New Zealand all-rounder] Chris Cairns. The problem was, we'd raised money for the Chris Cairns charity before, so some of the old guard didn't like it and sat at the other end of the ground. It was commented on in the New Zealand press, that there was a rift between the two Barmy Army factions. The New Zealand press just had nothing else to write about, but I guess you could say the Mad Caps had done a job.'

If England fans still had any hope of retaining the Ashes as they trooped to the ground on the first morning, the pre-match experience of Mark 'The Nun' should have been an omen for the filth and the fury to come. 'We'd all been out the night before and had an Indian and my tummy wasn't too great the morning of the match,' says 'The Nun'. 'Walking to the ground, I needed the toilet rather desperately and I didn't quite make it. So I ran to this pub, banged on the door and this woman let me in. I tidied myself the best I could and asked if her husband had any shorts, but she said she didn't have a husband and certainly didn't have any shorts that I could have. So anyway, my shorts were a little bit on the dirty side so when I got into the Gabba, I went straight to the souvenir shop to buy some, but they only had "large boys". I looked like Charles Hawtrey out of the *Carry On* films, or John McEnroe, with these tight shorts on that were cutting into my legs. I couldn't even sit down. Then, amazingly, it got worse from there.'

Ricky Ponting won the toss and decided to have a bat – and then came what will forever be known as 'that' first ball. After the considerable hype and hoopla, the on-field presentations, the pre-match interviews and the national anthems, Steve Harmison's first delivery was every bit as deflating as being caught short on your way to the ground and having to spend the day in a pair of undersized shorts. A colossal wide, the ball went straight to Flintoff standing at second slip. Up in the stands the Aussies laughed and pointed, in the press box the cricket writers were lost for words, while out in the middle Flintoff's grin spoke volumes: 'So now the secret's out, we're fatally undercooked . . .'

'That first ball is forever ingrained in my memory,' says Andy Thompson, who had also witnessed the first-day slaughter at 'The Gabbattoir' in 2002. 'I had a great view. "Harmy" came steaming in, let go of the ball and everyone was turning round to each other and saying, "Did that ball go to 'Freddie'?! At second slip?!" All the Aussies were laughing, even more so when they kept replaying it on the big screens. But the jarring thing for me was "Freddie"'s reaction, he was pissing himself laughing. That ball set the tone for the entire series. The contrast between that morning and the first morning of the first Test at Lord's in 2005 was marked – back in '05, Langer got hit, Ponting got hit, and even though we lost that Test match, you could tell we were up for the fight. But this time it was a case of, "What the bloody hell's going on?" There was just disbelief. My first ever Test with the Barmy Army was at Brisbane in 2002 and we got a hammering on day one after Nasser Hussain put them in. But we came back on day two, and although we lost the Test in four days, at least we showed a bit of fight. But there never seemed to be any fight in that Test, and it was quite clear from "Freddie"'s reaction what sort of series it was going to be. Much as we loved him, I thought, "Is he the guy to lead the country?"'

Some respected voices up in the commentary box also felt the series was pretty much lost then and there: 'It was a ghastly moment, betraying a desperate lack of confidence and form,' said BBC cricket correspondent Jonathan Agnew. 'From that moment, England were always trying to claw their way back into the psychological battle.'

Matthew Hayden, watching from the non-striker's end, agreed: 'The cricketing world was just mouth open,' said Hayden. 'Not to mention Justin Langer down that end, wondering is he on the wrong wicket. In a lot of ways it set the tone. You are going to have to play well in those first two hours of the game, it sets the whole competition up for the rest of the summer.'

'I froze,' conceded Harmison, who had rocked and rolled the Aussie batsmen on day one at Lord's in 2005. 'I let the enormity of the occasion get to me. My whole body was nervous. I could not get my hands to stop sweating. The first ball slipped out of my hands, the second did as well and, after that, I had no rhythm, nothing.'

Australia finished the first day on 346 for three, with Ponting making an unbeaten century, his sixth in Ashes Tests and his second in succession in Brisbane. Having been the first Australian skipper to lose the Ashes in almost twenty years in 2005, it must have been an enormously gratifying innings. Only Flintoff of England's seamers carried any real threat, with Harmison, Matthew Hoggard and James Anderson being treated with something like contempt. Harmison, who England's fans had hoped would be a real handful on Australia's hard, bouncy decks, was overlooked for the second new ball. 'England cannot retain the Ashes if Harmison fails,' noted the *Australian*, 'and he was horrid yesterday.'

On a positive note, up in the stands, 'The Fanatics' were

being routed: to the tune of Oasis' 'Wonderwall' went the Barmy Army refrain:

Today is gonna be the day that we're gonna sing a
    song for you,
By now, you should've somehow realised that's what
    we're here to do.
And I don't believe that anybody sings as bad as
    you ...

But anyone listening closely would have noticed the Barmy Army repertoire lacked its usual vim and vigour. 'I'd been playing all summer during the 2005 Ashes,' explains Bill 'The Trumpet' Cooper. 'Then, on day one at the Gabba, Paul Collingwood turned round on the boundary and said, "Come on, lads, make some noise," so I played a few tunes and nothing was said. But when I came back after lunch I knocked out the *Neighbours* theme and I was halfway through "Jerusalem" when I could feel someone peering over my shoulder, and there were two Aussie coppers standing behind me. I thought, "I've got to finish 'Jerusalem', I can't stop halfway through." And when I finished they took me out the back and the guy said, "We're going to arrest you." The policewoman decided that was a bit harsh, but they slapped me with a banning order and I wasn't allowed within five hundred metres of the Gabba for the next four days. Apparently I was disturbing the peace. It turned into this big media storm – one newspaper went with "TRUMPET-GATE: THE BIGGEST CRICKETING SCANDAL SINCE BODYLINE". I wasn't allowed to play at the Gabba at all, although I was allowed back without the trumpet after a couple of days.'

'You were more than welcome at the Gabba if you sat quietly in your seat, standing only to make your way to the extortionately overpriced food and drink outlets,' says Matt Williams. 'However, turn up with a rucksack, sing, chant, stand, join in with the Mexican wave, knock a beach ball around, play a trumpet, wave a flag, or generally attempt to have a good time, and you could be in a spot of bother. Assault by an unnecessarily aggressive and armed police officer, complete with foul language and threat of a possible fine, seemed to be the norm. Despite the strict laws imposed, it seemed that racist chanting was permitted, with many renditions of "I'd rather be a Paki than a Pom" heard from the broad-minded Aussie faithful. However, even the racism had been clamped down on by day three. Muzza, twenty-four, from Brisbane, had been ejected from the ground for using racially abusive language. His crime? Telling a West Bromwich Albion fan that his cricket team were rubbish and he might as well get himself off home to the Black Country.'

Burnham and the Barmy Army hierarchy were livid at the heavy-handedness. 'It seemed to me that Cricket Australia just wanted to win, full stop,' says Burnham. 'They believed the Barmy Army would help England win, so it just seemed like everything was geared to trying to make sure there was no fun in the game. We just wanted to come over and have a good time, not to be treated like schoolchildren.' Another gripe was the scattered seating allocation for English supporters, although Cricket Australia did not take the criticism lying down, arguing that 'Australia has a far more embracing attitude to UK fans than England does to Australian fans.'

The British press, however, came down firmly on the Barmy Army's side. 'The Barmy Army may not have been aware when they left home that Queensland is the kind of State with more rules than a 19th century boarding school,' wrote Martin Johnson in the *Telegraph*. 'Although if the Australians have any compassion at all [the trumpeter] will be allowed back in towards the end of the tour for a solemn rendition of The Last Post.'

'Threatening to boycott the rest of the series because their trumpeter was ejected is, on the face of it, hilarious,' wrote Kevin Mitchell in the *Observer*, '[but] any defections would eat into the $200m (£80m) they are estimated to be pumping into the Australian economy over the next couple of months. More pertinent to the job in hand, though, even a minor dwindling of their number or volume would detract from the atmosphere. Australians cannot provide it. This is not exactly the Bodyline crisis all over again, but it is no fiddling complaint. It is about attitudes, about social interaction, about not taking cricket or ourselves too seriously.'

However, some in the British media were uncomfortable with the amount of coverage the Barmy Army was getting, complaining – with no apparent sense of self-awareness, given that they were providing them with extra column inches – that the Barmies were now creating their own headlines. Wrote Barney Ronay in the *Guardian*: 'Large, sunburnt men attempt a slow-motion conga; someone waves a crumpled flag; depressed-looking people in funny costumes suddenly wake up and start punching the air on catching a glimpse of themselves on the big screen; and, yes, here he is again, Victor "Jimmy" Flowers, leader of the Barmy Army, also known as that skinny bloke in the singlet with the stringy blond highlights who keeps jumping around, drawing attention to himself and not really paying attention to the cricket. The army is now part of the spectacle. Its foot soldiers have begun to believe their own publicity. What fun could there possibly be at the first Test of a titanic Ashes series without a trumpet?'

BBC 5 live's Pat Murphy, writing in the *Birmingham Post*, was more scathing than most. 'The biggest bore associated with covering an England cricket tour isn't the guarded comments of the coach Duncan Fletcher or the inevitable paranoia from the team if it's all gone pear-shaped. No, the biggest pain in the backside is the Barmy Army. The Barmy Army are nowhere near as genial as they claim. After their trumpet player was ejected from the ground in Brisbane, their leader, Paul Burnham, whined, "We just want to come

over and have a good time, not to be treated like children."
Burnham doesn't seem to think that chanting the same
annoying rubbish and showing off to the TV cameras is
childish.'

Threats of a boycott proved unfounded as England fans
came back for more of the same on days two and three.
Ponting (196) and Hussey (86) amassed 209 for the fourth
wicket as Australia declared their first innings on 602 for
nine. Harmison finished with figures of one for 123 from
thirty overs. 'England's premier strike bowler did finally find
some semblance of direction towards the tail end of
Australia's first innings,' continued the *Telegraph*'s Johnson,
'albeit 550 runs later than his captain would ideally have
liked.'

In reply, the tourists collapsed to 157 all out, with Glenn
McGrath – who Ian Botham declared 'past it' before the
series started and had not played a Test since January – taking
six for 50.

Off the field, things were rapidly getting worse for the
beleaguered Barmies. The England and Wales Cricket Board,
who could never have been described as friends of the Barmy
Army, were now accusing them of breach of copyright, ques-
tioning the use of the ECB logo and the term 'Ashes' on
Barmy Army merchandise. 'The England and Wales Cricket
Board is just as perverse [as Cricket Australia],' wrote Greg
Baum in the *Melbourne Age*. '[The Barmy Army] supported
English cricket through its long, dark ages. For their pains,

they are facing legal action for unlicensed use of logos. The ECB's attitude is too typical. It should be thanking the Barmy Army. Instead, it is suing it.'

Burnham, meanwhile, was summoned for a summit with Cricket Australia chiefs. Three days into the series, he was wearing it from all sides.

Langer made an unbeaten 100 as Australia declared their second innings closed on 202 for one, a lead of 648. England were staring down the barrel at another mammoth Ashes defeat, although at least they showed some spunk on day four, Kevin Pietersen and Collingwood putting on 153 for the fourth wicket before Collingwood was stumped four runs short of his third Test century, coming down the track to Shane Warne. England began the final day five wickets down and hoping forecasts of thunderstorms would turn out to be true – but the rain never came and Australia's bowlers mopped up the England innings in ninety minutes. Empty stands at least allowed England's fans to congregate on the final morning. Problem was, they had nothing to sing about.

'For the intrepid English, the world champions of sports tourism,' wrote Paul Hayward in the *Daily Mail*, 'there is the added hardship of ridicule, the endless rain of scorn. The Vietcong had it easy. All they had to deal with in jungle hideouts were leaflet flurries and American choppers blaring out propaganda. Every second of an Ashes tour is a psychological assault on the Poms. They open their papers to see a Weet-Bix ad declaring: "Yesterday we also had the English for breakfast." As an Englishman, you hunker down, take your blows, and hope for a Freddie Flintoff hat-trick or Kevin Pietersen century to buy you some relief. Then you turn to the local papers with their "pathetic Pom" headlines.'

The usually cordial relationship between England's players and their fans was even showing signs of strain. During a 'naughty boy net' before the second Test in Adelaide, which was bizarrely open to television cameras, photographers and curious supporters, Harmison snapped at a Barmy Army member who was deemed to be invading the Durham fast bowler's space. In a peculiarly Barmy twist, said member was apparently shouting not abuse, but encouragement.

Meanwhile, in perhaps the most chilling sign that things could only get worse for the tourists, the Aussie players were singing the Barmy Army's praises. 'I am really looking forward to seeing what new songs they have come up with,' said wicket-keeper Adam Gilchrist. 'I get really excited by them shouting and singing for England, it's just so much fun to be out there.' That was one in the box for the Barmies.

Trumpet-gate took a truly bizarre turn during the build-up to the Adelaide Test. Mark Carroll, a professor and musicologist from Adelaide University and the Elder Conservatorium, emerged to announce that trumpets have 'a clearly defined place on the Ashes battleground, with cultural and historical significance'.

'Music in general, and wind instruments in particular, have long accompanied life's rituals like birth, marriage, work, death and so forth,' said Dr Carroll. 'The Barmy Army's use of the trumpet, however, seems to trace its origins to the use of the trumpet in war, as a kind of rallying cry for the troops. To some, the raucous trumpet sounds that accompany the Barmy Army's tour of duty to the antipodes during the current Ashes campaign are a mere irritation, but a deeper social and cultural significance can be attributed to the instrument.'

Officials from the South Australian Cricket Association were apparently not listening: Bill 'The Trumpet' was banned again. 'At Adelaide I wasn't allowed to play at all,' says Cooper. 'When I landed, two policemen approached me and said, "Are you Bill Cooper?" And I thought, "Oh, here we go again." And they said, "Oh, we just want to say, we're not like the people in Queensland, we'd like to take you on a guided tour of the city," and they took me out for lunch.' Ah well: if Bill Cooper was unable to blow his horn in Adelaide, at least the England team had the support of former players up in the press box, with Geoffrey Boycott predicting Flintoff's team would get 'murdered' in the rest of the series. That is the annoying thing about Boycott: he is so often right.

Flintoff won the toss and elected to bat first and England's batsmen made hay on a lifeless wicket. At 266 for three at the close, and with Paul Collingwood not out 98 and Kevin Pietersen not out 60, England were back in the series. Or so it seemed. On day two, England, although scoring slowly, continued to pile on the runs and finally declared on 551 for six. Collingwood made 206, while Pietersen made 158, although there were England fans who felt the Aussies had been let off lightly. 'I remember sitting there next to this middle-aged Aussie bloke, wearing a jumper when it was about thirty-two degrees, and I'm looking at him thinking, "What sort of a twat are you?"' recalls Andy Thompson.

'And when "Freddie" came out to bat, he biffed a few, and this bloke started saying, "You've got enough, mate, you've got enough." And I said "No, we're going to keep you out in the field, make at least six hundred, run you ragged and make sure you've got no way back." And almost as soon as I said that, "Freddie" biffed another four and walked off with his bat under his arm. And this bloke started shouting at me, "Aaah, what the fuck do you know about cricket, you Pommie bastard." Although I can't say I didn't think we had enough, I just thought we should have kept them out there a bit longer.' When Flintoff dismissed Langer shortly before the close, leaving the hosts on 28 for one, Thompson's argument seemed even less secure.

England made further breakthroughs on the third morning, Matthew Hoggard claimed two wickets to leave Australia tottering on 65 for three. But arguably the game-changing moment, as is often the case, seemed innocuous enough at the time. When Ponting was only on 35, he tugged a Hoggard long-hop down to deep square-leg, where Ashley Giles mistimed his jump and shelled the catch. Ponting steered his side to 105 for three at lunch and reached his thirty-third Test ton before tea, becoming his country's most prolific century maker in the process. At stumps, Australia were 312 for five, with the game seemingly meandering towards a draw. Ponting's men were finally dismissed for 513 after tea on day four, Michael Clarke taking his side to within 38 of England with a knock of 124 and Hoggard finishing with manly figures of seven for 109 on a heart-breaker of a pitch. 'In the local press they'd been slagging off the grounds-man, Les Burdett,' says Thompson, 'complaining about it being a featherbed and a batsman's paradise, and all the way through Les had been defending himself, telling everyone "Nah, mate, there's a result in that pitch." But you can't post 550 and lose, for crying out loud.'

'The few days before had been brilliant,' says James 'Beefy' Beare. 'We were all in the best ground in Australia, Colling-wood and Pietersen scored all those runs, it looked like we could win it at one point, and after day four it was a draw for all money. We were competing, we were back in the series. I remember emailing my dad before heading up to the ground on the final morning and I was saying, "It's gonna be a draw, it's petering out into nothing, but I think I'll go along anyway." And then it all went horribly wrong.'

'The final day's efforts were the hallmark of a team wracked with fear, self-doubt, negativity and a safety-first attitude,' wrote Dean Wilson in the *Mirror*. And he was one of the kinder ones. England had been rolled for 129, losing their last nine wickets for 60 runs, leaving the hosts a paltry

168 runs to win what only a few hours earlier had seemed an unwinnable game. 'I'll never forget that last day at Adelaide, it was probably the worst day I've had at cricket,' continues Beare. 'I remember Strauss getting a shocking decision off Warne's bowling, and once Warne gets his tail up, you're finished. Anderson got a shocker, too, which meant the Aussies claimed a couple of extra overs. Whatever could have gone wrong went wrong. Dejected is an understatement, it wasn't good, to be honest. On the outside we were trying to stay upbeat, but on the inside it hurt. We did our bit, but that hurt more than any defeat I can remember.'

'I was close to tears when Mike Hussey hit the winning runs [with three overs to spare],' says Andy Thompson. 'We were all just sat there in total disbelief. In Perth a couple of weeks later, when we lost the Ashes, we were all singing and making a big deal of it, staying behind when all the Aussies had gone. But in Adelaide it was a case of: "What the hell happened here? Can you remember anything worse than this?" If there was any singing I can't remember, I was just sat on The Hill with my head in my hands, dribbling into my beer.'

'It was a little bit depressing but we got exactly what we deserved,' says Barmy Army veteran Mark 'The Nun'. 'We should have never lost in Adelaide. We had "Freddie" declaring at 550 and you should never give those Aussies a sniff of winning. I actually had a bet with an Aussie bloke on day four and I said, "At least you're not going to drub us 5–0."

I had a real good day with this Aussie bloke, said goodbye to him on day four and then when they rolled us on the last day I thought, "At least I won't be bumping into him again." When I got in the pub that night he'd driven an hour and a half with a mate to come and rub it in. That was the lowest part of that tour – a game we couldn't lose, we absolutely bottled it.'

'England have been rocked to their very core by an Australian team that conjured a six-wicket win from the depths of cricketing hell,' continued Wilson in the *Mirror*. 'How the Ashes holders have managed to fall 2–0 behind after two Test matches Down Under is almost unbelievable. The hope this side had given the touring fans and millions back at home, that they could end 20 years of humiliation in Australia, has vanished within the space of a single day's cricket.'

'After that day I remember everyone thinking, "We're gonna get clobbered, I think we'll lose 5–0,"' says Beare. However, some of England's fans weren't going to let one of the most humiliating defeats in living memory get in the way of solid debauchery. Says Dave 'The General' Peacock, who clearly has a fairly relaxed attitude towards discipline among his troops, 'I maintain you go and watch England lose anywhere in the world at cricket and you're still going to have a great time. That's what the Barmy Army is all about.'

What had been a strange old tour got even stranger before the third Test in Perth. Ten Barmy Army members, fed up with the substandard Indian food on offer in Australia, shelled out £1500 for a takeaway to be flown in from Potters Bar in Hertfordshire. Remarkably, two waiters from the Bengal Paradise restaurant managed to smuggle the food through Heathrow customs, and it was only when they landed in Perth that their contraband was discovered, before being destroyed in an incinerator. Said Paul Burnham: 'Given the strength of the pound against the Aussie dollar, I'm sure the boys are not losing too much sleep over it.'

England coach Duncan Fletcher finally bowed to pressure and picked spinner Monty Panesar for Perth, and the decision paid immediate dividends. Panesar, in for Ashley Giles, took five for 92 and Harmison four for 48 as Australia were dismissed for 244 on day one. 'Fletcher finally brought Panesar in, and he bowled Langer with a wonder delivery – not quite a Warne ball, but almost as good – and for a moment we all thought, "Maybe we could come back from this." But no ...' England's first innings was wrapped up for 215 on the stroke of tea on day two, and it was all Aussie from then on. Ponting's men piled up 527 for five declared in their second innings, with Hussey and Andrew Symonds making tons and Adam Gilchrist weighing in with 102 from fifty-nine deliveries on day three, the second-fastest century in Test history. 'The Ashes were safely locked up by then,' wrote Ron Reed in the Sydney *Daily Telegraph*, 'Gilchrist simply threw away the key.'

On day four, Alastair Cook scored his maiden Ashes

century but it only delayed the inevitable. On day five, Flintoff's team lost their last five wickets for 14 runs as Australia romped home again. Warne, who had been taunted mercilessly by the Barmy Army throughout the series (one banner unfurled in the second Test read: 'Shane: I think I'm pregnant. Please call') was the top wicket-taker with four for 115. 'The Ashes gone after 16 succulent months,' wrote Vic Marks in the *Guardian*. 'Last time it took 18 years to get them back.' With two Tests remaining, Pietersen hoisted the white flag in his column in the *News of the World*: 'We will fight all the way but it is becoming increasingly clear our best is not good enough against this great Aussie side.'

'The Ashes over before Christmas,' laments James Beare. 'But we actually had a good time in Perth, even though the cricket wasn't going our way. They have the trots [harness racing] in Perth and after the game we'd go in and have a few drinks and a laugh. On the last day a Barmy Army bloke challenged an Aussie bloke to a race round the track for money. They kept saying, "You can't go on the track, you can't go on the track," and eventually they let them on there. Our bloke blew a gasket on the back straight and got eaten up by this Aussie. No real surprise there.'

Adds Andy Thompson: 'There is a sense that tours like that are the Barmy Army's greatest hours. There was a realisation that the Aussies were well up for it, we didn't seem to be able to match them and we were just getting beaten by a far better team, so it was a case of let's just have some fun, let's sing our songs and show the Aussies how a team should be supported. The Aussie fans are so fickle, you only have to see how they were in the last Ashes series. They turn against their own, and we never do that. We might get a bit frustrated when catches go down and players don't seem to be concentrating on the job in hand, but it's our job to get behind the team. And that's what we did at Perth.'

Not surprisingly given the triumphalism that followed England's Ashes victory in 2005, the Australian media and players showed little sympathy towards their downtrodden foes. 'You don't feel too much for them,' said McGrath. 'I remember standing at The Oval last year watching England celebrate when they won the Ashes. I'm sure everyone in Australia who met up with any England supporter since then has really copped it. So, no, we don't feel sorry for them. Order has been restored.'

One Aussie who did feel a tinge of compassion for the travelling fans was Gus Worland, a friend of the Hollywood film star Hugh Jackman, who had accepted the challenge to infiltrate the Barmy Army for a television series. Worland may have got more than he had bargained for – boozing every day of a Test from 11 a.m. to 2 a.m. and missing his wedding anniversary because he was trekking across the Nullarbor was presumably not stipulated in the contract – but that did not stop him from becoming a great admirer of the Barmy Army spirit. 'The camaraderie they showed in the face of defeat in Adelaide,' said Worland. 'I thought they would have been so upset with us, which they were for a couple of hours, and then they were resolute again. They leave their jobs and girlfriends to watch the cricket because the most important thing is to be on The Hill or in the grandstand and cheering for their team.'

Day one of the fourth Test in Melbourne was all about Shane Warne. After lunch, with England already in a precarious position at 101 for three, he bowled Strauss with a classic leg-break to become the first man to take seven hundred Test wickets. The Barmy Army, drenched to the bone by morning rain, rose as one to pay homage to the greatest cricketer most of them had ever seen. 'Everyone was up on their feet when Warne got his seven hundredth wicket in Melbourne,' says James Beare. 'You've got to take your hats off when it's due.' The Barmy Army serenaded Warne with a rousing rendition of 'We wish you were English', as they had done at The Oval in 2005. Warne, despite the dreadful barracking he had received down the years – a Barmy Army favourite in '06–'07 was 'Where's your missus gone' – was genuinely touched. 'When they sang that, it was unreal,' said Warne. 'After all the years of getting bagged, it was amazing to hear that.' Warne finished with figures of five for 39 as the tourists were skittled for 159, England's last eight wickets falling for 58 runs.

The opening day provided one darkly comic moment involving a St George flag and a rogue gust of wind. 'One of our party received a text saying there was a story in the Aussie papers claiming a racist comment was being displayed on an English flag,' explains Mark Watson. 'And then it occurred to us: we're Mansfield Town fans and at the time we were trying to get rid of the chairman, Keith Haslam, and so we'd emblazoned "Haslam Out" across the flag. But where the wind had curled it over, it looked like it might have read "Islam Out" instead. I rushed out to buy a copy of the paper – how could the Australian media be so thick? Luckily, the article led to some publicity for the campaign, and the newspaper carried an explanation about the original article the following day.'

'That Melbourne Test was the low point of what was, to be honest, a bit of a nightmare tour,' says Burnham. 'The authorities made selling merchandising very difficult, they tried to stop us selling outside the grounds; they tried to scupper our Christmas Day event on the Yarra River in Melbourne by appealing to the local council to try to stop us from getting together; they confiscated our magazines; they shut down our booth. There was also the Tonk A Pom campaign [endorsed by motor company Ford]; and we were asked to stop singing, otherwise we'd all be thrown out. Instead of taking it on the chin that they'd lost that 2005 series fair and square, they came back with excuses and one of those excuses was that the crowd have given them a hard time and they didn't like it.'

England hit back hard on the second morning, picking up the wickets of Ponting, Hussey and Clarke for 22 runs, before Hayden (153) and Andrew Symonds (154 not out) combined to take Australia from 84 for five to a dominant 372 for seven at the close. On day three, England shrivelled and died with barely a whimper: bowled out for 161, an innings defeat, the Test match over with six sessions remaining.

'I bumped into a lot of Barmy Army members when England got hammered 5–0 in Australia,' recalls former England captain Michael Atherton, now ensconced in the Sky commentary box. 'A lot of them were moaning because they felt they were being let down at that point. And I don't think it was the scoreline as much as the manner of the defeat. If they feel you're not giving your all, some will be pretty scathing, because they're spending good money on air fares and match tickets and all the rest. It's an expensive business and they demand, rightly, a player gives his all for them.'

However, Dave Peacock is quick to point out that, while some England fans might have voiced their frustrations in hotel lobbies and bars, those frustrations never spilled over on to the stands. 'We got rolled in three days in Melbourne, the weather was appalling, but I never remember the Barmy Army booing or anything like that,' he says. 'We didn't throw anything on the pitch, we didn't abuse the captain, we got behind Flintoff, who was still an iconic figure for us. And it was a dream come true to be in Australia watching England play cricket. The Barmy Army have never been angry, we were just disappointed. We're cricket supporters, pretty knowledgeable fans at the end of the day, and we knew that we were getting beaten by an unbelievable Australian side and we just weren't good enough. Deep down we knew after that first Test it was going to be 5–0, they were a phenomenal side.'

Adds Jamie Gavin, for whom Melbourne was his first Ashes Test down under: 'My abiding memories of the Melbourne Test were not of the cricket but of the Barmy Army: incredible support, given that their team had already succumbed to a heavy series defeat. The Army were there in full voice and in numbers, and the Australian public were genuinely bemused by their enthusiasm given the circumstances. Even on the day Shane Warne took his seven hundredth Test wicket, the Army comfortably embarrassed the home support in terms of noise.

'One of the most depressing things about that Test was watching England supporters queuing up at the MCG for refunds, some of whom had come out only for the one Test and for Christmas, only to see three days of cricket and their team humiliated. They were surrounded by gloating Aussies, but still the Army gave as good as they got. They genuinely lived up to the "barmy" tag during those few days in Melbourne: truly relentless support in the face of abject despair on the field. Even given all this support, I remember only one England player – Kevin Pietersen – who made his way over to the England faithful at the end of the three days to show his appreciation. It summed up a tour in which the support out-performed the players tenfold, and was a contrast to the player-supporter bond four years later.'

That England's fans were so sanguine is astonishing. England had not just been beaten, they had been embarrassed, emasculated, humiliated. Australia fans, already of the belief that their England counterparts weren't quite the ticket, were utterly bemused by the unconditional support Flintoff's team had received. 'The Aussies thought we were off our heads,' says Andy Thompson. '"Your team are a bunch of losers, mate, what are you still singing and shouting for?" But it's our team, win or lose we support our team. They didn't go out there intending to lose, they just came up against a better team and it all went to rat shit.'

Neither the Australian nor the British media could get to grips with it either. 'Only the bloody Barmy Army seems to have any life left in it,' wrote Mike Coward in the *Australian*. 'And if it is not to be demobbed before Sydney – hope springs eternal – it should add a dirge or two to its tiresome repertoire to give its heroes a sharp reminder of how they have failed their supporters and an expectant Australian public.'

Wrote Stephen Brenkley in the *Independent*: 'The nadir was reached in Melbourne. It was as embarrassing as it was dispiriting. There was an empty feeling, exacerbated by the fact the Barmy Army were still singing an hour after the horrible climax. And the band played on.'

As expected, the Barmy Army marched on Sydney in their thousands, hoping upon hope that Flintoff and his team would stave off the first Ashes whitewash since 1921. Instead, England got pummelled again. Flintoff at least gave the faithful something to shout about on day one with a muscular knock of 89, but England's second innings disintegrated again as the ruthless hosts romped to a ten-wicket win inside four days.

'Sydney was probably one of my least enjoyable Test matches ever,' says James Beare. 'The cricket had gone a long time before then, but it was the way the stewards treated everyone in the ground, they wouldn't let you in or out at lunchtime. They just treated everybody like children and I remember everyone being very pissed off. They didn't serve proper beer, there was hardly any food. I'd had enough of it by then, I was ready to go home. I think I spent the last afternoon in the pub.'

'The trouble is when England do well you get a lot of people joining up who, for want of a better description, have the football mentality rather than the cricket mentality,' says Graham Barber, whose first tour down under was in 1998–99. 'That was a big problem with Australia in '06–'07, it was full of football shirts and there was real aggressiveness between the two sets of fans. Because this new lot weren't used to seeing England lose so heavily, they took it a bit more personally. But cricket became such a big thing after we won the Ashes in '05, that was always going to be the case. The support was huge, but if not the wrong kind of support, it was a different kind of support, something we hadn't encountered before. Whereas before we knew most of the people we were in the stands with, suddenly we didn't know anybody. But it has to evolve, and there will always be new people coming in, in some cases for just one series, and then you'll never see them again.'

Nevertheless, while the authorities were determined to take away the Barmy Army's freedom and some of England's fans were set on lowering the tone, nobody could diminish the collective sense of fun. 'On the last day at the SCG, when England's humiliation/capitulation was all set to be completed, we kept ourselves amused by singing for each England player in the field to "give us a wave",' says Neil Rowe. 'Once that was achieved, we moved on to the two Aussie batsmen. Justin Langer, who, during the '02–'03 series had accused the Army of "drinking beer and being fifty kilos overweight" duly got into the spirit of the occasion and received a big cheer (his mood had improved over the years: at Edgbaston in '05, with thirty-five of us dressed as the Queen, waving our handbags at him, teasing him with "Seven Dwarves" songs, he bowed in deference and waved back). Matthew "Let's tonk a Pom" Hayden declined, to a chorus of boos, so we sang for the umpires, two Barmy Army favourites, Aleem Dar and Billy Bowden. Both joined in the fun, with Billy, as always, giving his full repertoire of extravagant gestures (in Sydney in 2011, Billy even gave us his rendition of "The Sprinkler" dance while standing at square leg!).

'As the inevitable denouement approached, Billy "The Trumpet" Cooper played "The Last Post", to which we doffed our caps, stood to attention and accepted our fate . . . and understood how it must have felt when the Aussies had won in England for the first time back in 1882. We'd shared some fairly dismal moments in recent years, but this series took the biscuit. The next time Billy was to play this anthem, the tables were turned: it was the last day at the SCG, January 2011. With impeccable timing, the notes rang out: Australia were 281 for nine, praying forlornly for rain, as Chris Tremlett came steaming in to Michael Beer – bowled! – and the payback was complete. It felt like a reward for following the team through thick and thin. What 5–0?!'

'It was over from the first delivery, the game was gone, the whole series was gone,' says 'Surrey' Mark Jacobs. 'We went in with hope and after that first morning you already knew, "Nope, it's not going to be this time." But I still enjoyed that tour. After all, they were the best team in the world, and we were far from it, so you almost forgave them. We were never expected to win, not really – although possibly a few people felt like we could – but even then we'd already won the Ashes in 2005, so maybe we didn't care as much. But I've never felt like I don't want to be there. Not once.'

'Once the Tests were over we dispersed, we didn't hang around for the one-dayers,' says Dave Peacock. 'The irony being we won the series but nobody was there to see it. It was really hard losing 5–0, especially having won the Ashes the series before. The Aussie fans were really getting stuck into us and when we got back home people were saying, "What a waste of money." They'd bring up Adelaide, but I'd think, "We were the lucky ones at Adelaide: brilliant day, sunny, went out and got pissed and forgot about it." Gutted, yes, but we were on holiday and you've got to get over it. And that's the thing, even though we got steamrollered, we can say we saw one of the greatest teams that's ever played the game. I'll never forget that Gilchrist innings at Perth, or watching Warne take his seven hundredth Test wicket. It was a privilege watching those guys, we'll never see their like again. And we knew that once those players had gone, they couldn't be replaced. And it's tours like that that make the winning ones that much sweeter. Even though I could never have guessed at the time how sweet the next tour down under would be.'

10

Victory at last ... Australia 2010–11

In April 2011, a miracle appeared in the pages of the *Wisden Cricketers' Almanack*. 'My opinion of the Barmy Army was not favourable when it began,' wrote its departing editor Scyld Berry, a cricket correspondent very much of the old school, 'because the songs contained foul language which should not have been imposed on children watching. But last winter their songs were no worse than bawdy, ridiculed senior Australian players rather than the juniors and were surprisingly tuneful, and the focus was on the cricket rather than on themselves.' After sixteen years of condescension, a prominent member of the cricket establishment had finally deigned to admit the Barmy Army might not be such a bad thing after all.

Berry even went as far as urging the England and Wales Cricket Board to make it easier for the Barmy Army to parade its support at home matches, by enabling fans to book more than a few seats in a row, as well as lowering prices. It was something that had been trialled, with great success, in the glorious Ashes series of 2005, but never repeated since.

It was England's triumphant Ashes tour down under in 2010–11 that triggered Berry's change of heart. When the reasons for that victory, England's first in Australia for twenty-four years, were being tallied, everyone seemed to agree that the vigour of the travelling support played a significant part. Of course, the fact the Barmy Army had been providing vigorous support for the previous four fruitless Ashes tours was conveniently ignored. Like veterans from long-forgotten military defeats, the Barmy Army's hardcore might have been forgiven for feeling unappreciated. And they might have done, if victory in Australia, when it finally came, had not felt so sweet.

The build-up to the 2010–11 series was feverish. Jonathan Agnew had been on every Ashes tour since 1990–91, so his hurt predated even the Barmy Army's. 'Had there ever been such a feeling of anticipation before a Test series?' wrote Agnew in his column for the BBC Sport website. 'This is my sixth Ashes tour, and I certainly have never felt anything like it. This huge excitement has been generated by the optimism among England supporters who genuinely feel that Andrew Strauss' men have a real chance of defeating Australia. At the same time, there is a serious trepidation in the Australian media and the general public that their great run of two decades without a home Ashes series defeat is finally coming to an end.'

Giles Wellington's first tour with the Barmy Army was the Ashes series in 1998–99, and he sensed the 2010–11 side was a far superior vintage. 'We arrived in Brisbane three days before the start of the series,' says Wellington. 'We were just acclimatising in Barmy Army HQ when we had the pleasant surprise of being joined by two members of the England team, Matt Prior and Stuart Broad. It was an excellent opportunity to showcase a few new songs, but we all felt it was refreshing and quite encouraging that the boys were relaxed enough to share with us details of their build-up, including the famous boot camp [the England team began their Ashes preparations with a bonding trip in a German forest]. It was clear they were focused and very confident, and that made us confident, too.'

Wellington – no relation to the Duke of, or not as far as I am aware – had been central to the planning of the tour, which was military in its precision. 'Most tours usually kick off the same way,' says Wellington. 'The majority of the Barmy Army meet up at the ground during the first day's play, and as the Tests progress the numbers increase, as does the noise, and banter and new songs develop organically. However, for the 2010–11 series things were different.

'Towards the end of the [English] summer, work had already started on new songs, the Barmy Army shirt design had been decided, seating and tickets had been confirmed after a lot of schmoozing of Cricket Australia, Bill "The Trumpet" had been permitted to play in all the Test grounds, which had been prohibited in 2006–07. It was said that the England team travelling to Australia was the best prepared in recent memory. Well, the same could be said for the Barmy Army.

'We are renowned for our vocal support but a common complaint is that our chants can be monotonous and a tad boring. So it was decided I would take on a new song based on an old one which was very successful during the New Zealand tour of 2008. Based on the Beach Boys' "Sloop John B", we came up with "Take the Urn Home":

'We came over from old Blighty
The Barmy Army and me
Around Australia we did roam (we did roam)
Six quid for a pint,
A grand for a flight
With Strauss our captain
We'll take the urn home.

Chorus (all)
Soooo hoist up the John B sail
See how the main sail sails
Call the captain ashore
Take the urn home

We'll take the urn home,
We'll take the urn home,
With Strauss our captain,
We'll take the urn home

Ricky Ponting's a broken man
Without Warne he has no plan
He tries to carry the team all on his own
He's losing his hair
But we don't care
'Cos Strauss our captain
Will take the urn home

Chorus
Soooo (etc)

Graeme Swann's a caring guy
Rescues cats in his spare time
Now he's gonna tear the Aussies apart
They can't read his spin
So England will win
With Strauss our captain
We'll take the urn home

Chorus
Soooo (etc)

'The guy who sang the song in New Zealand had an excellent, booming voice but he didn't make the trip to Australia, so I tentatively volunteered myself. The thing is, I was worried I wouldn't do it justice, so I shelled out for a crash course with a singing teacher (initially without telling my missus, and then swearing her to secrecy when she questioned my new-found obsession with laa-ing my scales around the house). After a slow start the song took off. Simon Hughes mentioned it in the *Telegraph* and then we had several thousand belting it out on the final day in Sydney. My crowning glory was duetting with Steven Finn at the Barmy Army end-of-tour party, with Graeme Swann and Alastair Cook also joining in. I'm not going to lie to you, the whole singing teacher episode was a little bit embarrassing, but who was laughing now?!'

'There is a little pub in Brisbane city centre by the river – a cracking little pub in fact – called the Pig 'N' Whistle,' says Jamie Gavin, who had seen England annihilated four years earlier. 'It was there that the Barmy Army gathered the night before the first day of the first Test, and I remember it being one of the most memorable scenes of the whole tour. The mood of expectation and optimism that night was tangible. The results of the warm-up matches [England won two and drew one] and the Australian media – who for once were more concerned about their own side than belittling the English team – gave the Army reason to believe.'

While the Pig 'N' Whistle may have been jumping, other pubs and hostelries were counting the cost of a sharp cut in the numbers of travelling supporters. In 2006–07 an estimated 37,000 England fans pumped approximately $320m into the Australian economy. That figure was expected to be down by a half in 2010–11 as economic uncertainty in

Britain and the strength of the Aussie dollar against the pound took their toll. Australia was no longer the bargain-basement cricket destination of old.

Well-drilled and pumped up with optimism they may have been, but if the Barmy Army members who did make the trip thought retaining the Ashes was going to be easy, a fired-up Australia team did their best to disabuse them of that notion on the first day of the first Test at the Gabba. England skipper Andrew Strauss, having won the toss and deciding to bat first, was out to the third ball of the game, cutting Ben Hilfenhaus to Mike Hussey in the gully. First blood Australia. Then, Jonathan Trott played all round a straight one from Shane Watson and was bowled through the gate. Alastair Cook and Kevin Pietersen took the score to 117 after lunch, before Pietersen edged to Ponting at second slip for 43. When Paul Collingwood fell to Peter Siddle before tea, the England innings was hanging off its hinges. After the interval, Siddle would rip it off completely with a hat-trick on his twenty-sixth birthday, only the second at the Gabba and the first in Ashes cricket since Darren Gough in Sydney in 1999.

From a comfortable-looking 197 for four, suddenly England were a distinctly fragile-looking 197 for seven. Bell played smartly for his 76, but a collapse of six wickets for 63 runs in 11.3 overs was completed when left-arm spinner Xavier Doherty bowled James Anderson for 11. England all out for 260, Siddle finishing with career-best figures of six for 54. Stick that in your optimism pipes and smoke it.

'To be honest, that wasn't really supposed to happen,' admits Swindon's Jason Cooper, who was in Australia when England were shredded 5–0 four years earlier. 'We'd all been having it in the Pig 'N' Whistle the night before until whatever o'clock in the morning and rocked up at the ground still half-cut, expecting England to roll them over. It was almost like Siddle knew what we'd been up to: "There you go, boys, celebrate this."'

England hit back after lunch on day two, taking four Australia wickets in the session for 72 runs. Skipper Ricky Ponting gave his wicket away softly, edging James Anderson down the leg-side to wicket-keeper Matt Prior for 10. Anderson swung it round corners in the afternoon session, suggesting he might be coming to grips with the Kookaburra ball used in Australia and might just have a big say in the series. However, Hussey and Brad Haddin rebuilt the innings and were both unbeaten at stumps, with the Australia total 220 for five.

Before start of play on day three, Geoffrey Boycott on *Test Match Special* called it 'the decisive day of the game'. It proved to be so topsy-turvy and full of imponderables, by the end of play no one could really decide whether it had been decisive or not. The rejuvenated Hussey, who saved his place with a hundred in a Sheffield Shield match for Western Australia, and Haddin piled on the runs in the first two sessions, taking Australia to 436 for five at tea. Wrote a somewhat previous Will Swanton in the Sydney *Sunday*

Telegraph: 'You could feel it when the Barmy Army began to realise their worst Ashes nightmare was becoming a reality and they became beautifully, wonderfully, terrifically submissive. Barely made a peep.' But the scorecard did not tell the whole story. In truth, England's bowlers could have rolled Australia over before lunch, with Anderson beating the bat on countless occasions. Australia also benefited from the Decision Review System, three words to put fear into the most unflappable umpire. However, the fact was Hussey (195) and Haddin (136) put on 307 for the sixth wicket, the third highest for Australia in Tests. Then, after tea, Australia's innings turned from granite to sand, the last five wickets crumbling for 31 runs. Pick the bones out of that, Geoffrey.

Still, England had it all to do on day four. And how they delivered. Strauss, who was lucky not to be out shouldering arms from his first ball the previous evening, and Cook both racked up tons as England made it to stumps on 309 for one. Their partnership of 188 was an England record at the Gabba. Strauss was the man out for 110, while Cook (132) and Trott (54) remained unbeaten. For Mitchell Johnson, in particular, it was a chastening experience. The Queenslander, playing on his home ground, had vowed to make Strauss 'crumble' under a barrage of bouncers before the series started. But bowling on a pudding of a pitch, Johnson endured a torrid day. In the same interview, Johnson admitted he let the fans get to him during the 2009 Ashes series in England. 'I was copping it left, right and centre,' he said.

'Then I just started thinking about too many different things. I'm happy to put my hand up to that.'

Big mistake. 'Johnson got a little bit of stick in '09 and really wore it in the last series,' says former England skipper Michael Vaughan, who was in the *TMS* commentary box in 2010–11. 'And, you know what? It's going to be even tougher in 2013, the abuse will get longer and louder because the crowd know they've got him. That's the one thing you don't admit to, that the crowd have got to you: you keep your gob shut and get on with it.'

'Basically, the Barmy Army are like sharks,' says Jason Cooper, 'but nice sharks. You leak a speck of blood and we'll smell it a mile off. In this internet age, any interview any player does with any outlet, the Barmy Army will sniff it out. So Johnson letting it be known we got to him during the previous series, that wasn't a wise thing to do.' While the Barmy Army songwriters would take until the fourth Test in Melbourne to compose their killer song, it would be brutal when it was unleashed.

Records fell like confetti on day five as Cook and Trott piled on the agony for Johnson and Co. Strauss declared England's innings on 517 for one, with Essex left-hander Cook 235 not out and Warwickshire rock Trott unbeaten on 135. After a harrowing first day for England, it sent a message to the Australia team and the Australian public: this England team is not like all the rest. Cook and Trott's partnership of 329 was the highest for any wicket for England in

Australia – the previous best was 323 by Jack Hobbs and Wilfred Rhodes for the first wicket in 1911–12; Cook's knock was the highest Test score at the Gabba, surpassing Don Bradman's 226 against South Africa in 1931–32; it was only the second time the first three batsmen in the order had scored centuries in a Test for England; and England's 517 for one declared was the highest total for a completed innings with only one wicket down in Tests.

Johnson, meanwhile, the leader of Australia's attack, finished with match figures of nought for 170 in forty-two overs, made a nineteen-ball duck, dropped a catch and missed a run-out. 'What to do with Mitchell Johnson?' said the Melbourne *Herald Sun*. 'The past four days at the Gabba have laid bare the demons lurking within.' Former Somerset skipper Peter Roebuck – by now referring to the Australians as 'us' – wrote in the Sydney *Morning Herald*: 'Australia have been cooked and served up for supper. The Barmy Army roared its approval and the locals were stunned into silence. It had been a long time since any Australian outfit, let alone its cricket team, was treated with such disdain by any opponent, let alone a bunch of Poms.' For melodrama, the Aussie newspapers made the *Sun* look like a hundred-year-old copy of the *Financial Times* by comparison.

And what did the Aussie players make of the Barmy Army's contribution? 'Bit annoying to be honest,' was Shane Watson's view. But Ponting's assessment was rather more revealing. 'I forgot where I was at times,' he said. 'It was like being back at The Oval in London. That's what's so great about the Barmy Army, they turn up no matter what is happening and support as much as they can.' You did not have to be a forensic scientist to read between the lines: it was barely concealed disgust that when the going got tough, his so-called supporters evaporated and there was no energy to lift his demoralised side. Johnson was even more explicit, if also slightly disingenuous: 'The Barmy Army hasn't bothered me,' he said. 'The only thing that bothered me was that I don't think we got the home support that we wanted at the Gabba on the last day.' Strauss, meanwhile, picked up on the Aussie paranoia. 'The support of the Barmy Army was outstanding,' said the England skipper. 'They have come a long way to support us and there'll be plenty more in Adelaide and if we can get off to a good start and get them in good cheer then it always has a slightly demoralising effect on the opposition.'

'Those last few days at the Gabba were important in so many different ways,' says Dave Wright, an Englishman living in Brisbane. 'But what I remember most about that Test wasn't England's second innings, astonishing as it was, but the reaction of the fans after day two, after Hussey and Haddin had put on that huge stand. At that stage, England looked like they were buried, yet the Barmy Army had to be ushered out by the stewards after the close, we just couldn't stop singing. It demonstrated England's was a united front. And then on that final day, there were only England fans in the ground –

the Aussies had melted away. Obviously it was going to be a draw, but we just couldn't understand that. You've got to support your team, through thick and through thin, yet they'd turned their backs and legged it at the first sign of adversity. If I was Ponting I would have been spewing, that last day he might as well have been playing at Edgbaston.'

Adds Jamie Gavin: 'My personal favourite chant of the final day was (to the tune of "He's Got the Whole World in His Hands") was "We've got one Aussie, in the ground", until another Australian fan was daft enough to stand up, then it would be, "We've got two Aussies, in the ground" and so on. It was an embarrassment for the home side, in every respect. So much so that Ricky Ponting finally responded to the chant of "Ricky, give us a wave". I think it even made a few of the Aussie tabloids the next day.

'There was even hope at one point that England would do the impossible and win the game, but once the match was beyond a result it turned into one big Barmy Army party in the Brisbane sun. New Barmy Army favourite Matty Prior even clapped along to a few of the songs and there was a sense the players and the Army began a close relationship that day which lasted throughout the whole tour. The detachment of 2006–07 was in the past and the players suddenly recognised they could feed off the Army, and, for once, vice versa. For me, days two and five at Brisbane were the two biggest days of the tour. Not only for the players, but also for the Army, who successfully quashed talk that they wouldn't be as strong this time around due to the strength of the Australian dollar and the recession.'

'I was at the Gabba on day five where England fans outnumbered Aussies by about a thousand to one,' says Paul Winslow, who wrote a syndicated column for Australian newspapers during that series. 'Seriously, the Australian support was about as weak as their lager, although now we finally understood where they got their inspiration from for that Lara Bingle [Tourism Australia] advert where she asked: "Where the bloody hell are ya?" That final day was a classic Barmy Army day. We can sing and chant through adversity (you've given us enough practice), but when things are going our way it becomes a lot easier.

'It also helped that we had a new pantomime villain in Ben Hilfenhaus. If you're going to field in front of the Barmy Army and show no sense of humour and for whatever reason not sign a young kid's bat, you're in for a long tour. We even offered to help him with the spelling of his name, but to no avail. Oh for the days when we had banter with Brett Lee.'

'England believes Australia's aura has gone,' said Shane Warne on the eve of the second Test in Adelaide. 'All eleven of the Poms are believers.' After one over's play at the Adelaide Oval, you could multiply the number of believing Poms by a hundred. On a smouldering morning, Australia were caught ice-cold. Simon Katich was run out by Trott from the fourth ball of the day, without facing a ball, and the next delivery Ponting edged Anderson to Graeme Swann at second slip: Australia 0 for two. When Michael Clarke was dismissed by Anderson, Australia were 2 for three. 'Anderson ran around the Adelaide Oval like he had slotted the winning goal in an FA Cup final,' wrote Andrew Webster in the *Herald Sun*. 'The Barmy Army, already more annoying than 1000 vuvuzelas, erupted. And it was only 10.44 a.m.'

It could have been worse. Hussey was dropped by Anderson off his own bowling for three, and the hosts limped to lunch at 94 for three. Hussey made the most of his let-off, compiling an unflustered 93, but Australia's last five wickets went down for 38 runs as they were all out for 245. England had struck a huge psychological blow.

The following day, England tightened their grip. Cook, in the form of his life, and Pietersen put on 173 for the second wicket as the tourists closed on 317 for two. Johnson and Hilfenhaus were unceremoniously dumped after the first Test, but it made no difference, and Jeff Thomson, who terrorised England batsmen in the 1970s, called it the weakest Australian attack for thirty years. It did not take much, it seemed, for Australian to turn against fellow Australian. It was more of the same on day three, with Pietersen making an unbeaten 213 and Ponting's hair must have been coming out in clumps.

Ponting described the Barmy Army as 'the best fans in the world' during the 2009 Ashes in England (as a *Financial Times* editorial pointed out at the time, 'Being insulted by a drunk Yorkshireman in a polyester replica shirt is not normally counted as one of the highlights of a visit to England, but if the Australian team do not object to the abuse, do the rest of us have any right to complain?'). The Barmy Army repaid the compliment by kicking him while he was down, booing him all the way to the crease and launching into a whole new repertoire:

Yesterday, Ponting's troubles seemed so far away,
Now Ben Hilfenhaus is here to stay,
McGrath and Warne were Yesterday;
Suddenly they're not half the team they used to be,
Will he lose Ashes number three?
Yesterday came suddenly;
Why 'Haydos' had to go I don't know,
Langer wouldn't say, Adam Gilchrist's gone,
Now Ricky longs for Yesterdayyyyyy . . .

Strauss declared England's innings closed on 620 for five before lunch on day four. The stand of 173 for the second wicket between Cook and Trott was an England record for the Adelaide Oval, while Pietersen's knock (he was eventually out for 227) was the highest score by an Englishman on the ground. Now it was time for Swann, who up until then had been strangely mute, to join the party, removing Katich and Ponting in the afternoon session. When part-time tweaker Pietersen dismissed Clarke with the final ball of the day, England were poised to move in for the kill. 'The last time we were there, losing 5–0, was miserable, it really was,' says Bill 'The Trumpet' Cooper. 'By the end I was looking forward to coming home, the Aussies were just so cocky. But I'd actually started feeling sorry for them at Adelaide, they just looked like such a downtrodden outfit.' So sorry, in fact, that Cooper was presumably crying all over his horn as he ran through his Aussie-baiting repertoire on the final day.

'These days we've got tunes for all different players,' says Cooper, who had become such a fixture on England tours by that stage that he was being invited to give talks at corporate events ('I was talking at functions alongside cricketing legends, sandwiched in the middle of Nasser Hussain and Ian Healy. It was nice to do, but at times I was thinking, "What the hell am I doing here?"). I've got a repertoire, but any tune I know how it goes I can play. People seem to like singing "Livin' on a Prayer", so if we're halfway through the day or halfway to a total we might start singing "Oh, we're halfway there ..." I play the *Bullseye* theme tune when someone gets a fifty; "I will score 500 runs, I will score 500 more" when England score 500, to the tune of The Proclaimers' "500 Miles". That was quite rare until the last Ashes series, when it seemed to be happening every Test. But every day at the cricket I try and do something I haven't done before. People will just come up and say "What about this," and they'll request old TV themes and old pop songs. If I know it I'll play it, although there are times people will say, "It's my dad's birthday today, can you play his favourite song?", and it will be some 1950s easy listening number I've never heard of.'

'Jimmy Savile' was, of course, England's other cheerleader on that tour, as he had been on the previous two down under. Real name Vic Flowers, from Oldham, and a carpenter by trade, he had become the Barmy Army's *de facto* leader in the stands, always resplendent with George Cross vest, top hat and flag. But having been raised in defeat, physically attacked at Port Elizabeth and Kingsmead and ejected from venues across the globe, he might have found this England dominance a little difficult to deal with. 'Having a name like Victor, as in victory, for the past twenty years it seems quite inappropriate,' he says. 'I've never won anything. One of life's biggest losers, tragedy my whole life, marriage, divorce . . .'

It was during the Melbourne Test in 1998 that 'Jimmy' found his calling, although it was at Port Elizabeth the following year, when under attack from some local hoodlums, that the Barmy Army took him under their wing and made him their lightning rod. And while to those around him England cricket tours are a break from their jobs, to 'Jimmy' they are his job. 'I don't spend a lot of time in England [when he does, he is often to be found on Burnham's sofa], I spend a lot of time on a small Greek island, I have a lovely little place. But you can't just wallow in self-pity when there's a whole world out there. So that's what I did. But that's the thing about the Barmy Army, we're just not used to winning.'

Says Mark 'The Nun', a fellow Oldhamer: 'He's a great fella and a very, very good friend of mine. In a short space of time his mum and dad died, leaving him a bit of money, and he got separated from his wife and kids. That obviously hurt him a bit, and I think his life is the cricket. He sold his house and said, "I'm not going to work for a living, I'll travel and see where life takes me." I first met him in Brisbane in 2002, even though I knew him vaguely through the Oldham connection. Before you know it he's this Barmy Army folk hero. The one thing about Jimmy is he's genuine, although he hasn't got a brilliant cricket brain. I remember David Lloyd went up to him in South Africa and said hello and Jimmy turned round and said "I don't know you, do I?" He's that kind of level, but David Lloyd was rolling about laughing, he thought it was hilarious. Fame hasn't gone to his head, he's still got time for anyone who wants a picture taken with him, gives out the leaflets, and when we're in Oldham he can walk round and no one would know who he is.

'But you put that gear on him and he's a different bloke, very, very passionate. When he's not in Oldham he rents a room above a bar in Greece, sits on the beach all day and when "Leafy" [Paul Burnham] gives him the call, he jumps on a plane, slips on the gear and off he goes again. "Leafy" looks after him, pays for all his flights and everything. "Jimmy" brings the Barmy Army to the fore, when he stands up and starts singing everybody listens. It's all a bit damp when he's not in town, there's a buzz when he is. The Barmy

Army would be lost without him and "Leafy", they're the two that make it tick.'

On the bright side, 'Jimmy' found himself slung out of the Adelaide Oval for anti-social behaviour on day three. And this action had the support of one of the wise old owls of the British press pack, the *Independent*'s James Lawton: 'There is still a view prevailing in some quarters that the Barmy Army are an unending source of good cheer and enjoyment and entertainment on their travels around the cricket world. The Adelaide Police Department seem, at least in this quarter, to have got it just about right.' Perhaps Lawton is not on speaking terms with the *Sydney Morning Herald*'s Greg Baum, but his Aussie counterpart would have put him right: 'The last time England won by an innings in this country was at the MCG in 1986,' wrote Baum. 'One afternoon, a section of Bay 13 amused itself (and many others) by making monkey noises and throwing bananas at England bowler Gladstone Small. Sad to relate, neither peers nor authorities moved against them.'

Song-wise, day five at the Adelaide Oval was largely about Graeme Swann. Fuelled by the strains of 'Swann will tear you apart again' (to the tune of Joy Division's 'Love Will Tear Us Apart'), the Nottinghamshire spinner finished with five for 91 as the Aussies slumped to their first innings defeat by England for twenty-four years and the first at Adelaide since 1891–92. For the Aussies, a burst of Joy Division's 'Atrocity Exhibition' might have been more apt. The Aussie pressmen were merciless in their appraisals of their team. 'Strong and reliable, he suddenly looks the best bowler in the country,' wrote Robert Craddock of Ryan Harris in the *Melbourne Herald Sun*. 'Mind you, being Australia's best bowler is a bit like being the nation's best sumo wrestler. The competition is not great.'

'The Ashes are all but gone,' wrote the *Australian's* Malcolm Conn. 'So too, it appears, are the last vestiges of Australia as a Test force after England's imposing second Test victory in Adelaide.' The *Herald's* Peter Fitzsimons even called for Ponting to be sacked as captain and replaced by Shane Warne, a suggestion that had the backing of former skipper Mark Taylor. 'He's the sort of guy who gives them a bit of aggro, and that's exactly what they need,' said Taylor.

From the Adelaide Oval, England's fans took their celebrations to P.J. O'Brien's, the official Barmy Army Adelaide HQ. 'That was quite a night,' says Dave Wright. '"Jimmy Savile" leading the singing, everyone going absolutely mental, it was a good day to be an England supporter. It might have been the greatest day in the history of the world. Ever. That night, I was so pumped up I felt like I could have pulled anything, I was like Barry Sheene and James Hunt rolled into one.' Phil Tufnell may not have been there, standing on the table singing 'if you've all shagged an Aussie clap your hands', as he did in Adelaide back in 1994, but, for all the cosmetic changes, little in the world of the Barmy Army had changed.

Some of the chat emanating from the Aussies prior to the

third Test in Perth was downright bizarre. Explaining the decision to recall Johnson in place of Doug Bollinger, selector Greg Chappell said they had simply been rotated. Meanwhile, former Australia wicket-keeper Rod Marsh announced Michael Clarke was not fit to captain his country because he had tattoos. Things got even stranger when it was announced that Michael Beer, who had played only five first-class matches for Western Australia, had made the Australia squad.

Strauss won the toss and, encouraged by a grassy WACA wicket, made the brave decision to put Australia in to bat. It proved to be the correct one. Australia slid to 69 for five before lunch and, despite recovering to post 268 all out, it was England's day again. By this stage, the Aussie media had pretty much given up. 'If the fat lady sings any louder for Ponting,' wrote Robert Craddock in the *Herald Sun*, 'she will shatter a window.' What Craddock had forgotten was that fight is the key protein in an Australian's DNA.

On day two, Mitchell Johnson, of all people, dug his side out of what was becoming a very big hole, taking six for 38 as England were skittled for 187. And what did Johnson put the turnaround in form down to? Blame the Barmy Army. 'It was a dreadful time for me,' said Johnson of his horror show at Lord's in 2009. 'Everything that could possibly go wrong did go wrong. And the crowd got to me. Usually you can block them out but they were pretty boisterous, revelling in my problems and that was unsettling me. I could hear them laughing and jeering and that just made things worse. I do feel I have unfinished business with England and their supporters. I'm getting tired of watching them celebrate.'

Australia posted 309 in their second innings before England were humbled again, this time being bowled out for 123. From the high of Adelaide, the Barmy Army were now left to reflect on a massive 267-run defeat. Still, Dave Wright was not going to let a crushing defeat on the pitch get in the way of more swordsmanship. 'The Barmy Army HQ in Perth was a bar called the Lucky Shag, on the Swan River,' says Wright. 'That had to be the most appropriately named bar in Australia.'

If the Barmy Army was momentarily becalmed by the crushing defeat in Perth, they were back on form during the build-up to the Boxing Day Test in Melbourne, doing what they do best: annoying the Australian cricket team. 'Christmas Day involved a tremendous event held at the Crown Casino in Melbourne,' says Giles Wellington. 'About two hundred Barmies paid out for a four-course meal and – wait for it – as much booze as you could drink between noon and three o'clock. What could go wrong? Well, nothing for the Barmies, who drank and sang their hearts out. But for the Australian team and their families, who were in the adjoining room trying to have a quiet Christmas lunch, it was a little bit different. Ricky Ponting looked particularly sour when asked to pose for a photo. Which seemed a bit off, considering we were all serenading him at the time . . .'

'On Christmas Day, I was with two friends enjoying a quiet beer in Base Hostel, St Kilda, near Melbourne,' says Jamie Gavin. 'All of a sudden the Australian DJ put on "Love Will Tear Us Apart" – little did he know what he had unleashed. Within thirty seconds the dance floor had filled with fifty or so people belting out "Swann will tear you apart". This was followed by a run-through of the full Barmy Army repertoire long into the Christmas Day night. Someone produced an England flag from somewhere, people were stood on tables, the lot – the hostel workers had never seen anything like it.

'Many like us hardly had a penny to our names by the time we reached Sydney, and while members of the official Barmy Army tour enjoyed their hotels, a large bulk of the unofficial Barmy Army – which must have been bigger than ever on that tour – stayed in hostels, eating pasta every night and having no choice but to watch every cent they spent. The contrast between the strength of the Australian dollar in 2007 and 2010 was ridiculous – it was about five or six quid a drink.'

Despite Gavin's (relative) hardships, there were those within the 'official' Barmy Army hardcore who believed the 'unofficial' Barmies were the ones doing things the right way. By 2010–11, Paul Burnham's operation was a slick one, far removed from the outfit's rather shambolic and spontaneous beginnings sixteen years earlier. 'People supporting England will always be there and I like to think the Barmy Army would carry on,' says Graham Barber. 'But I'm always wary of over-commercialisation. There's no harm in selling a few T-shirts, but the ethos of the Barmy Army used to be very much that you did your own thing, and then you just sort of bumped into people in the pub when the Test started or at the cricket ground.

'A lot of people now are after that Barmy Army "experience" from the time they arrive at Gatwick or Heathrow until they get back again. Because they're all coming along as part of Barmy Army tour groups, for me it's all a bit over-orchestrated, that old ethos of just turning up and joining in has gone. It's become almost too organised. I still organise all my own flights, I do what I want to do when I want to do it, but there are people who want that safety net a package holiday provides. But are they really getting the real feel of it? And then it becomes the responsibility of the people organising the tour to make sure they do get the real feel of it. I don't want to knock it, it's just not my idea of what it was and what it can be.'

But Nicky Bowes, who worked for the Barmy Army between 2004 and 2007, says a more structured approach was a necessary evil. 'I can understand why it's become so organised and perhaps in some people's eyes over-orchestrated,' says Bowes. 'But basically it just became too big for itself and the issue Paul was having was that everyone and anyone was using the name Barmy Army in the media, often about people who were behaving like idiots. And he was thinking, "That's our name you're besmirching, we need to be a little more structured," so he brought in membership,

315

and in doing that you are going to cut out some of the random element.'

Adds Katy Cooke: 'It's a fair cop to say we lack spontaneity, but sometimes it's necessary. The players basically dictate the way we behave. Someone like [seam bowler] Ryan Sidebottom would literally turn round and say, "Come on, it's bloody hot out here, help me out." Graeme Swann always wants help. When they're batting, not so much, we try to stop it from happening, because that's what the players have told us they want. Obviously after tea on any given day, when more liquids have been taken, it gets louder and louder. And we would have rested "Jimmy" and Bill "The Trumpet" during the break so they can come out and gee up the crowd. But it's not like they sing the songs in a particular order, they just go out and do their thing. Bill is class, his comedy timing as a musician really brings the crowd together. And it's never contrived, because he has people shouting at him all the time, "Do this one, do that one," and he makes decisions based on the situation.'

'People have said it's not spontaneous,' says Paul Burnham, 'but it is almost coordinated spontaneity, if that makes sense. We make sure we have the right people there – "Big" Graham Barber will sing his song, Giles Wellington will sing his song, we have Bill "The Trumpet" and "Jimmy" and numerous other people – and then we just let the day evolve, almost grow off these central figures. It is a case of making sure there is always one of the central figures there at any given time just in case the Aussies pipe up. But more so it is a case of maximising the support for the England cricket team, which is all we can do, because we can't go out and play.'

The effort to rein in, or detach itself from completely, some of the more unruly elements of England cricket fandom has gone down well with some members of the British media, and partly explains the more positive coverage during that series. Says Jonathan Agnew: 'The hardcore element love their cricket and where there are issues I don't think it's to do with the regulars, it's the add-on element, and that's the danger with the Barmy Army: that they can attract the wrong sort of people. But I have noticed over the past couple of years they do seem more regimented and it appears they have made an effort to make it a little more orderly. They have changed a bit in that they don't do so much chanting until later in the day and the trumpet has added a bit to it, made things more melodic.'

'I listen to *Test Match Special* and it's nice to be accepted by that lot and not to be seen as, "Oh God, here's that bloke again,"' says Bill 'The Trumpet' Cooper. 'It is very surreal at times. On the one hand, I'm trying to be a serious classical trumpeter by day and the next I'm standing in the crowd at the MCG, six pints down, banging out the *Neighbours* theme tune. I do a little bit of teaching with kids, and they say, "Sir, you always tell me to hold the trumpet like this, but I saw you on TV holding it with one hand and a pint in the other one."

'But without trying to sound too pretentious, I take my role very seriously. Over the years the cricket authorities have realised I'm not going to ruin the Test match for everyone and that I can ensure people aren't singing anything too inappropriate. If swearing starts creeping in and things start going too far, I feel a weight on my shoulders and try and stop it. The whole ground were singing something in Sydney in 2007 and it was all about Shane Warne being up to no good and the message came down from upstairs, "You've got to stop them singing this, Warney's threatening he won't come out to play any more." I don't know how serious that was, but I had to try to deflect them back to the cricket. You almost end up being crowd control, which is not so fun. Sometimes some lads will turn up and start singing football songs and I'll try to play over the top of that with cricket stuff instead. That's why I try to keep it varied and make sure it's not incessant. You're trying to keep the Barmy Army happy, everyone else in the ground happy and the owners of the ground happy, because in a lot of cases I'm given special dispensation to bring my trumpet in. There are a lot of boxes to tick and a lot of different groups to keep on side.'

If the Barmy Army – both official and unofficial – had been pacified by the sterile display of their team at the WACA, they were silenced for a completely different reason in Melbourne. 'After that first day at the MCG, there was a strange, quiet feeling surrounding the England fans,' says Jamie Gavin. 'It had been one of the greatest days in the history of English cricket, and the Barmy Army, for once, were stunned into silence by their own team. I don't think anyone could believe what they had just witnessed. Although things picked up later on in the bars of Melbourne, the English fans walking away from the MCG that day were so in awe of the performance that few had words, or songs, that could describe it.'

Australia were all out for 98 before tea, their lowest score at Melbourne and their lowest against England since 1936–37. Now savour the irony of Ponting's pre-match comments: 'When you walk on to the [MCG] field on Boxing Day morning and stand up for the anthem and the ground is full, it is an amazing place. You almost feel like you are bulletproof if you are an Australian.' Chris Tremlett, who replaced the injured Stuart Broad in Perth, took four for 26 and Anderson, who moved the ball prodigiously, four for 44. For the Barmy Army, the day got even better from there, with Strauss and Cook taking England to 157 for nought at the close. While the official attendance was 84,345, the number must have been half that when stumps were drawn. Proof, if proof was needed, that Aussies do not find anything funny about losing. Especially Mitchell Johnson.

'During England's first (and only) innings at the MCG, when England's batsmen were putting Australia to the sword, the Mitchell Johnson song was born,' says Jamie Gavin:

'He bowls to the left, he bowls to the right –
That Mitchell Johnson, his bowling is shite.

'It's sung with hands in the air while swaying from side to

side. He was horrendous that day, going to all parts, and with every over, every wide and every run he conceded it just grew louder and louder.'

'When everyone was getting on Mitchell Johnson, that was special,' says Bill 'The Trumpet' Cooper. 'In Melbourne I piped up with a version of *The Addams Family* theme tune, which referred back to the row his mum and his fiancée had had [during the 2009 Ashes series according to the press, Johnson's mum accused his fiancée of 'stealing' her son]:

'Your mother hates your missus,
Your missus hates your mother,
You all hate each other,
The Johnson family.

'Everyone was clapping along and at one point he stopped in his run-up, turned round and started giving out to us. We really got to him on that tour. I remember him batting one day at the MCG and he was standing at the non-striker's end and the whole stand was rocking from one side to the other singing at him. We had a drink with some of the players after that Test and I said to Jimmy Anderson and "Swanny", "Could you actually hear what we were singing?" And they said, "Too right."

'Apparently, every ball Kevin Pietersen was saying, "can you hear what they're singing, Mitch? They think you're shit". It's not nice in a way to see someone falling apart, but getting on top of him was good for the England team because he was supposed to be such a vital bowler for them.'

'To be fair to the Barmy Army they've seen it all,' says Jonathan Agnew. 'The last time England had won an Ashes series in Australia, the Barmy Army didn't exist. They were still on good form when England were getting thrashed in 2006–07, so they've probably earned the right to enjoy themselves. I thought the Mitchell Johnson song was hilarious. Every time he started an over at the MCG, a whole end was just swaying, it was fantastic. I will defend the right for any Englishman to fill his boots having seen what we'd seen on the previous five tours. And it definitely got to him, there's no doubt about that.'

England's batsmen poured on the pressure on day two. Cook, Strauss and Pietersen made fifties before Trott and Prior put on 158 for the sixth wicket, Trott finishing unbeaten on 141 and Prior on 75. With five wickets remaining, England led by 346 runs. Even better for the Barmy Army, Ponting lost his rag, just as he had done when things were unravelling at Trent Bridge in 2005.

'That was a smashing moment,' says Graham McNulty, who had never witnessed England win an Ashes Test before that game. 'I think that was the moment we knew we were going to retain the Ashes: when their skipper is rowing with and pointing fingers at umpires who have done nothing wrong, you know things are falling apart. The Barmy Army went through the entire Ricky Ponting repertoire that day. There was "Who Do You Think You Are Kidding Ricky Ponting?":

'Who do you think you are kidding Ricky Ponting
If you want the Ashes back
We are the boys who will stop your little game
We are the boys who will make you bat again
Ali Cook comes into bat position number one
Not out in the evening and he's got a double ton
So who do you think you are kidding Ricky Ponting
If you think old England's done!

'Then there was "My Name Is Ricky Ponting" (to the tune of "My Old Man's a Dustman"):

'My name is Ricky Ponting
I want the Ashes back
But there is just one problem
My team can't bowl or bat
And when I hurt my finger
And I can play no more
I hand the team to Clarky
We still can't flaming score.'

The attendance was down significantly on day two, prompting Greg Baum in the *Melbourne Age* to write the following day: 'Yesterday's attendance was nearly 70,000 and at least half of them were exultant Brits. Australia has been re-colonised. Rarely since the First Fleet dropped anchor has Australia been so comprehensively claimed for England.'

Noted Agnew: 'There were times when it felt more like England were playing at home rather than in Australia. And that was down to the Barmy Army – they were loud, they were funny and their acerbic wit got under plenty of Australian skins. Realistically, I think, they contributed rather more than some of the old stagers might like, and the players certainly fed off the atmosphere generated by the ever-present and noisy Army. That day in Melbourne when Australia were in the field all day, getting slogged around and knowing they were going to lose, the Australian fielders were gradually getting picked off by the Barmy Army. There was nowhere for them to hide. From an Australian perspective, it was very intimidating.'

England wrapped up their second innings victory of the tour before lunch on day four, meaning the Ashes were retained. With Bill 'The Trumpet' Cooper bashing out Christmas standards throughout the day, Australia were dismissed for 258, Tim Bresnan weighing in with four for 50. The final wicket of Hilfenhaus sparked wild celebrations among the travelling faithful.

'I genuinely don't think there's ever been a better day in the history of the Barmy Army,' says Jamie Gavin. 'Nor might there ever be. There was a woman behind us who was there the last time England had triumphed in Australia and she wept as Bresnan took the final wicket as the emotion of the achievement took over.'

'The Sprinkler' dance, rather ironically, had been a fad in Australia in the 1980s, was rediscovered and dusted off by all-rounder Paul Collingwood and adopted by the England team as they prepared for the Ashes series. But it was Graeme Swann who brought it to the public's consciousness, performing the dance on one of his wildly popular video diaries. The 'moves' involved holding one arm out and imitating the motion of a garden sprinkler, and the group rendition on the MCG's hallowed turf after England's spanking victory sparked a dance craze to rival the Macarena. Even Jonathan Agnew promised to perform the dance if England sealed the series in the final Test in Sydney – something he would live to regret. '"The Sprinkler" had become the secret handshake, the salute which would be performed as if to say "You're here for the same reason as us,"' adds Jamie Gavin. 'And I think what really hurt the Aussies the most was when "Swanny" and Co. took the biscuit by performing it in front of the Barmy Army. Not that there were any Aussies in sight, but it made pretty much every front page of the Aussie papers the next day.'

For Barmy Army co-founder Dave 'The General' Peacock, who had witnessed England lose fifteen Tests down under and win only three on four previous tours, victory in

Melbourne was the culmination of a lifetime's ambition. 'Without a doubt it was made all the sweeter by what had happened on the previous tours, especially the whitewash in 2006–07,' says Peacock. 'That was hard. We put on a brave front and we sung our songs and we backed the England players through every single session, but it's hard to lose and it's hard to get thrashed 5–0. So the celebrations at Melbourne were the best thing I've experienced watching sport around the world in all my life. I've been to every football ground in England, on countless cricket tours, but to see the players all run over and do "The Sprinkler" in front of the Barmy Army was just the best. No words were said but it was the ultimate mark of recognition, it showed the passion they had for us, as well as us for them. That was the players saying thank you, it said everything. It made us laugh, it made us proud, and we could see their appreciation.'

'The great thing about the early wins in Adelaide, Melbourne and Sydney is that they left the Army pretty much the whole of the rest of the day to celebrate,' says Jamie Gavin' In Melbourne large swathes of England fans – after the almost stunned silence of the first day – were ready to have what must have been the biggest English party abroad in a long time. This is what I imagined it would be like if England ever won the football World Cup. Another lasting, and recurring, image of the series was when jubilant, slightly merry England fans met everyday Australians going about their business during the Christmas holidays. The trams were a picture, rocking from side to side as we belted out the Mitchell Johnson song. Nothing was bad-natured, it wasn't intimidating, it was just a sheer release of joy after all those years of Ashes hurt down under. The England fans were determined to make the most of it, and they did, long, long into the night.'

Says Giles Wellington: 'The post-Melbourne Test celebrations were legendary. We took over a bar in north Melbourne and things were already rocking when a cab pulled up and out poured five of the England team – Paul Burnham told about eighty of us where to go and then got word to the players that's where we were going to be. They made their entrance while singing the Mitchell Johnson song, doing all the actions as well. It was a night those that were there will remember for the rest of their lives.'

'I went out at the last minute, not knowing if we'd see any play even, and arrived for the last hour and a half of the win at Melbourne,' says Nicky Bowes. 'After the match we had a colossal party and "Swanny" had us playing credit card roulette for rounds of Jägerbombs – you buy a round of ten or twelve Jägerbombs, everyone puts their credit cards in a hat and the last one picked out has to pay for the round. Bresnan, Anderson, Finn and Prior were also there. There was a lot of "Sprinkler" dancing going on, and as the cricket had finished so early, by ten o'clock most people were on the floor.'

That Melbourne Test also saw a major sea change in coverage of the Barmy Army by the British press. Of course, the boo-boys remained, including long-time critic Matthew Norman, who wrote in the *Telegraph*: 'I refer to the self-styled Barmy Army, that desperate coalition of saddoes who are the sons not only of Thatcher, but of Dave Lee Travis as well. The Barmy Army soldier's true self is the respectable, law-abiding IT operative in Swaffham, accountant from Wilmslow or stockbroker from Virginia Water, and not even turning up at the Gabba or Sabina Park in fancy dress – as Wonderwoman, Bertie Bassett, a Khmer Rouge deathcamp guard, or whatever – can begin to disguise that. Quite the contrary, it serves only to highlight the conformity.'

But the words of Jim White in the same newspaper were more typical: 'Even the doyens of *Test Match Special,* who have harrumphed about the Barmies' raucous presence for years, acknowledged the part they played. This is the glorious point of the Barmies – indeed, of this nation more generally: lovely as triumph might be, the purpose is not the pursuit of winning. The blokes pinking up in the Victoria sun represented a strain of sporting support that is gloriously, wonderfully and uniquely British.'

'There was a big-style change in the press coverage on that tour,' says Nicky Bowes. 'When I worked for the Barmy Army I used to have to scour the newspapers to see what people were saying about us and there really was hatred from certain people. But something has changed. I think perhaps it's trickled down from the players, who are always quick to thank us at the end of each game. The players enjoy it more than ever now, and there's also more youth coming through in the media, and ex-players like Michael Vaughan and Phil Tufnell in the *TMS* commentary box as well.'

As one of those ex-players in the press pack, former Glamorgan batsman Steve James, pointed out: 'Say what you like about the Barmy Army's often droning noise, but they're keeping Test cricket alive.'

In stark contrast, the Aussie pressmen were inconsolable. 'Darkness dawns on Australian cricket,' rumbled the Brisbane *Courier Mail*; 'Our darkest day in 133 years,' thundered the Sydney *Daily Telegraph*; 'They're gone,' whimpered the *Northern Territory News*.

After the mental disintegration applied to Mitchell Johnson during the Melbourne Test, the fifth Test provided an opportunity for the Barmy Army to display its softer side. The first day of the Sydney Test was in honour of Glenn McGrath's late wife Jane and even the Barmies were decked out in varying shades of pink, the colour of the McGrath Foundation, a breast cancer charity. The Barmy Army alone raised more than $35,000. But then the Barmy Army had always had a compassionate side.

'In New Zealand in 2002, during the Wellington Test, we found out from Jonathan Agnew on the radio that Ben Hollioake had died in a car crash in Perth,' says Paul Burnham. 'There was an eerie silence around the whole ground and we collectively decided to start singing "Oh Benny, Benny – Benny, Benny, Benny, Benny Hollioake".

The England players were in tears on the pitch and we got criticised in the British media for upsetting them. Then, in turn, people got upset by the media's reaction. "Freddie" Flintoff, all the Surrey boys – "Butch", "Thorpey", "Ramps" – they were all crying their eyes out, everyone got very emotional. He was part of a new generation of players, could have been bigger than "Freddie". We were singing his name all day and all night, and that's without a doubt the most emotional thing that's happened, certainly on tour.'

While the Ashes were already retained, Strauss, his team and its fans were desperate to become the first England side to win a series down under for twenty-four years. Only outright victory would go some way to erasing all that pain. Ponting missed the final Test because of a fractured finger sustained in Perth and was replaced by vice-captain Clarke, while Australia handed debuts to two players: New South Wales batsman Usman Khawaja came in at number three, while spinner Michael Beer, who had never even been to the SCG before, let alone played there, came in for seamer Ryan Harris. On an opening day curtailed by bad light and rain, Australia closed on 134 for four. The following day the hosts were bowled out for 280, Anderson taking four for 66, despite Johnson and Hilfenhaus combining for a fine ninth-wicket stand of 76. In reply, England were 167 for three at stumps, leaving the match in the balance.

However, the tourists took the game away from Australia on day three, Cook falling eleven runs short of a double hundred as England closed on 488 for seven. For Cook, it was a truly remarkable series, especially as there were those questioning his value to the team before the tour began. In total, he spent thirty-six hours and eleven minutes at the crease and scored 766 runs at an average of 127. Bell, too, made a hundred, making the most of a let-off when on 67. Australia thought they had him when he was caught off what appeared to be an inside edge, but the batsman called for a review and umpire Aleem Dar was forced to overturn his original decision on the evidence of Hot Spot. The problem was, a few minutes later Snickometer, which takes longer to process the information, revealed he probably had hit the ball. When Bell did reach three figures, none of the Australian players applauded, which left rather a sour taste. You might have thought the crowd would have been incensed as well, if it were not for the fact that about half of it was English.

'Even though the SCG was full of pre-booked ticket holders on day three, there was a glorious Barmy Army moment,' says Jamie Gavin. 'It occurred after the Army had hushed for the now familiar rendition of "Sloop John B/Take The Urn Home", somewhere in the middle of the final session. There were pockets of English fans all over the place by this point, and one such pocket started off "Stand up for the England". The most unwitty, simple of songs but every England fan in the whole ground – young and old – stood up, and it became apparent that about forty or fifty per cent of the SCG crowd was supporting the away side, a truly remarkable feat for a regular day's play. It was a mark of appreciation from the supporters for the efforts of the team – which for once had matched, and even exceeded, those in the stands.'

Before play began on day four, Paul Collingwood announced he would be retiring from Test cricket after the game. With the England fans in carnival mood as Australia slipped to another crushing defeat, he chose a good day. 'First Matt Prior reached his hundred in England's total of 644, but – sorry, Matt – that wasn't the best bit,' says Gavin. 'The best bit came when the wicket of Brad Haddin in the final session brought Barmy Army favourite Mitchell Johnson to the crease.'

Says Jonathan Agnew: 'In came Johnson to a roof-raising rendition of the Mitchell Johnson song. Bellowed in perfect unison, complete with thousands of swaying arms to the left and then to the right, it is an astonishingly hostile entry for an Australian to make on one of his home grounds. The poor man looked absolutely shattered and was promptly bowled first ball.'

Adds Gavin: 'Cue the wildest scenes of celebration of the whole tour. Bar none. For me, it was the best moment of the whole series. It was like your side scoring in a cup final, I ended up about three rows down from where I started, beer everywhere, arms and legs all over the place. And when it had all died down, everyone picked themselves up and went straight into another rendition of "He bowls to the left ..."

This was, of course, followed by the announcement that everyone would be admitted to the following day's play for free. As England took the extra half hour, to no avail, most fans were quietly hoping no more wickets would fall – which they didn't – so they could have one final day in the sun.'

The England players could barely have imagined the commitment of some members of the Barmy Army to the team. Gavin worked on a rubbish tip to save up for the trip, returned to England for two and a half days after the Perth Test for a job interview, before flying back immediately for the fourth Test in Melbourne. Bill 'The Trumpet' Cooper, meanwhile, passed up several career-advancing opportunities that winter in favour of getting behind his team. 'Over the Christmas period I can earn more than in the whole of January, February and March,' says Cooper. 'So I've had a few missed opportunities down the years where I've thought, "If I'd done that I might be established here". But that's life, I wouldn't change it for the world. When you've got Matty Prior turning to you at the SCG, clapping his hands and telling you to gee up the team, it's all worthwhile. And a lot of people are very jealous of what I do.'

And then there was the human moose. Explains Jamie Patrick: 'I'd been doing an internship in the spirits industry in Sydney for the previous four months and somehow found myself with an old friend from school, two moose outfits from work that had actually been meant for a Canadian Club promotion and two seats right in the middle of the Barmy

Army for the fourth day's play. And while I'd always hated the muppets who stood around waving on the big screen, we spent that whole day mugging for the cameras, doing "The Sprinkler" dance in our moose outfits, in heat that was pushing thirty-eight degrees. Shame most people watching, including David Lloyd commentating on TV, thought we were bears. Less happy to see us on television were my bosses back at the office, who had been informed I was taking the day off "sick". All of a sudden their mooses were dancing around with the Barmy Army, gloating at the demise of Australia.

'But the real fun came after the final day at the Bristol Arms Retro Hotel. It really was an honour to meet the likes of Swann, Bresnan (the cheeky northern lad tried to run off with the moose head), Finn, Cook and Bell in our furry states. Weeks later there appeared in *The Times* an article entitled "Swanny's Best Ashes Moments". When asked what his "favourite drunken moment" of the whole tour had been, his answer, to my shock and horror was, "Rugby tackling a six-foot moose in a bar with the Barmy Army after the Sydney Test." And there was an accompanying photo of yours truly. I say "to my shock and horror", in truth it was one of the best things that's ever happened to me.'

On day five, the Barmy Army, crammed into the Trumper Stand, had the ground virtually to themselves. The Aussie fans had melted into the background, and given that their side had been utterly marmalised, you could hardly blame them. 'There wasn't the sun we had hoped for,' says Gavin, 'but the Sydney rain wasn't about to dampen anyone's day. In another surreal experience there were thousands of fans in the ground over an hour and a half before the start of play. As the England players emerged for their warm-up, they looked shocked at the volume of fans already in the ground and every catch during fielding practice was greeted with loud cheers. Even the most pessimistic England fans knew the game was won and a series victory ensured – and a few rain delays later it was. In another stand-out moment, the trumpeter played "Singin' in the Rain", and the Barmy Army were doing just that when Tremlett took the final wicket of Beer. Perfect.'

*

'When "Colly" was doing his lap of honour, having announced his retirement, he came up to me and sang my song back at me, which was a bit of a giggle,' says Graham Barber, whose party piece is a falsetto version of 'The Lion Sleeps Tonight', rendered deliberately high to shatter the window of barracking from the Australian supporters. Why 'The Lion Sleeps Tonight'? Barber cannot remember either. (Des Kelly of the *Daily Mail* described Barber's performance thus: 'He led the crowd rendition with a voice so piercingly high it sounded as if he had his testicles trapped in a vice.'). 'It's not cheap what we do,' adds Barber. 'But we don't worry about it, we just want to support the team. But when you get something back off the team, some sort of recognition, that's great. It's nice to know they appreciate you and want you to be there. That was really highlighted on the last tour, just how much the guys in the middle could hear what was coming from the stands.'

Barmy Army HQ for the Sydney Test was the Paragon Hotel on Circular Quay. A couple of hundred yards from the Opera House, England's fans staged one last monumental party. 'England fans celebrated inside the pub and outside in the beer garden,' says Jamie Gavin. And once again, Australian locals and other tourists, who were just going about their everyday business, looked utterly bemused. But then it was quite a unique sight: hundreds of England fans bouncing up and down in the mid-afternoon sun singing "Cheer Up Ricky Ponting" in the shadow of one of their iconic buildings. In truth, it must have stung a bit.

'Another sign of how slick the Barmy Army's commercial arm had become was the fact they had printed "Cook conquers Australia again" T-shirts with the exact score of each Test on the back, including the one which had finished that morning. These were being flogged for $40 each in the bar, and everyone was biting. Chris Tarrant, Michael Vaughan and [television analyst] Simon Hughes all popped in to the bar to a heroes' reception, with Tarrant joining in with the Barmy Army songs – it didn't matter who you were, everyone was in awe of what Strauss's team had just achieved.

'The last thing I remember was walking down George Street with five or six mates, singing all the way back to our hotel on the other side of the city. England fans we walked past would join in from time to time, again all good-natured, but surreal nonetheless. Sydney had been reclaimed by the English all over again, there were battalions of Barmy Army marching down every street, hanging out of every pub and bar, gathered on every corner.'

However, for Graham Barber, who had witnessed England being mauled on three previous Ashes tours, this new sensation of winning – and winning so big – brought with it mixed emotions. England had become only the fourth team to make four totals over five hundred in the same series in all Test history; they had inflicted three innings defeats on Australia in the same series for the first time; no Australia batsman in the top four of the order had made a century in the series; England had amassed nine centuries in the series and five English batsmen had averaged more than 50. With stats like that, the Barmy Army just did not seem as barmy any more.

'We were called the Barmy Army in the first place because we were so bad, so winning the series like we did in 2010–11 was a weird sensation after losing so often for so long,' says Barber. 'In a way it's ruined it. We enjoy being underdogs, we just don't care. My biggest dilemma now is, "Now we've won in Australia, what have I got to look forward to?" We're never going to repeat what we did last time. There were a lot of us sitting there thinking, "Will we ever come back to Australia?" But come three years' time, we'll all be back there again.'

Adds 'Surrey' Mark Jacobs: 'The problem with that tour was that it wasn't the Australia team of old – there was a sense of "there's no Shane Warne or Glenn McGrath, it's not that great team", so we were expected to win out there, and I'd never experienced that before. And the Aussie fans were quiet, they didn't speak to you, just ignored you, except in Perth. Previous tours you'd be walking down the street and they'd give you abuse, "Pommie this and Pommie that", but on that tour it was as if we didn't exist for most of the time.

'But from a personal point of view, I'd had enough of Australia, and I'd say a lot of people would say the same. It was just so expensive and it was wearying, travelling around the whole country, doing the same things. You couldn't go out as much, people were taking beers back to their hotels, which is a shame, because you want to go out and experience it all. And there was definitely that feeling that now we've climbed Everest by beating Australia in Australia, we might as well not go back – we've pretty much done everything now, having also beaten Australia at home after all those years back in 2005. Obviously, once the dust has settled, we'll all go back, but the need to go back has gone.'

Dave Peacock, however, has no time for any negativity. 'Winning at home was nice, but winning on Australian soil was everything I'd dreamed of,' he says. 'My view might be different from Graham's because we started the Barmy Army with those thirty backpackers in '94–'95, we helped put following England abroad on the map. It's always been about having great fun in another country, and whether you win or lose or draw it's the holiday of the year and, for many, the holiday of a lifetime. Of those thousands of England fans who were there in 2010–11, for a very large percentage that will have been the first tour they've ever been on and it would have been the best time of their lives. That is the ultimate for any sporting fan and nearly all of them would be proud to associate themselves with the Barmy Army.

'On days three, four and five at every Test match, all the England fans grouped together, and not just the young lads from the backpackers, but people on tour with Gullivers and other tour groups. They all left their seats and came and joined us to be part of the atmosphere when we won. The vast majority were proud to be part of an England victory overseas, and realised it's far more fun to be with us singing the songs than it is to be sat on your own. Some of the guys, like Graham, prefer the smaller tours, with a hundred and fifty people instead of ten thousand, where they get to know the players and make great personal friendships. But as far as I'm concerned the more people who support England the better and the more people who associate with them the better.

'I didn't cry after that Sydney Test, I just went and got absolutely hammered, just as I'd always done. We went straight from the ground to the Fox and Lion pub next to the ground and we hosted a party back in town. We had eleven hundred fans, some of the players – Ali Cook and his girlfriend, "Swanny", Ian Bell, Steve Finn and Tim Bresnan, and it went on until the early hours. I was proud as punch I'd organised it and the players had turned up. And in that way nothing had changed, we were organising parties in 1994–95 that players were turning up to. You can call us too commercialised or say we lack spontaneity or whatever, but the essence of the Barmy Army remains the same.'

'The way that people watch sport has changed and I suppose the Barmy Army is a reflection of that,' says Jonathan Agnew. 'My opinion of the Barmy Army hasn't actually changed very much in that I've always viewed them as being fiercely loyal, very devoted followers of cricket. They bring a certain colour and ferocious support to the game, and for the most part they behave themselves. I've always taken the view that they're good entertainment and good value – as long as you're not sitting beside them, in which case they can actually be quite annoying. And I say that from experience – I've had Test matches in South Africa where I've been sat right beside them and they make broadcasting extremely difficult and, frankly, tedious.

'I would like to think there is an opportunity for everybody to watch cricket however they would like to watch it and generally now the Barmy Army have become more accepted and acceptable. "Johnners" [former *Test Match Special* commentator, the late Brian Johnston] would have said the same as me. He would have just been happy that people were going to watch cricket and watching it the way they want to watch it.'

'Two performances stood out as England completed a comprehensive Ashes victory at the SCG,' says Australian commentator Jim Maxwell. 'Throughout the series the Barmy Army chorused every moment of play. They should have been given free entry because they were so entertaining, rapturously encouraging the dreaded Poms, and alternately mocking the Aussies. The Barmy Army had earned the right to celebrate because Andrew Strauss's team played better cricket than any England team in Australia for at least fifty-six if not seventy-eight years.'

'The Barmy Army adds colour to any day's cricket, and that is why the Aussie media will always welcome it to our shores,' adds Scott Heinrich of the Fox Sports website in Australia. 'The truth is they really are no trouble. As supporters, they are giving and unconditional. When I covered what I call the "Redemption Ashes" in 2006–07, England fans had very little to cheer. But a lasting memory is staying back late to file copy at Adelaide and Melbourne, two harrowingly bad Tests for the Poms, and seeing not Australian fans loitering at the ground to bask in victory but members of the Barmy Army, singing along as if nothing had happened, as if to say, "Is that all you've got?" Crushing defeat after crushing defeat would not ruin their mood. In many ways, that *is* support.'

'The amount of positive press that came out of the last tour of Australia was amazing,' says Graham Barber. 'It was a long time coming but we were actually being accurately reported on for once. The majority of the press went out there with an open mind rather than a closed mind. I think some of it must have filtered down from the team, because they're always quick to thank the Barmy Army now. It just didn't make sense any more that the press were slating us and the team were always thanking us for their support. Even the older establishment people, like Scyld Berry, started writing nice things about us, and that never would have happened before.'

For Paul Burnham, one of the three small acorns (along with Dave Peacock and Gareth Evans) planted in 1994–95 from whom a mighty oak has formed, that 2010–11 series was reward for sixteen years of almost incomprehensible support for the England team.

'That series was testimony to the planning everybody did,' says Burnham. 'You had Giles Wellington having singing lessons, we went to great lengths to make sure Bill "The Trumpet" and "Jimmy" were there for all five Tests, to make sure the singing was more varied and inspiring for the team, and that all came out of the Barmy Army coffers. We have a role to play in the Ashes and I'm convinced we couldn't have done it any better – maybe it increased England's performance by one or two per cent, who knows, and that's all we ever wanted to do. We never planned to be called the Barmy Army, we were just there to support the team, but I think after five tours we finally got it right.

'The Aussies were struggling with injuries and retirements,

which is something we'd had to deal with down the years, but never been allowed to use as an excuse because we'd just get called whingeing Poms. So it was good to be able to call them whingeing Aussies, because that's all they'd moan about, the fact that Warne and Gilchrist and McGrath had retired. Actually, we probably did too good a job at putting them in their place because they stopped turning up. They've had years and years of success and to not turn up the first time it doesn't go right for them, to not show they're behind their team whatever happens on the field, just summed up the difference between the two sets of fans.

'It's something that's unique to the British. Maybe it's all to do with this Dunkirk spirit, this never-say-die attitude. We seem to like backing underdogs, we seem to struggle when we're favourites and when we are really good at something we don't like to shout out about it. If it went on for ten years, there would be a danger of our support becoming triumphalist, but that's not going to happen; the Australian mentality won't allow it and we'll never be that dominant. But we didn't change the psyche of the British sports fan, the psyche was there already: even when we're winning, we don't put out songs about winning, we're still taking the mickey out of our own players, just like we were when we were losing. We're more into the participation than the excellence.'

Burnham is no longer that young swordsman who arrived on Australian shores in 1994 hungry for sun, sea and sex. Oh, and cricket. As such, he has started allowing himself to contemplate the previously unthinkable: a Barmyless future. 'I don't want to grow old with the brand,' says Burnham. 'It's a young man's game – early starts, late finishes, non-stop boozing and partying, and the old body's not what it used to be. The knees have gone and I'm a diabetic nowadays, which is definitely self-induced. A lot of the guys have all got old together within the Barmy Army, and while they'll always remain friends, they won't be piling off to the same place again and again because other things happen in your life.

'It's great fun, but difficult, and you've probably only got a lifespan of ten years – I'm already sixteen years in and I think I need to start taking things a little bit easier. So, yeh, I guess I'm looking around for some heirs – and I stress the plural, because I wouldn't want it to come across that it's just me who runs the show. There are various people working tirelessly behind the scenes to make the Barmy Army what it is. It's a group thing, and I'm confident some new blood will come through. There were a lot of younger guys on the '10–'11 tour for whom it was the best holiday of their lives – I lost track of the number of times somebody came up to me on that tour and said that – and they're the next generation of Barmy Army leaders.'

But Burnham is not ready to pack away his board shorts and flip-flops just yet: as always with the Barmy Army, there are still horizons to be conquered. 'A lot of people will be heading over to India in 2012, where England will hopefully be playing a Test in Calcutta for the first time,' says

Burnham. 'But before then there's the series against Pakistan in Abu Dhabi and Dubai, where we've never played Test cricket before. A lot of people will want to tick that off. But my ultimate goal now for the Barmy Army is to retain the Ashes in Australia in 2013–14, to show it wasn't a one-off – or regain them, depending on what happens in England in 2013. And then there's the World Cup in 2015, and with Alastair Cook now in charge of the one-day side – he quite likes playing in Australia – we might have a pretty good chance of winning it. That would be a nice time to finish because that would mark twenty years of the Barmy Army. So that's where I'm heading to – but at a slower rate than the first sixteen years.'